Geoffrey Chaucer

The Canterbury Tales
IN MODERN VERSE

GEOFFREY CHAUCER

The Canterbury Tales
IN MODERN VERSE

Selected and Translated, with an Introduction,
by Joseph Glaser

Hackett Publishing Company, Inc.
Indianapolis/Cambridge

For Carol Ann

Copyright © 2005 by Hackett Publishing Company, Inc.

21 20 19 18 17   3 4 5 6 7 8

For further information, please address:

Hackett Publishing Company, Inc.
P.O. Box 44937
Indianapolis, IN 46244-0937

www.hackettpublishing.com

Cover art: Illustration of the Prologue to *The Canterbury Tales* from John
Lydgate's *The Seige of Thebes* (c. 1455/62). Courtesy of Art Resource.
Cover design by Brian Rak and Abigail Coyle
Text design by Chris Downey
Composition by Agnews, Inc.

Library of Congress Cataloging-in-Publication Data

Chaucer, Geoffrey, d. 1400.
     [Canterbury tales. Selections]
     The Canterbury tales in modern verse / Geoffrey Chaucer ;
selected and translated with an introduction by Joseph Glaser.
          p.   cm.
     Includes bibliographical references.
     ISBN 0-87220-755-2—ISBN 0-87220-754-4 (pbk.)
     1. Christian pilgrims and pilgrimages—Poetry. 2. Canterbury
(England)—Poetry. 3. Storytelling—Poetry. 4. Tales, Medieval.
I. Glaser, Joseph. II. Title.

PR1870.A1G58   2005
821'.1—dc22

                                                      2004060693

ISBN-13: 978-0-87220-755-4 (cloth)
ISBN-13: 978-0-87220-754-7 (pbk.)

Contents

INTRODUCTION

CHAUCER'S LIFE

Geoffrey Chaucer was born in the early 1340s though no one knows the exact year. Both his parents belonged to rich merchant families, and his father, John, had served as an officer of the royal court. He was educated in London, possibly at Saint Paul's Cathedral, and later in the great aristocratic courts, where he played a variety of roles. Although a commoner, he moved in the highest circles, beginning as a page in the household of Elizabeth, Countess of Ulster, the wife of Prince Lionel, one of the sons of King Edward III. There he came to know John of Gaunt, another of Edward's sons and father of the future King Henry IV.

Before he was twenty, Chaucer took part in a military expedition to France, one episode in the Hundred Years' War that smoldered with episodic flare-ups throughout his lifetime. He was captured near Reims and promptly ransomed along with other prisoners. Though this was the beginning and end of his military career, he later came to know parts of Europe well through extended trips to France, Spain, Flanders, and Italy, generally on government business.

In 1366 Chaucer married Phillipa de Roet, a court lady from northern France whose life, like his, intertwined with the English royal family's. She was lady-in-waiting to the queen and later to Constance of Castile, John of Gaunt's second wife. Her sister, Katherine Swynford, was John of Gaunt's mistress and later his wife.

In his twenties Chaucer was recognized as an esquire, the first degree of knighthood though still somewhat below the aristocracy. He may also have been studying then at one of the Inns of Court, the London law societies that governed the legal profession. There is no record he ever attended Oxford or Cambridge, the two British universities of the time.

In 1372, still only about thirty years old, Chaucer traveled as part of an embassy to Genoa and later visited Florence, where he might have met Petrarch and Boccaccio, two famous poets he draws on repeatedly throughout his work.

Soon after, he was appointed controller of duties on wool for the port of London, a critical post he held for the next dozen years. Wool was England's chief exchange commodity, and the export tax on wool was a vital source of government funds. As controller, Chaucer saw to it that the tax collectors were honest. When he wrote about graft and corruption, as he often does in *The Canterbury Tales*, he undoubtedly understood precisely what he was talking about.

Edward III died in 1376, but Chaucer continued to prosper under Richard II. In 1382 he became controller of customs on wine and other goods as well as wool. But not long after that his life began to change, partly in response to political upheavals in both Parliament and the court. Phillipa died, apparently in 1387, and by 1388 Chaucer had quit the customs post and was living in nearby Kent, where he was elected to the House of Commons.

In 1388 a dissatisfied faction in Parliament executed several of King Richard's supporters, including three who were associated with Chaucer. Chaucer survived the purge and went on to be appointed clerk of the king's works, responsible for special projects and royal properties including Westminster Palace and the Tower of London. Three years later, he became deputy forester for North Petherton, where he was involved in overseeing forests, commons, villages, farms, roads, and rents in a large tract of Somerset.

In 1399 Henry Bolingbroke, John of Gaunt's exiled son, returned to England, overthrew King Richard, and was recognized as Henry IV. Chaucer was in London that year, living on the grounds of Westminster Abbey. Once again he weathered the political storm handily. Henry IV confirmed his royal grants and even added to them.

According to an inscription carved on his tomb many years later, Chaucer died on October 25, 1400. He was buried in Westminster Abbey, where his grave became the nucleus of the famous "Poets' Corner."

Other records of Chaucer's personal life are generally sketchy. He and Phillipa had two sons, Lewis and Thomas, and probably two daughters, Agnes and Elizabeth, who became a nun. Thomas enjoyed a brilliant career as speaker of the House of Commons and envoy to France. His grandson— Chaucer's great-grandson—was later Earl of Lincoln and designated heir to King Richard III before the king was killed at Bosworth Field.

In 1380 Chaucer was released from legal actions concerning the *raptus*, or rape, of an heiress, Cecilia Chaumpaigne. The event sounds more dramatic than it probably was. Chaucer may have been involved in helping the girl elope or in abducting her to marry someone else. In 1324 his own father had been abducted for the same purpose.

Six years later Chaucer was called to testify in a dispute about a coat of arms, and in 1388 he was sued for debts left over from his customs days. This does not mean he was poor; probably, like the government that paid him, he was just slow to settle his accounts. Finally, in 1390 as royal clerk, he was robbed and apparently wounded, presumably while carrying royal funds for wages or building materials.

CHAUCER'S WORLD

Although he traveled widely throughout his career as a court functionary, diplomat, and administrator, Chaucer was essentially a Londoner, growing up in a merchant enclave near the Thames and living in and around the city the rest of his life. With only about 40,000 people, London was a small town by modern standards, but it was also the cosmopolitan center of a diverse and energetic nation. As a wine-importer's son, Chaucer met foreigners from all over Europe. He must have known at least a few well enough to learn their languages, especially Parisian French and Italian, which were not taught in schools.

Chaucer's London teemed with a variety of people and professions. Tradespeople tended to live and keep shops in neighborhoods associated with their crafts or guilds—goldsmiths, clothiers, stationers, butchers, and so on—so a short walk would present a kaleidoscope of sense impressions, especially within the city walls, which still stood in Chaucer's days. Outside the walls to the west ran The Strand, a mile-long thoroughfare lined with law courts and palaces he would have passed as he went to conduct business at the royal court in Westminster. This to-and-froing between the lively, mercantile city and the aristocratic court provides a good emblem of the diversity of Chaucer's experiences and his own ambiguous social standing.

Away from London, where Chaucer must often have gone as royal clerk and deputy forester, the countryside quickly became rougher and wilder. Villages like Chaucer's "Bob-up-and-down" on the way to Canterbury stood close together along the road, which was sometimes no more than a muddy track. Most were quite small, perhaps only a huddle of poor houses around a village pond and communal green. Market towns were spaced at wider intervals among a patchwork of manors, woodlands, chases, parks, and commons. Estates belonging to noble lords or monasteries controlled much of economic life through the labor of serfs who worked for just their keep or villains who tended plots that they rented for a portion of their crops. Both groups were bound to the estates they served. In good years they led a hard-scrabble life like old Janicula in "The Clerk's Tale" or the widow in the Nun's Priest's. In bad years many starved.

Overseas, as Chaucer had several occasions to observe, new ideas were in the air. In northern Italy the Renaissance was already stirring in city-states like Florence, then more than twice the size of London. Dante and Chaucer's later favorites Petrarch and Boccaccio led the way in literature, while Giotto set a new standard of realism in painting. France excelled in music, largely through the *Ars nova* compositions of Guillaume de Machaut, whose poems Chaucer translated. The leading thinker of the age, though he was often in disgrace, was the revolutionary William of Ockham, an Englishman who spent most of his life on the Continent. Like other progressives of the time, Ockham mistrusted elaborate systems based on untestable principles such as natural law. He tried to make sense of the world on the simplest possible terms using direct experience. Closer to home, John Wycliffe, an Oxford theologian, called for a new simplicity in spiritual life, sending out "poor priests" to beg and preach. Wycliffe also denied the doctrine of transubstantiation, which he thought insufficiently grounded in the Bible, and started a movement to translate the Bible into English so that people would be less dependent on priests to tell them what it said. Though they came at the issue in different ways, both Ockham and Wycliffe sought to flatten the religious bureaucracy that had grown up between ordinary people and God. In particular, both opposed the vast wealth and convoluted hierarchy the Church had acquired over centuries.

Although his era in England is usually thought to belong to the Middle Ages, Chaucer clearly felt a new world coming into being and responded to it in his writings, especially in *The Canterbury Tales*. In spite of the turbulence and misfortunes of the time—the historian Barbara Tuchman called it "the calamitous fourteenth century"—people were increasingly interested in breaking with the past and assuming greater control of their lives. In this, as in many ways, Chaucer was a leader. Even when his work is based on medieval forms like the romance or fabliau, its spirit is crisply modern—critical, innovative, diverse, and strongly interested in individual identity and experience.

CHAUCER'S TIMES

The 14th century was calamitous indeed. Two cold, wet growing seasons in 1314 and 1315 led to The Great Famine, in which not only peasants but also churchmen and nobles died across Europe. I have already mentioned the Hundred Years' War, 1337–1453, an ugly, interminable contest between England and France. A succession of English kings considered they had a claim to the French throne and pursued it through a series of brilliant battles, such as Crécy and Poitiers. But each victory was swallowed up by long periods of stagnation, and the war settled nothing until well after Chaucer's death. In the meantime, conscription, taxes, destruction, and lost crops eroded economic and civic life, especially in France, where most of the fighting took place.

This was the period, too, of the Avignon Papacy, 1305–78, when for over seventy years popes ruled the Catholic Church not from Rome, but from Avignon in France and in a way generally friendly to French interests. If there had ever been a doubt that secular politics could shape church policy, Avignon is where it died. From 1378 to 1414 matters deteriorated even further during the supremacy of *two* popes, one at Rome and one in France, each putting the other and his supporters under excommunication. Between consternation in Rome and Avignon at the top, a thoroughly un-Christlike accumulation of wealth in the middle, and widespread corruption at the bottom, no other era has been more damaging to the credibility of the Church.

Another defining event of Chaucer's time was the Black Plague. In the middle of the century (1348, with later outbreaks), this epidemic stood social and economic life on its ear. After plague carried off a third of the population of Europe—more in crowded cities like London—labor grew scarce, threatening the cherished privileges of the aristocracy and the Church. At the same time, talented professionals like Chaucer himself began to blur the line between commoner and aristocrat in one direction and, because the Church no longer held a monopoly on learning, between commoner and cleric in the other.

In the second half of the century worries associated with the social and economic implications of these developments brought a backlash from the propertied interests—who tried to curb the new independence of those beneath them—and a violent counterbacklash in the form of the 1358 Jacquerie uprising in France and the Peasants' Revolt of 1381 in England, when Wat Tyler and his rebels marched on London and beheaded the Archbishop of Canterbury in the Tower, only a short walk from where Chaucer lived at the time.

THE CANTERBURY TALES

With all the turmoil of his times swirling around him Chaucer could easily have been a different writer, wringing his hands in uncertainty or looking for targets to rail against. In fact he is nothing like that. In place of uncertainty, he appears to have been exhilarated by the new possibilities in the air. Instead of combativeness, he seems eager to take characters at their own estimate. Located between commoners and aristocrats; moving between high culture on the one hand and tax receipts on the other; interested in everything along the way; familiar with the classics, but also popular English literature and contemporary trends in France and Italy; he became one of the most inventive and unpredictable writers in the English canon, and this is nowhere more evident than in *The Canterbury Tales*.

Start anywhere you like and Chaucer surprises you. His idea of a series of tales within a frame narrative was not new, but only he would think to draw the tale-tellers from all over England and from a variety of economic and social classes, giving his stories and narrative framework a vitality and social relevance no other collection approaches. The first Canterbury story, "The Knight's Tale," is a courtly romance, but its stylized action and noble sentiments—fine as they are—are followed immediately by a racy fabliau (a comic story of everyday life) that the Miller insists on telling out of order. While there is no way of knowing for sure how Chaucer meant to arrange the tales, it is probable that many of them would have arisen from outbursts between individual pilgrims like the Wife's quarrel with the Friar or the Miller's feud with the Reeve.

Chaucer writes in prose and poetry, using couplets, rime royal, ballade stanzas, and other verse forms in eight-syllable to ten-syllable lines. His stories range from fabliaux to saints' lives, from beast fable to courtly romance, from the popular jingle of "Sir Thopas" to the Parson's monumental sermon. Even more diverse are the modes and conventions found *within* the tales: dialogue, set speeches, myth, theology, biblical and classical allusions, natural and allegorical description, dreams, visions, astronomy, alchemical recipes, philosophical arguments, and insults, to name a few. Sometimes Chaucer goes out of his way to upset readers' expectations, as he does in "The Wife of Bath's Tale," a notably un-Arthurian Arthurian romance in which fighting ability is irrelevant, women hold all the power, and ideas count more than actions. Variety is everywhere, from the burgeoning springtime setting to the shifting scenes along the pilgrims' route to the exchanges among the pilgrims themselves and the complex play of different viewpoints between their tales. The Monk's dismal stream of tragedies is cut off not just because it is depressing but also because it saws away at the same theme. No author since Ovid valued variety as highly as Chaucer or was so ingenious at injecting it into his work.

Griselda is a monstrously long-suffering wife; the Wife of Bath will butt heads with anyone. Husbands can be sweet and understanding, or they can box you on the ear. The Church is God's kingdom on earth for the Parson or Saint Cecelia, or a flagrant swindle in the hands of the Summoner or the Pardoner. Humans have free will in one place but are bound by God's foreknowledge in another. What they think is based sometimes on the stars, sometimes on the state of their bowels. They range from unthinking hedonists like Alison in "The Miller's Tale" to stern pillars of morality like Virginius in the Physician's. The Clerk is steeped in book knowledge; the Cook seems utterly unlearned. The Parson is a saint; the Shipman a murderous pirate. Chaucer's imagination contains them all, and he considers all their tales worth retelling, refusing to be bound by any one poetic style or philosophical vision.

With few exceptions Chaucer seems more concerned to understand his characters than to judge them. Even a charlatan like the Pardoner is called "a fine ecclesiast," because he no doubt appeared no less than that in his own eyes. There is irony in such descriptions, as when the narrator tells us how the generous Friar paid for the weddings of girls he had debauched, but there is generally a note of fellow-feeling too. For all his deplorable opportunism, the Friar's eyes sparkle with the joy of life. Listening to the Wife of Bath's story of her life shows us with perfect clarity how she became what she is. Even the repellant January in "The Merchant's Tale" can see that his obsession with May is irrational, and when he discovers her in the pear tree with Damian he lets out a cry "as mothers do when babies die." No one who lived through the plague years could have made that comparison without feeling a degree of compassion for the wicked old sensualist.

All this diversity and the lifelike roundness of his characters define Chaucer's sort of realism, a poetic vision especially in tune with a time when old assumptions were passing away, hurried along by skeptical thinkers like Wycliffe and Ockham. Ockham in particular thought human minds impose a system of meanings on things that may or may not correspond to what they really are. Particular rocks and houses and trees exist. But they would exist as well if they were called something else and thought of some other way. The categories "rock," "house," and "tree" are human inventions, and so, of course, are all institutions, which would include things such as monarchies and organized religion. Grant Ockham's arguments and the implications for any entrenched form of government or special privilege are enormous. Longstanding customs mean nothing. Social arrangements and beliefs might just as well be reinvented every other week. Experience, not received opinions, is the touchstone of truth. For Ockham, the world order, which had occupied much of medieval philosophy, is a mere construct, far less interesting than the individual beings within it.

While there is no evidence that Chaucer knew Ockham's work, there is often a similar spirit in *The Canterbury Tales*. The old hag in "The Wife of Bath's Tale" comes close to Ockham when she insists that nobility means acting nobly *yourself*, not just occupying a slot in a system that declares you noble. In the same vein, *old* and *poor* and *mean* are merely words society has come to condemn. Look at the realities they represent, she says, and they may be worthy of celebration instead.

Chaucer's pilgrims are types—the Knight, the Monk, the Summoner, and so on—and sometimes little more than that. Everything he says about the Yeoman or the Franklin, for instance, is rooted in conventional stereotypes. But other figures, including some of his most notable ones, are so individual it is as if the type were being shattered from within to let a real person rise out of it. The secretive Reeve indulges himself, out of character, with an especially good horse. Chaucer also reveals that the Reeve was trained as carpenter and that his disposition is remarkably vengeful and smutty, unanticipated details that make him a person, not just a reeve. The spaces between the Wife of Bath's teeth may be a conventional sign of lechery, but who would have guessed her incessant talking, which is part of the antifeminist caricature of a mettlesome woman, would be driven by a respectable degree of learning, which is not?

Chaucer's diversity and realism come through just as clearly in his style, or rather his styles, for his language is beautifully responsive to his matter, so that, to take the opening of "The Nun's Priest's Tale," for example, he can sound like a dispassionate sociologist talking about a needy widow:

> She kept three sows, for breed, not slaughter,
> And three thin cows and Moll, the sheep.
> Her house was sooty, hard to keep.

From this dry treatment he passes seamlessly to sympathetic irony:

> And there she served, despite her wishes,
> No piquant sauce nor far-fetched dishes.
> No dainty morsels passed her throat;

To a mock-heroic celebration of Chanticleer, the cock:

> His voice outdid the ample organ
> That rang out when the Mass began.

To the language of scientific objectivity:

> He knew the stations of each sphere
> Above that town throughout the year.

To a parody of the avid descriptions of the heroes in popular romances:

> His comb was red as brightest coral
> And scalloped like a castle wall.

It would be hard to name another writer (though once again Ovid comes to mind) whose poetic voice moves so deftly between different registers.

OTHER WORKS

Though little in Chaucer's life records hints that he was a poet, he must always have had a project or two going on throughout his adult life. He needed to have in order to compile such a distinguished literary record while also pursuing a government career that would have been a full life's work by itself.

Around 1370, when he was about thirty, Chaucer translated part of one of the most influential works of the time, *The Romance of the Rose,* an unfinished allegory of courtly love by the French writer Guillaume de Lorris. The same period gave birth to *The Book of the Duchess,* a dream-vision elegy based on the death of Blanche of Lancaster, John of Gaunt's first wife, in 1368.

In the later 1370s it is likely Chaucer wrote the story of Saint Cecilia that became "The Second Nun's Tale" and also some of the tragedies rehearsed by the Monk. *The House of Fame,* another dream-vision poem, also dates from the 70s, and so does *Anelida and Arcite,* an unfinished narrative set in ancient Thebes.

The 1380s saw Chaucer complete *The Parliament of Fowls,* a dream-vision of birds discussing the nature of love and perhaps a tribute to young Richard II's marriage in 1382. "The Knight's Tale" also dates from this period, along with the unfinished *Legend of Good Women,* Chaucer's first poem in iambic pentameter couplets.

But Chaucer's signal achievement of the 80s was *Troilus and Criseyde,* his greatest single poem—over 8,000 lines of rhyme royal stanzas on infatuation, morality, betrayal, and free will that also manages to be a brilliant narrative of events associated with the Trojan War. No one has ever written about the triumphs and agonies of love with more psychological insight, a gift highly evident throughout *The Canterbury Tales* as well.

The idea for the *Tales* seems to have come to Chaucer in the late 1380s, when he wrote the General Prologue and some early tales. The bulk of the work, though, dates to the last decade of his life, and he was probably still working on it when he died in 1400.

All through his career Chaucer wrote short lyric and occasional poems, many of them now lost. He also produced untraceable works such as the *Book of the Lion* he mentions in the Retraction to *The Canterbury Tales.*

Two other threads to Chaucer's career as a writer are *Boece,* his translation of *The Consolation of Philosophy,* the best-known work of his favorite philosopher and frequent authority, Boethius (d. 524), and *A Treatise on the Astrolabe,* addressed to "Lyte Lowys [little Lewis] my sone." The *Treatise* is an introduction to the astrolabe, an instrument used to make astronomical sightings and calculations. Chaucer may also have written the *Equatorie of the Planets,* a more advanced work in the same field.

A NOTE ON THE TEXT

Although Chaucer wrote well before the advent of printed books in England, his work was popular throughout the century after his death. Over eighty manuscripts of *The Canterbury Tales* survive, about fifty of them relatively complete—enough to show that Chaucer was well known, given the distribution methods of those times.

Once book printing got underway in England, Chaucer took his place at the center of the enterprise. *The Canterbury Tales* was the first nonreligious book printed in England, probably in 1476, the year William Caxton set up his press in London. Caxton went on to produce another edition in 1483, and two other English printers produced early editions as well: Richard Pynson in 1492 and Wynkyn de Worde in 1498.

However, no copy of *The Canterbury Tales* dates to Chaucer's lifetime or carries his indisputable authority. Modern editors generally draw their texts from two carefully prepared manuscripts produced about ten years after Chaucer's death: the Ellesmere Manuscript in the Huntington Library and the earlier but less complete Hengwrt Manuscript in the National Library of Wales.

Another complication for Chaucer editors is that the tales are unfinished, so that often the author's final intentions can only be guessed at, supposing he knew them himself. He may not have. At the beginning of "The Shipman's Tale," for instance, the narrator is not the Shipman, but a woman who sounds suspiciously like the Wife of Bath. Details like this seem to show that Chaucer was still working on the collection and even reassigning tales when he died.

According to the Host's plan, each of the pilgrims—about thirty of them, though Chaucer never pinned the number down exactly—was to tell two stories on the way to Canterbury and two on the way back, for a total of about 120 tales, only 24 of which were actually written. So, like much of what Chaucer wrote, *The Canterbury Tales* remains radically incomplete. The Cook's and the Squire's tales were never finished, and they and the rest exist as ten fragments[1] whose order is often unclear.

This translation is based on *The Riverside Chaucer*, edited by Larry D. Benson and others, which in turn is based largely on the Ellesmere Manuscript.

A Note on the Translation

Chaucer's robust language is one of the major delights of English literature, once you catch onto it. But catching on is a chore for most readers, at least at the start. Here are the famous first eighteen lines of *The Canterbury Tales'* General Prologue as they appear in the current standard edition:

> Whan that Aprill with his shoures soote
> The droughte of March hath perced to the roote,
> And bathed every veyne in swich licour
> Of which vertu engendred is the flour;
> Whan Zephirus eek with his sweete breeth
> Inspired hath in every holt and heeth
> The tendre croppes, and the yonge sonne
> Hath in the Ram his half cours yronne,
> And smale foweles maken melodye,
> That slepen al the nyght with open ye

---

1. These are not physical fragments—separate documents—but units defined by internal references. Thus the General Prologue looks forward to "The Knight's Tale," which is explicitly linked to "The Miller's Tale." These two go with "The Reeve's Tale," which refers to "The Miller's Tale," while the Cook's prologue says his story follows the Reeve's. These five elements make up Fragment 1, and so on. Except for Fragment 1 with its General Prologue and Fragment 10, which includes the Retraction, no one can say for sure what order the fragments themselves should take. Most editors follow the Ellesmere Manuscript, where the fragments all occur together for the first time.

(So priketh hem nature in hir corages),
Thanne longen folk to goon on pilgrimages,
And palmeres for to seken straunge strondes,
To ferne halwes, kowthe in sondry londes;
And specially from every shires ende
Of Engelond to Caunterbury they wende,
The hooly blisful martir for to seke,
That hem hath holpen whan that they were seeke.

Squint a bit, read some footnotes, and the lines begin to look more comprehensible. But *The Canterbury Tales* is longer than *Paradise Lost,* and the effort mounts up over time. Without a strong incentive, most readers never find out how well Chaucer repays those who can read him fluently. An anonymous Internet reviewer probably speaks for many disgruntled readers: "Unless you are a lit major or have a lot of free time on your hands, . . . buy anything else."

I have tried to head off such reactions by making this the most readable translation available, partly in hopes it will give readers an incentive to tackle Chaucer himself and partly because, for reasons I'll get to in a moment, *The Canterbury Tales* deserve better than they have had from translators. Scholars and critics disagree about the exact depth of Chaucer's religious feeling, his belief or disbelief in the science of his day, and his real attitude about women; but everyone who knows him acknowledges that most of the tales are fun to read and reread—witty, informed, and generally fast paced and entertaining. I believe a good translation should be the same.

That's why I've shortened Chaucer's ten-syllable lines to eight syllables, at least in the tales written in couplet form. For a variety of reasons Middle English is looser in its syllable count than the language we speak now. Not only does Chaucer's English abound in spoken endings that have since disappeared, but many borrowed words were still pronounced in a more polysyllabic, Continental fashion (for instance, *condition,* which was four syllables for Chaucer: *con-di-si-own*). As a result, what Chaucer took ten syllables to say often sounds more natural in eight or fewer today. Consider the first two lines of the prologue cited above:

Whan that Aprill with his shoures soote   *ten syllables*
The droughte of March hath perced to the roote,   *eleven syllables*[2]

2. Or maybe twelve syllables if the final *e* in *droughte* was pronounced. To simplify a vexing topic, Chaucer seems to have held himself free to pronounce or not pronounce final *e*'s to suit the meter of a given line.

"Whan that" is an idiom no longer with us. We say "when." Likewise "soat-uh," "pierc-ed," and "roat-uh" are one-syllable words for us: *sweet, pierced,* and *root.*

A very literal translation would be

When April with his showers sweet   *eight syllables*
The drought of March has pierced to the root,   *nine syllables*

Trying to put those lost syllables back into a Modern English version almost inevitably makes for stodgy, congested writing, the exact antithesis of the elegance and rapidity of Chaucer's own verse. You might wind up with something like this:

When gentle April with his dulcet showers,
Supplants the drought of March with flowers,

Here extra syllables make the meter come out right, but they also muffle the meaning and slow the reading for no worthy reason.

I hope my version of the first eighteen lines and the several thousand that come after them is sharper and brighter, more like Chaucer himself:

When April's fruitful rains descend
And bring the droughts of March to end,
Bathing each vine in such sweet showers,
That young buds burst and unfurl flowers,
When West Wind too, with his mild airs
Inspires in fields and hidden lairs
Fresh-minted leaves, and when the sun
Halfway toward the Bull has run;
When small birds sing for all they're worth,
Wide-eyed all night with reckless mirth,
Mad for love in trees and hedges,
Why, then folks go on pilgrimages
And pilgrims yearn for foreign strands
And distant shrines in sundry lands.
In England, from every plot or skerry,
They make their way to Canterbury,
Seeking the shrine of great Saint Thomas,
To pay for sins or keep a promise.

Eight-syllable, four-beat lines like these are common in English poetry going back hundreds of years before Chaucer. In fact they are more in keeping with native English tradition than ten-syllable, five-beat couplets, which Chaucer invented, working from Italian and French models. Chaucer himself chose four-beat lines for major undertakings like *The Romance of the Rose, The Book of the Duchess,* and *The House of Fame;* and four beats are standard in alliterative English verse, including superb (though un-Chaucerian) narratives like *Beowulf* and *Sir Gawain and the Green Knight.* But the real justification for shortening Chaucer's lines, I hope, is that it works. Four-beat lines make for a leaner, quicker, more direct and gripping Modern English version of *The Tales,* and to that extent come closer to the effect Chaucer must have had on readers and hearers of his own time.

Two other points can be made more briefly. I have abridged or summarized some of the tales to save space. The prose tales and the little-read "Canon's Yeoman's Tale" and "Manciple's Tale" are summarized, and I've shortened "The Knight's Tale," "The Man of Law's Tale," "The Clerk's Tale," "The Squire's Tale," The Franklin's Tale," and "The Monk's Tale." I hope there is enough here to give the flavor of the originals.

Finally, I've imitated Chaucer's poetic form exactly in the tales not written in rhyming couplets. The rhyme royal tales—the Man of Law's, the Clerk's, the Prioresse's, and the Second Nun's—share a religious feeling that seems suited to this austere stanza form, which is another of Chaucer's introductions. "The Monk's Tale" uses a French ballade stanza of eight ten-syllable lines rhyming *ababbcbc.* And the delightful beginning of "Sir Thopas" imitates popular romances of the day, in general alternating eight-syllable couplets and six-syllable split rhymes in the pattern, *aabaab,* though Chaucer introduces some strange variations in later stanzas that incorporate a "bob" of shorter lines at the end. As these stanza forms show, Chaucer was a determined and resourceful rhymer. The best evidence of this is undoubtedly the envoy that follows "The Clerk's Tale," thirty-six lines with only three rhyme sounds between them!

THE RELIGIOUS ESTABLISHMENT
IN *THE CANTERBURY TALES*

As one of the three great "estates"—the aristocracy, church officials, and workers—that were still considered to make up society in the 14th century, the religious profession of Chaucer's day was more important and recondite than it is now. Nine of the twenty-nine pilgrims mentioned in the General Prologue are religious figures of one sort or another, and their standing and duties can be confusing to readers today. The Church was a recognized career path for surplus aristocrats and ambitious commoners in Chaucer's day, and church service offered them a wide variety of roles to occupy.

Chaucer's Monk represents a tradition reaching back to Saint Benedict (d. 543) in Italy. By Chaucer's time there were other orders besides the Benedictines, but all monks were attached to a monastery where, according to the original conception, they were to work and pray. By work, Saint Benedict meant work. Monks labored away at farming, milling, woodworking, and other jobs. For centuries, copying manuscripts was one of their most important tasks. Monks were originally expected to stay within the monastery grounds and do manual labor at least seven hours a day.

Prayer for monks included daily Mass and prescribed readings for each of the canonical hours—Vespers, Matins, Lauds, Terce, Sext, None, Prime, and Compline today, although the number of hours and their timing has differed over the centuries. These prayers and readings were meant to remind monks and others who used them to dedicate themselves to God throughout the day and night. Monks took vows of poverty, chastity, and obedience. Their aim was to retire from ordinary life to a world without distractions that might draw them away from Godly work and contemplation.

By the late Middle Ages, however, many monasteries had grown rich and were involved in far-flung business arrangements—rather like today's universities. The monasteries Chaucer knew might own commercial properties (not just farms, but mills, warehouses, ships, breweries, and rental shops and housing) that required oversight from outriders like the Monk on the pilgrimage to Canterbury. The endowments they accumulated from donors and government grants over time needed to be invested and managed. Large monasteries influenced rents and wages and could be deeply involved in business dealings and politics.

Unlike monks, friars were supposed to live among the common people, begging for their living and donating anything they had left over to the poor. The founders of the movement, saints Francis (d. 1226) and Dominic (d. 1221), stressed social service and preaching. At first friars were supposed to own nothing either personally or collectively, but by Chaucer's time friars in convents like the one mentioned in "The Summoner's Tale" aggressively sought property and wealth. Competition between neighboring convents led to establishing exclusive territories where each group was allowed to beg. Sometimes, as with the Friar himself, competition within a convent led to specific territories for specific friars. At any event, when Chaucer's

Friar roisters in taverns while avoiding lepers and homeless wretches, he is not just a bad priest but a traitor to the founding principles of his order.

Fourteenth-century nuns tended to follow the monastic pattern, living in communities apart from the world and committed to a life of work and prayer. As Chaucer's Prioresse shows, however, reality was often more complicated than this. From her coquettish name—better suited to a romance heroine than a nun—to her ambiguous motto, Madame Eglantine seems far more attached to the world than she ought to be. As a younger or unmarriageable daughter of good family, she might have been placed in the convent for the convenience of her guardians, not for any religious vocation she felt. In the same way, she became prioress—the chief nun of her convent—not necessarily because of her piety or ability but because that was part of the arrangement when she came into the order. As a bride of Christ she would have brought a dowry to the convent, in her case no doubt a substantial sum. Well-off families often used such dowries to secure privileges for girls they offered up to the Church.

Like monasteries and friaries, convents of nuns could become rich and worldly. Chaucer's Prioresse heads the convent of Saint Leonard, an actual Benedictine house in what is now part of London. Saint Leonard was home to ten to thirty nuns at various times and controlled water mills, estates in several English counties, rental properties in London and Cambridge, shops in Southwark, and several churches, one of which involved the sisters in a dispute with the nearby staff of Saint Paul's Cathedral, circumstances not entirely favorable to a contemplative life.

With monks and nuns retired from the world, at least in theory, and friars roving about their territories to beg, preach, and serve, the bulk of daily church work fell to the secular clergy, usually commoner-priests ordained by bishops and appointed or approved by whoever controlled local churches, most often a bishop or local lord. Absenteeism was common. A well-connected priest, perhaps associated with one of the universities or the court, would be given a church "living" but would farm out the ecclesiastical duties to a less-wealthy priest for a portion of the parish income, which came from rents, farming parish lands, donations, and tithes. Everyone in the parish was obliged to tithe, that is, give a tenth of his or her income to the Church. A third of the combined income commonly went to the bishop, a third to maintaining the church building and helping the poor, and a third to the incumbent, the priest-of-record, who might return only part of it to the parson, the man who actually served the parishioners by preaching, counseling, offering the sacraments, and visiting the sick.

Chaucer's Parson is one of these local priests, not deeply learned or well connected but wholly faithful to his calling. Unlike the Monk or the Friar, the Parson is held up as an ideal example of what a priest ought to be: simple, humble, generous, but unbending in matters of religious principle even though his livelihood depends on the local powers that be. While the Monk and the Friar have taken vows of poverty, the Parson is actually poor. In this he resembles the bulk of his parishioners and also, as the old hag in "The Wife of Bath's Tale" points out, Christ himself.

The Pardoner represents the medieval minor orders—officials who could not say Mass but were appointed to lesser duties. His job was to go from parish to parish offering spiritual indulgences for a price, part of which he was supposed to remit to his employers, the Hospital of Rouncivale in London, a house of Augustinian friars. Because he also had to pay a licensing fee to each diocese he worked, the Pardoner needed to raise a lot of money through his inflammatory preaching to have any left over for himself. He was apparently doing very well.

According to Catholic teaching, only true contrition and the sacrament of penance can gain sinners moral forgiveness, but not even these excuse them from suffering punishment in Purgatory before being admitted to Heaven. The Pardoner's chief wares—signed indulgences—were supposed to reduce or eliminate this Purgatory obligation. They were not exactly for sale, but everyone understood that it took a substantial offering to obtain the benefits they promised. The Pardoner also peddled spurious relics with miraculous properties, a sideline that may have been especially profitable since he was not obliged to share those takings.

The Pardoner is still a cut above the Summoner, a layman who went about his diocese sniffing out or inventing sins for which parishioners could be hailed before an ecclesiastical court. Because these courts could impose church sanctions, fines, and even physical punishment for such offenses as adultery, fornication, sorcery, blasphemy, working on Sunday, or withholding tithes, the Summoner was in an ideal position to extort money or favors from his victims in return for suppressing his charges against them.

The Canterbury Tales

THE GENERAL PROLOGUE

When April's fruitful rains descend
And bring the droughts of March to end,
Bathing each vine in such sweet showers,
That young buds burst and unfurl flowers,
When West Wind too, with his mild airs
Inspires in fields and hidden lairs
Fresh-minted leaves, and when the sun
Halfway toward the Bull has run;   *the constellation Taurus*
When small birds sing for all they're worth,
Wide-eyed all night with reckless mirth,   10
Mad for love in trees and hedges,
Why, then folks go on pilgrimages
And pilgrims yearn for foreign strands
And distant shrines in sundry lands.
In England, from every plot or skerry,
They make their way to Canterbury,
Seeking the shrine of great Saint Thomas,
To pay for sins or keep a promise.

    And thus in Southwark one spring day   *across the Thames from London*
At the Tabard, where I lay,   20
Ready to journey from the place
And seek the holy martyr's grace,
A merry group arrived to dine,
A mounted crowd of twenty-nine.
Pilgrims all of every station,
And every corner of the nation,
Riding toward Saint Thomas' shrine.
The rooms were good, the food was fine,
The fires were warm, the wine went round,
And by the time the sun was down,   30
I had agreed with every one
To join their fellowship anon.
The next day we'd begin at dawn,

The tale I'll tell you further on.
 But first grant me a little space
Before I stir another pace,
To set forth, as an author should,
The qualities, both bad and good,
These pilgrims showed a man like me,   40
What each one was, of what degree,
Even the outfits that they rode in,
And with a knight I will begin.
 A KNIGHT was there, a worthy man,
That from the time he first began,
Devoted himself to chivalry
And truth and blameless courtesy.
His name was held in high repute
In every camp without dispute.
In every pagan or Christian nation   50
He won the greatest acclamation.
He watched as Alexandria fell,
Presided at the citadel,
First knight among the troops in Prussia,
And fought in Lettow and in Russia,   *Lithuania*
The hardiest man of his degree.
He smote the Moors with savagery
In hot assaults from southern Spain
To the parched Moroccan plain.
From western seas to Turkish towns,
He followed war with great renown,   60
Attending fifteen mortal broils.[3]
In Africa for Christ, and spoils,
He met picked champions of the Alcoran
Three times and always killed his man.
Once he upheld a Turkish lord
Against another pagan's horde,
With no loss to his reputation.

---

3. Chaucer mentions here a number of other places where the Knight had campaigned (Granada and Algeciras in Spain; Ayash, Atalia, and Balat in Turkey; and Benmarin [Morocco] and Tlemcen in North Africa). He means to show that the Knight has fought on all three fronts facing Western Europe in the 14th century: in the Baltic States with the Teutonic Knights facing forces from the east, in the Middle East confronting Islam, and in North Africa and Spain warring against the Moors.

Yet he made little of his station.
As meek and mild as any maid,
He practiced no deceit nor said ⎤
Insulting words or words of spite. ⎮
He was a true and perfect knight, ⎮   70
Not overweening or contentious. ⎦
His horse was good but unpretentious.
He wore a shirt of homespun stuff,
Armor-rusty, coarse, and rough,
For he had lately been abroad
And rode to make his peace with God.
    Beside him rode his son and SQUIRE
A lovesome, lusty bachelor,   80
Whose locks were crisped as in a press—
Some twenty years of age I guess.
His build was of the middling sort,
Well knit and apt for every sport,
He too had been in chivalry
In northern France and Picardy,
And served well in that little space
To win a certain lady's grace.
In robes like meadows, as we said,
Picked out in flowers of white and red,   90
He sang and whistled all the day,
As fresh as is the month of May.
His gown was short; its cut was fair.
He sat his horse without a care,
Inventing songs and poems at will,
A handy lad with lance or quill,
A lover too, warm blooded, hale,
And sleepless as a nightingale.
Yet he was courteous. He knew his part,
And served his knight with courtly art.   100
    A YEOMAN, their subordinate
(They fared abroad with little state),
Went with them in a hood of green.
A sheath of arrows, bright and keen,
Rode at his belt, beside his hand.
There was no yeoman in the land
Whose tackle made a finer show,

From polished straps to mighty bow.
Short-cropped hair, a creased, brown face,
A horse well suited to the chase,   110
An archer's guard upon his arm,
A sword and shield to ward off harm,
A silver dagger on his haunch,
To part a joint or rip a paunch,
A Christopher upon on his breast,   *Saint Christopher medal*
A horn, a baldric, and the rest,
Proclaimed him woodsman, and the best.
    A nun there was, a PRIORESS,
Her smiling seemed a harmless folly,
Her strongest oath was "gosh" or "golly."   120
They called her Madame Eglantine,   *name suited to a heroine of romance*
And claimed her singing was divine,
Tuned through her nose with elegance.
She used the tongue and airs of France,
But used them with outlandish features,
As taught to her by English teachers.
At meals she coyly sipped or nibbled,
And never missed her mouth nor dribbled.
Her fingers barely skimmed her sauce,
Transporting food without a loss   130
To slide or trickle down her chest,
And mar the manners she professed.
She wiped her lips with such great pain
That in her cup no drop remained
Of grease when she had sipped a drink.
Her grace made common people shrink!
Behaving well with such facility,
She seemed far nobler than nobility,
All dignity, the height of fashion.
But let me mention her compassion: 140
Holding all God's creatures dear,
She could not watch without a tear
A mouse, even, if she saw it suffer.
Her lap dogs' lives were scarcely rougher,
She fed them roast and fine white loaves,
And wept if one should die, or oafs
Walloped it and made it smart—

All conscience and a tender heart.
Her wimple styled the latest way,
A well-formed nose and eyes of gray,   150
A dainty mouth, pursed soft and red,
And over them a broad forehead—
About a hand's-breadth wide, I own.
You'd hardly call her undergrown.
Her cloak was soft and finely napped;
And round about her arm was wrapped
A rosary of coral and green.
Its golden brooch, fit for a queen,
Showed a proud, crowned *A* without a flaw,
Then *Amor vincit omnia.*   *"Love conquers all."*[4]
    With her came her secretary,
And three tame priests to fetch and carry.
    A forceful MONK rode near the front,
A chief and master of the hunt,
A manly man, fit for an abbot,
But horseman first by choice and habit.
His bridle's jingling was as clear
And sounded sweetly on the ear
As church bells tolling to the people
Around his little chapel's steeple.   170
The holy Rule of Benedict,
Because he thought it somewhat strict,
This Monk was eager to renounce
And live instead among his mounts.
He wouldn't bet a half-plucked hen
That hunters aren't holy men
Or that a monk who hunts and shoots
Is pointless as a fish in boots—
That is, a monk out of his cloister.
Such maxims aren't worth an oyster.   180
I found his logic ironclad;
Why should he study and go mad, ⎤
Through ceaseless reading in his cell, ⎟
Or work until he grew unwell, ⎟
As Augustine bids? What a dunce! ⎦

4. A secular motto that could also have a religious meaning.

Let Augustine labor if he wants!
This Monk rode with all his might.
His hounds were swift as birds in flight.
At his pet pastime, hunting hare,
There was no outlay he would spare.   190
His sleeves were lined, and warm as felt,
With the finest squirrel pelts.
To gather his hood beneath his chin,
He wore a well-wrought golden pin.
This love knot held the fabric fast.
His head was bald and shown like glass,
As did his features, red and gleaming.
He was full fat and hearty seeming,
With glaring eyes, a bit bloodshot,
Fierce as the fire beneath a pot.   200
His proud steed, preening like a pigeon,
Did further credit to religion.
This Monk was no one's bloodless ghost,
A fat swan was his favorite roast.
His horse was brown as any berry.

    A FRIAR there was, wanton and merry,
A beggar of most rare dispatch.
No friar anywhere could match
The way he flattered girls and flirted,   *negative*
Made free with them and then diverted   210
Funds to wed them at his expense.
He was a man of consequence,
Well beloved and widely known   *positive*
· In neighborhoods he called his own.
On wives he made a great impression
For he had power of confession,
Far greater than a lesser cleric,
A brand-name shriver, not generic.
He'd crown the grossest peccadilloes,
With admonitions soft as pillows   220
And a gentle penance at the close
If you were rich, for Heaven knows,
Fat offerings against perdition
Bespeak a most sincere contrition.
A penitent dispensing alms

Earned this Friar's smoothest balms.
For many have a stony heart
And cannot weep although they smart,
And therefore in default of weeping,
Place silver in the Church's keeping. 230
This Friar's hood was packed with knives
And pins to offer pretty wives,
And he could sing and strum a chord
To start a dance or please a lord.
His ballads brimmed with piquancy.
His neck was white as fleurs-de-lys.
Bullish as a champion,
He knew the bars in every town
And thought more of a tavern schlepper
Than any homeless wretch or leper, 240
For such a worthy man as he,
In keeping with his dignity,
Must hold himself above the gutters
In every act and word he utters.
Fie on the sickly, unwashed hordes!
Give him the moneyed class and lords.
That was where his profit lay.
He filled his role in every way,
Begging well enough to be
Awarded by his friary 250
A rich, exclusive territory,
A princely mendicant signore
A widow without board or batten
Encountering his euphonious Latin
Would give, despite her indigence.
His income trebled his expense.
And he could gambol like a pup,
Step in and make a quarrel up.
He was no skinny anchorite
Nor shared a scholar's squalid plight.
No, he went proudly like a pope. 260
Of double worsted was his cope,
Creased like a bell from careful pressing.
He lisped to sound more prepossessing
And mince the English on his tongue.

I noticed when he harped or sung,
His eyes shown from his head as bright
As stars do on a frosty night.
Huberd was this worthy's name.

    Next a bearded MERCHANT came;   270
In parti-colored clothes he sat,
Beneath a Flemish beaver hat.
His boots were of the finest sort,
His proclamations round and short
And mostly of the deals he made
And growing threats to foreign trade
Up and down the English coast.
A financier, to hear him boast,
His eyes were turned beyond the seas
Manipulating currencies   280
And leveraged debts and deals in kind.
No one could sound his bottom line.
He was a worthy man, I guess.
I missed his name, though, I confess.

    There was an Oxford CLERK as well,
A logic student unexcelled,
Astride a horse built like a rake
And lean, himself, as any snake,
Hollow looking, a bit remote.
All threadbare was his overcoat.   290
He had no sinecure in Kent,
Parish ladies, lands to rent,
But lined up books around his bed
Twenty tomes in black and red,
Of sober Aristotle's teaching,
No fancy robes or fiddle screeching.
He relished only ancient learning
Although it rarely led to earning.
The pittances his friends provided
He spent on books, although they chided,   300
And prayed for them in shrines and churches,
For underwriting his researches.
With all those axioms in his head,
He seldom looked about or said
A needless word, but still you knew

That he had thought things through and through.
Careful reading shaped his speech.
He was glad to learn and glad to teach.
　A MAN OF LAW was on our jaunt,
Well known in every lawyers' haunt,   310
A fount of ancient legal fribbles,
To tie up courts with lawyers' quibbles.
His wit was deepest, opinions wisest,
A frequent justice of assizes
By royal appointment and commission.
His standing and his great ambition
Brought streams of gold in gleaming spate
Which he deployed in real estate.
Confronting such a legal idol,
No one would dare dispute his titles.   320
He made the air around him buzz,
Yet seemed far busier than he was.
He knew each law and precedent,
How it applied, and what it meant,
Since William's reign—each lawyers' fix
Dating to 1066.
No instrument this man dictated
Had ever been invalidated.
He rode in a silk-belted coat
With stripes, but nothing else of note.   330
　Beside the lawyer rode a FRANKLIN,   *a prosperous landowner*
A snow-white beard adorned his chin.
With ruddy cheeks and shining head,
He broke his fast with wine and bread.
He'd long enjoyed a life luxurious,
For he had found with Epicurus,
Abundant pleasure, not simplicity,
The truest measure of felicity.
A potentate in his locality
And patron saint of hospitality,   340
His bread and ale were unsurpassed,
The holdings of his cellar, vast.
His table groaned with smoking dishes
Of roasted game and seasoned fishes.
The house snowed first-rate meat and drink,

With delicacies to make you blink,
Pegged to the season of the year,
From berry pies to autumn deer.
He raised fat partridges in runs
And served up perch and pikes well done.   350
Woe to the cook if the sauce was bland:
"Hot and sharp!" was his command.
His board stayed mounted in the hall
Spread like a food seller's stall.
As local justice, he'd been sent
By his home shire to Parliament.
A short sword and a purse of silk
Hung at his belt as white as milk.
A sheriff once, and court commissioner,
He was his borough's prime parishioner.   360
    A CARPENTER and a TRINKET BUYER,
Two WEAVERS, and a PIECE-GOODS DYER,
Rode solemnly and fitly horsed
In livery their guilds endorsed.
Each item of their gear was new.
With finest silver, bright as dew,
Their knives were trimmed and pouches filled.
Each one was burgherhood distilled.
They knew each scrap of local trade,
Sat in their merchants' hall and weighed   370
The latest deals, who lost or won,
Each rumbling like an alderman.
Their properties and rents spread wide;
Their wives surveyed the town with pride,
And well they should. They knew their worth.
Ladies by custom if not by birth,
They ruled at large in their domains,
With serving boys to bear their trains.
    A COOK was there, the very man
To braise a chicken in a pan   380
With marrow bones and sweet-sour spices,
Or quaff, left to his own devices,
Good London ale, or poach or fry,
Or heat a hash or bake a pie.
He had, although it seemed a sin,

A runny ulcer on his shin,
For his white mousses were the best.
   There was a SHIPMAN from the west.
From Dartmouth or nearby, I guessed.
Bouncing on a low-bred nag,   390
His wool gown drooping like a bag.
His knife hung from a sailor's lanyard,
And he was as brown as any Spaniard
Where the sun had burned his skin—
A thruster with a wolfish grin,
The first upon his ship who crept
To sample the wine while the shipper slept.
Remorselessly, beneath the waves,
He sent sea captives to their graves.
He knew the lore of winds and tides,   400
And currents, rocks, and reefs besides,
Harbors, moons, and navigation,
No better man in any nation.
He faced the blackest storms at sea
With perfect equanimity,
No sea-borne danger made him falter
From Oslo down beyond Gibraltar.
Each inlet town from France to Spain
Had seen his ship, the *Magdelaine*.
   Next came a prominent PHYSICIAN,   410
A proper medical patrician.
His dosages and surgery
Were grounded in astrology.
In fact, he treated all his cases
By the stars' great wheeling traces,
Interpreting the sky's aspect
With charts and figures to detect
The hidden causes of each malady,
Whether hot or cold or moist or dry,
Where it grew and what it fed on,   420
So he could stop its progress head on.
When he knew the cause for sure,
He'd prescribe the proper cure,
And if the patient was unwary,
He'd also pick the apothecary.

For years they'd greased each other's palms
With graft and kickbacks, merchant's alms.
Aesculapius, Dioscorides,   *two thousand years' worth of medical*
He knew the best authorities,   *luminaries from Greece*
Each pill purveying theory spinner   *(Aesculapius and Dioscorides)*
From Hippocrates to Avicenna,   *to England (Gilbertus*
Through every modern theory, thus   *Anglicus)*
Down to Gilbertus Anglicus.
Seldom lavish at his meat,
This doctor's food was plain and neat,
Moderate dishes, healthful, fit.
He took no joy in Holy Writ.
His clothes matched any of our crew's,
Rich taffetas in reds and blues.
Yet he'd got most of them for free   440
From sufferers, to settle fees.
Gold is good for many an ill,
So he sought gold with all his skill.
     A WIFE OF BATH rode in the crowd,
Half deaf, unless your voice was loud.
The trade she drove in woven stuffs
Surpassed the Belgians right enough.   *famous cloth makers*
No wife, however fond of glory,
Preceded her to Offertory,   *the offering at Mass*
Or if one did, then she would vow   450
An awful vengeance on the cow.
Her coverchiefs would weigh, when starched,
Ten pounds apiece and grandly arched
Each Sunday high above her head.
Her stockings were of scarlet red,
Shaping the calves above her shoes.
Her looks were bold and ruddy too.
Her taste for fights and bold carouses
Had quite undone her first five spouses
And sundry boyfriends in her youth.   460
(To mention these would be uncouth.)
On three trips to the Holy Land,
She mastered hardships like a man.
She'd gone to Rome and to Boulogne,   *pilgrimage sites*
Galicia and then Cologne.

Love was her life's leitmotif,
As shown by gaps between her teeth. *a mark of lechery*
Upon an ambling horse she sat,
Wimpled well beneath a hat
As broad as any soldier's shield. 470
Below her waist a robe revealed
Sharp, gleaming spurs. She was
A boon companion, but one with claws,
And knew as well as any dance
Each stage and gambit of romance.
    A PARSON of a town came next,
Poor in gold, but one suspects
Richer than most in holy works.
He was a learned man, a clerk.
Deep gospel-lore informed his preaching, 480
And daily life and moral teaching.
He was benign and diligent,
Even tempered and content,
Though life for him was seldom blithe.
He'd curse no one who couldn't tithe,
But gave out food and clothes and more—
All that he could to help the poor—
Drawn from the Church and his own savings.
Long temperance had quelled his cravings.
Although his flock was widely scattered, 490
Storms or distance never mattered:
Near or far, great or small,
He'd visit anyone at all,
Tramping on foot the direst traces.
He put things in their proper places,
For, "First he wrought, and then he taught
Because the Gospel said he ought."
He had another motto too:
"If gold rusts, what will iron do?"
If a priest is foul, with souls in trust, 500
Why should a layman curb his lust?
This sight must make the angels weep:
A shepherd shittier than his sheep.
A priest's commitment should be ample
To lead his people by example.

This Parson never hired a curate
To tend his parish and secure it,
While he himself besieged the Church
For an easy job that he could shirk
Or a post as chaplain to some guild.   510
No, he stayed home to watch and build
Against the wolf, lest sheep miscarry,
A shepherd, not a mercenary.
But though a priest of sterling worth,
He spurned no other man on earth
Nor took a domineering tone.
Indeed, his fellow-feeling shown
In every word, for saving souls
Was always first among his goals.
But faced with hardened, stiff-necked scoffers,   520
However placed or full their coffers,
He'd prick their wicked hides, I'm bound.
No better parson could be found,
A lowly man and free from vice,
Not finely dressed nor over-nice,
But like Christ's humble first attendants,
In Heaven's light he shone resplendent.
    Next came a PLOWMAN, the Parson's brother,
Who shoveled dung like any other.
An honest laborer was he,   530
Living in peace and charity.
He worshipped God with all he had
On all occasions, good or bad,
And loved his neighbors selflessly.
He had no faults that I could see.
For he would freely plow and more
For Christ alone to aid the poor,
He paid his tithes without a question,
Ten percent of his possessions.
He wore a smock with ragged sleeves.   540
    Next came MILLER and a REEVE,
A SUMMONER, a PARDONER,
A MANCIPLE, and, at the rear,
Myself, the last of all the party.
    The MILLER was both stout and hearty.

He used his brawn and piston thighs
In wrestling and won each prize.
He was broad, short-shouldered, thick—
Unhinging doors was his pet trick,
Or breaking through them with his head!   550
His outspread beard was foxy red
And broad and solid as a spade.
The skin upon his nose had made
A wart, crowned with a tuft of hairs,
Red as the bristles in an old sow's ears.
His nostrils were hairy, black, and wide.
He bore a short sword at his side.
His mouth gaped open like a cauldron,
Spewing language that appalled one,
All japes of sin and harlotry.   560
He doubled every rightful fee
And weighed out flour with a golden thumb.   *That is, he used his thumb*
In white and blue clothes, all and some,   *to depress the scales.*
He clamped a bagpipe between his lips
And led us forward on our trip.

   The MANCIPLE labored, by report,
Purchasing goods for an Inn of Court,   *one of several legal societies*
A model man in these affairs,   *in London*
Buying food or wine or wares
In such a wily, complex fashion,   570
He always got his private ration.
Now isn't it an act of God,
When such a plain, untutored clod
Can bilk a canny, learned crew?
For all his thirty masters knew
Every law from *A* to *Z.*
Most were fit to keep the keys
And deftly manage large estates
For any lord, however great,
And make him dwell within his means   580
And pay his debts and cool his spleen,
To live as sparsely as they said—
Or they could lead a shire instead
Through any crises or mishaps—
And yet this scamp set all their caps!

The choleric REEVE was next to pass.
He scraped his cheeks as smooth as glass
And trimmed his hair on front and sides,
Like a poor priest's coif down to the hide.
His legs were lean as any staff,   590
Straight sticks without a trace of calf.
His record keeping was arcane,
So no one else could count his gains,
Transforming nature's starts and stops
To meat and hay and milk and crops.
Whole herds of cows and other stock
From sheep to pigs and poultry flocks
Were solely in this steward's hands.
All things had run at his commands,
Since his lord came of age at twenty.   600
No one had seen him steal a penny.
No underling on his estate
Could hoodwink him. He ruled their fate,
And kept them honest out of fear.
He owned a fine house standing near
Upon a stately, shaded plot.
He could afford it. His lord could not.
He hoarded up his secret riches,
And sometimes scratched his lordship's itches
With funds he skimmed from the estate;   610
Or else he let the young lord wait.
In youth he'd learned a trade aright,
He was a carpenter, a wood wright.
He rode a stylish dappled gray
Named Scot. This was his one display.
His surcoat was a dark blue shade,
Hung with a poor, rust-pitted blade.
A man of Norfolk, as I heard tell,
Near a town called Baldeswell,
He tucked his skirts up like a friar,   620
And trailed behind in this attire.
    The SUMMONER with us in that place
Bore a fire-red cherub's face   *Chaucer's reference here is obscure.*
With raging acne, puffy eyes,
A flaming lecher by his guise.

His scaling brows and scabby beard
Made up a visage children feared.
No lead-based salve or keen attar—
Brimstone, borax, cream of tartar—
No paste with sharp astringent bite   630
Could tame his pimples, red and white,
Or dry the pustules on his cheeks.
He lived on garlic, onions, leeks,
And wine as strong and red as rubies—
Too strong at least for this poor booby—
For when the wine had seized his reins
Scraps of Latin filled his brains,
He knew some terms, just two or three,
That he had plucked from some decree,
Words he encountered every day.   640
(Of course you know a brainless jay
Can call out "Walter" like the pope.)
But then he soon ran out of rope.
We saw his lack of wit for sure as
He bawled his nonsense tag, *"Quid iurus?"*   *"Which law [applies here]?"*
He was a loose, confiding fellow,
A veteran barfly, kind and mellow;
For no more than a quart of wine,
He'd let you keep a concubine
Twelve months and then excuse you for it.   650
He liked himself to pluck a pullet.
As he would tell his fellow sinners,
Fear of the Church is for beginners
Unless your soul is in your purse,
For gifts will trump a deacon's curse.
"You pay to play," was his pet line.
At worst you'd pay a church court's fine.
(But I rejected all he said.
Myself, I hold the Church in dread.
Church curses are the spirit's bane!   660
Church courts can lock you up in chains!)
He kept young girls beneath his thumb.
They did his will to keep him mum,
For he could publicize each sin.
Now strong ale made him reel and grin.

A tavern garland crowned his head;
He bore a shield, a loaf of bread.
    Beside him rode a PARDONER
Of Rouncivale, his friend and peer.   *a religious institution in London*
This man, though lately come from Rome,   670
Sang all the latest songs from home.
The Summoner caught the beat and thumped it,
And sang along, loud as a trumpet.
This Pardoner's hair was pale like wax
And hung as limp as beaten flax,
Spreading across his back in hanks,
Damp, oily locks, and stringy ranks.
Though it was thinning, he was vain;
He wore no hood in sun or rain,
But rode uncovered mile on mile   680
In what he thought the latest style.
His head was bare but for a cap.
His glaring eyes would dart and snap.
His badge recalled Veronica's veil.   *with its image of Christ*
His wallet bulged like a pouch of mail,
Brim full with pardons signed and sealed.
His fluting treble voice revealed,
A girlish nature. He never shaved
And never had to. He behaved
Much like a gelding or a mare.   690
Still, in his pardoner's craft nowhere
Was anyone with more audacity.
A pillowcase, by his mendacity,
Became Our Blessed Mother's veil.
He had a piece of that same sail
Saint Peter raised the day he tried
To walk the sea at Jesus' side.
He rattled a brass cross full of stones
And a fusty jar of moldy bones.
With tools like these to gain him entry   700
He fleeced the country clods and gentry,
Clearing enough in just one day
To match two months of parson's pay.
His lurid talk and phony treasures
Made money flow in at his pleasure.

For one of his distrusted caste,
He was a fine ecclesiast,
A great hand for a psalm or story,
Still better singing Offertory.
Because he knew when this was done   710
It would be time to file his tongue
And preach to win a great oblation,
He sang with rare anticipation.
    And so I have described for you
The state and nature of our crew—
How we met and joined to ride
From Southwark by the mild Thames' side
At the Tabard, near the Bell.
Now it's time for me to tell
All the plans we settled on   720
Before we left the inn at dawn.
And then I'll undertake to say
What fell to us along the way.
But first, I beg your courtesy.
Good friends, don't count it villainy
If I speak plainly in my tale;
I have to, or my work will fail!
I must convey the things I heard
And tell my stories word for word.
An author who is conscientious   730
Must be objective, not tendentious.
Every word must be related
Or he can justly be berated
For telling lies or feigning matters,
Leaving honest truth in tatters.
He must spare no one, not his brother,
Noble pa, or saintly mother.
Christ himself spoke plainly in
Holy writ, condemning sin.
Plato adds, if you can read,   740
Words must be brother to the deed.
To head off other criticism,
I'm hardly preaching social schism
By putting pilgrims out of order.
I'm not their marshal—just recorder.

Our HOST drew us into accord
As we assembled round his board
With food and smiles, a nod, a wink,
And all the wine we cared to drink.
A seemly man in form and feature,   750
The perfect after-dinner speaker.
He ran the house to suit his whims,
The finest landlord on the Thames—
The life and breath of any party,
Bold and witty, warm and hearty,
And in all ways a merry man.
Just after supper he began,
When we had paid our reckonings,
To speak of mirth and other things,
And said, "Now, gentle people all,   760
You're surely welcome in this hall.
I tell you, and I never lie,
I've seen no finer company
Assembled this year at my inn.
Seldom have my feelings been
So well engaged. Now, if I might,
Let me propose a plan tonight.
    "You go to Canterbury—good, Godspeed;
Saint Thomas help you in your need!
But nothing makes the way seem short   770
Like travelers' games or other sport;
All it takes to make you drag
Is sitting dumbly like a bag
Of senseless rocks. Ah, you agree!
Why then, my friends, attend to me.
Pledge one and all to join my plan,
And put yourselves at my command.
If you do everything I say,
Tomorrow, riding on your way,
I swear by my dead father's name,   780
You'll think this journey's just a game.
Show your hands if you assent!"
    We gave unanimous consent.
No one wanted to debate it.
We were too jolly and elated,

And begged him to expound his scheme.
"Friends," he said, "I'd never dream
Of drawing out my words in vain.
I'll say my piece both short and plain.
Swear each of you will tell two tales   790
Along the Canterbury trail;
Two more as you come back again.
Four tales won't tax the lightest brain;
Just tell of old things from the past.
The pilgrim we shall judge at last
Preeminent in storytelling—
The one whose tale is most compelling—
Will have a supper at our cost,
'Our' meaning all the folks who lost.
The journey finished, by Our Lord,   800
We'll reassemble at my board.
And with you I myself will ride;
I'll pay my way and be your guide.
Anyone refusing my behests
Must bear the costs for all the rest.
Tomorrow, if this concord suits,
We'll all set out along your route."
       We relished all he said and swore.
That done, we asked him one thing more:
That he would oversee the contest,   810
Assign the tales, judge which was best,
And set the winner's bill of fare.
We would honor, for our share,
All his commands. Thus by accord
We took our landlord at his word.
More wine was brought. We shared a toast.
Each pledged the others and our Host,
And then we yawned our way to bed.
       Next morning when the east was red,
Our wakeful Host—he was our cock—   820
Drew us together in a flock,
And led us at an ambling pace
Out to a pilgrims' watering place.
There he stopped and peered around.
"Friends," he said, "I've always found

It's best to reaffirm a contract
The morning after. If our pact
Survived the night, now I will name
The first tale-teller and start our game.
This is where your pledge commences.   830
Comply, or pay the rest's expenses.
Draw straws, and let shortest win.
The one who holds it will begin.
Sir Knight," he said, "respected lord,
Draw first to honor our accord.
You next," he told the Prioress,
"And then the Clerk and all the rest."
We weren't shy; we crowded near;
Compared our straws with lively cheer;
And in truth, it turned out well   840
For what we wished was what befell:
The Knight had plucked the shortest straw.
I swear that no one rigged the draw.
But we all thought it for the best
The noblest man should lead the rest.
That should be plain to anyone.
When the knight learned he had won,
We knew he'd do just as he should,
And tell the finest tale he could.
He said, "I shall begin the game,   850
And nothing loath, in God's great name!
So listen now to what I say."
We set our horses on their way,
As he began with pleasant cheer
To tell his tale, as you may hear.

THE KNIGHT

THE KNIGHT'S TALE

The Knight tells a long story based on Il Teseida, *an Italian poem of Boccaccio's. The great Athenian hero Theseus has defeated the Amazons and married their queen, Hippolyte. Returning to Athens, he meets a company of Theban ladies grieving because the dictator Creon killed their husbands and will not allow the bodies to be buried.*

Enraged, Theseus sacks Thebes, kills Creon, and returns the bones of the slain husbands to their wives. Meanwhile his pillagers find two royal cousins half alive among the wounded, the young Theban knights Palamon and Arcite (Ar-SEET). Theseus transports these two to Athens and locks them, without hope of ransom, in a tower overlooking the palace where he lives with Hippolyte and her lovely sister Emily.

Until one blooming dawn in May
Emily stepped forth like a queen,
Soft white amid the gardens' green,
As fresh as any flower that grows.
Her cheeks could match the chastest rose;
No eye could choose between the two.
That day, as she was used to do,
The girl walked out to take the air,
For May allowed no sluggards there.
That month unlocks each gentle heart   10
From winter with resistless art,
And says, "Arise, and honor me!"
Swift to heed sweet May's decree,
Young Emily rose in reverence,
And clothed herself without pretense.
Her hair, coifed in a golden braid,
Hung down a yard behind the maid.
Outdoors she watched the mild sun rise

And strolled the walks and fed her eyes,
Gathering flowers of white and red   20
To weave a garland for her head,
And singing with an angel's grace.
A great tower loomed above the place.
The castle's strongest keep and ward,
Where captives languished under guard—
The young knights' prison, stark and tall.
This tower adjoined the garden wall
Where Emily relished every flower
Unfolding in that sunlit hour.
No sun could cheer young Palamon;   30
Still, he had risen up and gone
To peer out high above the town—
The garden too, where, looking down,
Among the shining branches there
He might have seen a sight more fair.
As Emily paced upon the lawn,
This wretched prisoner, Palamon,
Stalked his chamber to and fro,
Forgotten, hopeless, racked by woe.
He wished for death, called out, "Alas!"   40
But then at length it came to pass
That through the window and its bars
(Black, heavy iron ones, thick as spars)
His wandering eye found Emily.
He blanched at once and cried, "Ah, me!"
And felt her beauty pierce his heart.
Arcite sat upright with a start,
And said, "My cousin! What's amiss!
How pale you look! Now, by my bliss,
Why such a cry? Because we're bound?   50
That's just the way our fates are wound.
Our outlook's bleak. I know it too.
Ill luck wronged me as well as you.
A bad aspect or evil station
Of Saturn or some constellation
Destroyed our prospects here on earth.
Malign stars doomed us at our birth.

We must endure. Coz, that is plain."
　　But Palamon answered with disdain,
"Truly, cousin, that's our plight,　　　　　　　　60
But I can bear it like a knight.
This prison didn't cause my cry.
No, I was wounded through the eye,
Stabbed to the heart, as God's my law!
A shining lady that I saw,
Among the garden paths below,
Has plunged my very life in woe.
Lady? Say, rather, she's divine—
Venus herself, unless I'm blind."
He fell in prayer upon his knees.　　　　　　　　70
"Goddess," he said, "since you are pleased
To show yourself to me this way,
Oh, rescue us without delay!
Free us from this wretched fate
Or if the gods hold us in hate
And we must die here in this fashion,
Please show our city your compassion,
Deliver Thebes from tyranny!"
And now Arcite edged round to see
The girl his cousin thought a goddess.　　　　　　80
He looked—and, lo! she seemed no less.
If Palamon was wounded sore,
Arcite was hurt as much or more.
He sighed and called out piteously,
"Her beauty slays me suddenly.
My mistress, she who roams below,
Has tendered me a killing blow.
I cannot live without her love,
Or sight of her here from above!"
　　Palamon heard his cousin's cry　　　　　　　90
And answered with a flashing eye:
"Say, do you speak in truth or jest?"
　　"Brother," said Arcite, "as I am blessed,
My statement was entirely earnest."
Palamon's brows knit at their sternest.
"Cousin," he said, "you go astray

To mock my love or else betray
Me, your cousin and your brother,
When we are sworn to aid each other.
We pledged—I hope you didn't lie—   100
To help each other till we die,
To put our friendship well above
All earthly things, like women's love,
And work together as we should.
You swore to this and thought it good.
That was the oath we made each other.
You won't foreswear it, will you, brother?
You know I'm struck, without a doubt.
Will you renege and creep about
To love the lady I adore   110
This instant and forevermore?
Ah, Arcite, don't be my foe!
I loved her first and told you so
In perfect trust, upon my head!
I hold you fast to all you said.
You pledged your honor as a knight.
Help me now by all that's right,
Or shall I say that you're foresworn?"
    Arcite regarded him with scorn:
"Ha! Palamon is false, not I.   120
Let me show you how and why.
I took her for my paramour,
An earthly creature, well before
You guessed that she was not divine.
While you were kneeling at her shrine,
I loved her with a lover's passion,
And said so in a downright fashion,
Assuming you would give *me* aid.
But say you loved her as a maid.
Don't you know that old clerks' saw,   130
That lovers are above the law?
Love's urgings cancel other vows.
I love her—that you must allow.
If this is lawless, well, abhor me.
Others have done the same before me.

Men must love despite their pledges,
No matter what the world alleges,
Even if she's someone's wife.
Yet think! Can you in all your life
Obtain her grace? No more can I.   140
No matter how we rail and cry
We'll die right here. That's all and some.
No clemency for us, or ransom.
We're like the dogs who found a bone,
And squabbled till their chance was flown.
A kite, when they had fought all day,
Flew down and snatched their bone away!
You know when kings hold court, my brother,
Each man competes with every other.
Give her your heart, and let me too;   150
For now that's all that we can do.
No prisoner's love suit advances.
So love alike and take our chances."

This remains the cousins' situation until Theseus' friend Pirithous, who had known Arcite in Thebes, arranges for the young knight to be released but banished from Athens. Arcite's reaction is anguish. With no hope of seeing Emily, he's actually unluckier than Palamon. A prisoner prays for deliverance, he muses, and when it comes he's devastated:

"Oh, who can tell why folks complain
As if God's plans for them were vain?
They get their wish, and it denies
What might have saved them otherwise.
A man who prays for heaps of wealth
Succumbs to thieves or ruins his health.
A wretch in prison seeks release.   160
His household slays him at a feast.
Endless harms arise from this.
We have our will, yet run amiss.
We act like one drunk as a mouse.
He knows right well he has a house
But can't remember how to find it,
And slips and slides like one who's blinded.

Thus men seek good, but then obtain
Mere worldly ends that prove their bane."

*Palamon feels even worse. He's certain Arcite will raise an army and return to
win Emily. His loss, he thinks, must be a punishment from heaven:*

"Cruel gods ordained this for my ill,   170
For all things happen by their will.
They rule the future, they alone;
Their words are heavy, set in stone.
What are we human folk to them,
But cowering sheep whom they condemn?
For men, like any beasts, are slain
Or locked away to live in pain,
And find their health or fortune spilt
Through random chances, not through guilt.
    "What species of foreknowing god   180
Could beat the righteous with his rod,
And then, to make their anguish worse,
Subvert their nature with this curse:
To thwart for his sake their own will
Just where a beast may his fulfill?
Then too, a dead beast feels no pains
But when men die their souls remain
To suffer, though their lives were bitter.
That's what we face, and nothing fitter.
And why? Let theologians say;   190
Their answers won't drive pain away.
Alas, a snake or slinking thief
Who's brought the finest men to grief
Now goes at large, up hill, down dell,
While Saturn pens me in this cell,
And savage Juno hounds me too,
With further ruin for Thebes in view,
Although its walls are scattered wide,
While Venus wrings my other side,
For fear now that Arcite's at large."   200

*So Arcite is free but banished from Athens, and Palamon can glimpse Emily from
time to time in the garden but is confined as hopelessly as ever to his cell. Who*

has the better lot? Part Two of the tale follows Arcite to Thebes, where he pines
away for love of Emily.

He couldn't sleep; food made him sick,
As brittle as a dried-up stick.
His face was grim and hollow eyed,
Yellow looks from ashen hide.
He slunk about or lurked alone
And walked out late to wail and moan.
If he heard music or someone sang,
It gave his heart an added pang.
Relentless weeping, sunken spirits,
Consumed his voice, if you could hear it.   210
No one would know him by his sound.
In every way he trailed around,
Not just as one whom love is burning,
But like a man whose wits are turning
As melancholy bile and fumes
Flood his sick brain's deepest rooms,
And hopeless sorrow, hot despairing,
Destroy his aspect and his bearing.

After a year or two the god Mercury sends Arcite to Athens, where, Mercury says,
his sorrows will end. Arcite complies, realizing he is so altered by grief that no
one in Athens will know him anyway. This proves to be the case. Calling him-
self Philostrate (PHIL o STRAIT) he finds a place as Emily's page of the cham-
ber, serving her so well he is eventually appointed Theseus' squire and makes him-
self indispensable to the duke.

Meanwhile Palamon languishes seven years, until one May he drugs his
keeper and escapes into the woods nearby. He means to make his way to Thebes,
raise an army, and win Emily by force, as he once thought Arcite would. Pala-
mon is hiding in a thicket when Arcite happens along, gathering flowers at
dawn:

The busy lark, announcing day,
Sings to salute the morrow gray,   220
And fiery Phoebus flames so bright
The eastern sky laughs in his sight
As he strews sunbeams and retrieves
The brilliant dewdrops from the leaves.

Although Palamon doesn't recognize him at first, Arcite falls into a brown study,
as lovers will, and loudly complains against Juno and fate, identifying himself
and recounting his love for Emily. Palamon is close enough to hear all this.

Near his heart
He felt a gliding, icy sword.
He shook with ire; his pulses roared
When he had heard the other's tale.
A crazy man, wide eyed and pale,
He bolted from his hiding place,   230
Exclaimed, "Arcite! So false, so base?
You love my lady as you say,
For whom I've suffered to this day.
You share my blood and knew my mind,
Sat nodding by as I repined.
And now you've duped Duke Theseus,
Changed everything about you thus!
Well, surely one of us will die
Before you gain my Emily!
We'll settle this before you go,   240
You see here Palamon, your foe.
Though I've no weapon in this place,
But just escaped the tower by grace,
I'll fight you naked as I came.
Now die or quit your wicked claim!
Take your choice; you won't escape."

Because Palamon is unarmed, the cousins agree that Arcite will gather two suits
of armor and return to the woods the next day for a fight to the death. When he
arrives . . .

Straight, without a word of greeting,
Each armed the other for their meeting,
As brothers might. They donned their gear,
And then at once each grasped a spear,   250
Two stout ash shafts they could rely on,
And Palamon lashed out like a lion,
Well matched with tigerish Arcite.
They crashed like boars in violent heat;
With frothing mouths they slashed and tore,

Ankle-deep in crimson gore.
Now leave them fighting as they must,
And let me tell of Theseus.
    Great destiny, God's minister
Rules high and low, as clerks aver,   260
And shapes all things to his foreknowledge
So strictly, though the world allege
A thing won't happen, come what may,
Yet it observes its chosen day,
If only once each thousand years.
In truth, for all our hopes and fears,
War and peace and hate and love
Are destined in God's sight above.
    The heart of great Duke Theseus
Was filled with so much sporting lust,   270
And most for hunting harts in May,   *stags*
That in that month there dawned no day
But he was dressed and hot to ride
With hunt and hounds in joyous pride.
Stag hunting was his chief delight,
And nothing cooled his appetite
For coursing in the boldest manner,
For after Mars he served Diana.
    The day was fair, as I have said,
The duke rode out and with him led   280
Hippolyte, his sovereign queen,
And Emily, clad all in green,
To summon forth the royal chase.
Within a grove quite near the place
His scouts had spied a noble hart.
With small discussion they depart,
The duke to wait beside a glade
Along a trail the stag had made
And where he'd flee pursuing hounds
To ford a brook upon the grounds.   290
The duke could run at him at will
Or turn him for the dogs to kill.
    But when the lord took up his stand,
The clearing was already manned,
For stout Arcite and Palamon

Had picked that plot to scrimmage on,
Clashing like two rival boars.
Their swords enforced their hot amours
So stoutly that their lightest stroke
Seemed stark enough to fell an oak.   300
Not knowing who they were at first,
The duke spurred forward with a curse
And urged his mount between the two.
He drew his sword and shouted, "Hoo!
No more of this, or lose a head!
By Mars, that man shall tumble dead
Who strikes again without my word!
Who are you now, and why so stirred
To battle in these woods alone,
Unwitnessed, save by trees and stones,   310
As if you fought in royal lists?"
     Palamon stood forth to answer this.
"Great Duke," he said, "conserve your breath,
We each deserve a sudden death.
We are your enemies and captives,
And both are weary of our lives.
Since you're our rightful judge and lord,
Sire, put us wretches to the sword.
But slay me first for charity.
Just kill this hound along with me.   320
Or kill him first. You little know
That this is false Arcite, your foe,
And banished hence on pain of death.
Don't let him draw another breath.
He made his way inside your gate,
Insidiously, as Philostrate,
And hoodwinked you as he wound higher
And rose to be your trusted squire.
He loves your sister Emily.
This is my day to die, I see.   330
My lord, receive a true confession,
For I am luckless Palamon.
I broke your prison wickedly.
I am your foe. Lord, punish me.
My love to Emily the bright;

Extinguish me within her sight.
It's only fit that I should die.
So should this varlet standing by.
We both deserve that penalty."
   Duke Theseus answered wrathfully: 340
"Let it be so! You, Palamon!
Your words, however woebegone,
Have damned you. No need to seek
A torturer to make you speak.
You'll die indeed, by Mars the Red!"
   But then his queen for womanhead
Began to weep with Emily
And ladies of the company.
They thought it pity, one and all,
To see so harsh a chance befall   350
Two gentlemen of high estate,
Betrayed by Love to such debate.
The lovers' wounds, now gaping wide,
Melted the ladies so they cried:
"Have mercy, Lord, we pray you, please!"
And threw themselves upon their knees
And would have kissed his Lordship's feet.
Their pleading made his wrath retreat.
How pity wells in gentle hearts!
Though indignation made him smart,   360
The angry duke now sheathed his claws,
Reviewed the trespass and its cause.
And though stern ire swelled in his breast,
His reason laid rash thoughts to rest,
For well he knew a man in love
Will find a way to serve his dove
Or wrest himself out of a cell,
And in his heart he weighed as well
The women weeping at his knees.
To placate them and keep the peace,   370
He said unto himself, "Now, fie!
A lord's no lord who'd grace deny,
But lion-like gnash every foe.
Why treat each adversary so,
As if he were a stiff-necked man,

Resolved to end as he began?
A lord should have much keener vision
And weigh his judgments with precision
Smite pride, but foster humbleness."
And shortly as his ire grew less,　　　　　　　　380
He felt his fit of passion clear
And spoke aloud for all to hear:
　　"Don Cupid, benedicity,　　　　　　　*bless us*
Ah, what a mighty lord is he!
He treads our best defenses under;
Well is he called a god of wonder.
He holds each one of us at will
And shapes our course for good or ill.
Lo, this Arcite and Palamon
Escaped from me and might have gone　　　390
To live in Thebes in pleasant ease.
No hope to soften or appease
My fixed resolve to see them dead,
And yet that god has pinned them here
To lurk unknown in constant fear
And steered them to this mortal fight.
Say who can doubt the love-god's might!
What fool can match a man in love?
Here in the sight of gods above,
Look how they bleed! Ah, well arrayed!　　400
Thus has the god of lovers paid
These two for their obedience!
Yet lovers claim it's perfect sense
To live for love, beneath his yoke.
And, lo, here is a greater joke,
That she for whom they act this way
Can laugh with us at their display.
She knows as little of this pair
As daft cuckoo or staring hare!
Yet men must try both hot and cold　　　410
And act the fool though young or old—
There was a time, a long way back,
I languished under love's attack.
And thus I know how lovers feel
And how love summons them to heel.

Because I struggled in that snare,
Let amnesty absolve this pair
To please my queen, who's kneeling here
And also Emily, like dear.
But they must swear without reserve
To live in blameless peace and serve
My wishes and our country too.
Swear, younglings, as I urge you to,
And I'll forgive your every crime."
Each swore with scanty loss of time,
Implored his lordship for his grace,
And he complied with an embrace,
Then spoke of a yet nearer match:
   "For royalty and high estate,
Each one of you deserves a mate
Of sovereign rank or courtly standing,
Your place in life is that commanding.
But for my sister Emily,
For whom you feel such jealousy,
In truth, she cannot wed you both.
You must admit, however loath,
Fight till a thousand years have passed,
She must have one of you at last,
And one must whistle through a leaf.
One's triumph is the other's grief.
A maid may marry just one knight,
No matter how they squawk and fight.
Thus let me issue a decree
So each may have his destiny
As God intends. Now in this wise
Receive the plan I have devised.

Theseus allows the rivals fifty weeks to prepare for a tournament in Athens, one hundred men to a side. Emily will go to the knight who kills his opponent or drives him from the lists. The cousins are delighted.

Who beams with joy but Palamon?
Who capers now but bold Arcite?
Already burning to compete,
They shared the duke's view of their case

420

430

440

450

And thanked his lordship for his grace.
By now latecomers ringed the field.
They praised the duke's largess and kneeled,
But lowest bowed the rival knights.
And thus with hopes buoyed to the heights,
They rode to gather gear and friends
In ancient Thebes to serve their ends.

*Part Three opens with Theseus preparing royal lists for the tournament. The field
he set out was a mile around, walled, moated, and surrounded by a ring of tiered
seats rising to a height of sixty yards. This coliseum boasted shrines to Venus, Mars,
and Diana.*

In Venus' temple you might see,
In paintings grievous to behold,
The sleeplessness and quaking cold,   460
The sacred tears and lamentation,
The greedy fires of expectation,
That everyone in love alleges,
The broad assurance of their pledges—
Pleasure, Hope, Desire, Foolhardiness,
Beauty, Youth, Wealth flanked by Silliness,
Charm and Force, Lies, Flattery,
Expense, Solicitude, and Jealousy,
Who stood there with her marigolds,
And cuckoo, bane of jealous souls.   *symbol of cuckoldry*
Then feasts and music, winsome dancing,
Lust and clothes, the antic prancing
Of those whom pricking love enthralls,
Appeared in order on the walls,
With many pleasing, amorous scenes
Exalting Love and Love's great queen.
That mountain was portrayed as well,   *Cithaeron*
Where Venus and her minions dwell
Among its pleasant scenes collected.
Lax Idleness was not neglected,   480
Who kept the gate, nor was Narcissus,
Nor Solomon, still drunk on kisses,   *Solomon had 700 wives and 300*
Nor Circe, nor great Hercules,   *concubines.*
Nor fell Medea, now at ease,

Nor Croesus, made a servant late.   *Lydian king and servant to Cyrus,*
These showed that neither wit nor state,   *his conqueror*
Not beauty, sleight, or hardiness
Can stand against the heart's behests.
Dame Venus has the sovereignty,
For as she deigns, the world must be.   490
Count up the victims in her snares.
They won't go free for all their prayers.
Her exploits live in tales and lore.
I could rehearse a thousand more.

   Her statue showed her rising free,
In naked glory from the sea.
From navel down, green crystal waves
Half hid her form from gawking knaves.
She held a cittern in her hand,   *a stringed instrument*
And on her hair a pretty band   500
Of tender roses, fresh and sweet.
Around her head soft doves' wings beat.
Cupid faced her with his stings,
His marble shoulders sprouting wings.
Though he was blind, as often seen,
His bow was strung, his arrows keen.

   Why shouldn't I go on to tell
About the other shrines as well,
Beginning here with Mars the Red?
Mars' temple pictured scenes of dread,   510
Resembling that grisly place,
The famous shrine of Mars in Thrace,
Where, in that icebound, misty region,
His warlike devotees are legion.

   Around the walls a forest ran,
Stark wilds, devoid of beast or man,
With knobby, twisted, barren trees
And snapped-off stumps like shattered knees.
The wind roared constantly, so grim
It seemed to threaten every limb.   520
Beneath a hill, beside a slope,
The shrine of Mars, the soldier's hope,
Gleamed bright with steel. Its entryway
Was low and dark in plainest day

And vented such a howling gale,
The gateway shook as if to fail.
Cold northern rays spilled in the door,
To light the place, and nothing more,
No windows shown from sides or front.
The doors were made of adamant,   *stone of mythical hardness*
Crosshatched with hardened iron bands.
The stoutest work of human hands,
Barrel-like pillars braced the nave,
Cold, burnished iron that never gave.
   And there I saw the darkest schemes
Of Felony; the unhinged dreams
Of Anger, red as glowing coals;
The pickpurse and pale Dread-of-Souls;
The smiler with the secret knife;
The stable fired; the hidden strife   540
Of treasonous Murder in the bed;
Then War itself where deep wounds bled—
Cruel War with grating blades and sighs—
The darkness breathed out groans and cries.
A suicide was standing there—
The heart's blood stiffening in his hair—
A skull pierced by a hammered nail,
And cold Death gaping wan and pale.
Amidst the temple sat Mischance;
Dire anguish warped his countenance.   550
And I saw cackling Madness too,
Where armed Complaint and Outrage flew,
The thicket where a slit throat bled,
A thousand slain, and none in bed,
The tyrant glutted with his prey,
The village shattered in a fray,
Storm-tossed burning ships and wares,
A hunter torn by savage bears,
A sow that ate a child in cradle,
A scalded cook who cursed his ladle.   560
Each Mars-caused mishap bore a part—
The teamster crushed beneath his cart,
Pinned beneath the iron wheel,
And tradesmen wearing great Mars' seal:

The surgeon, butcher, and the smith,
With blades to taste the bone's red pith.
Above them all, shown on a tower,
Sat Conquest, splendid in his power.
A sharpened sword above his head
Hung quivering upon a thread.   570
The lives that Julius Caesar spilled,
The teeming crowds whom Nero killed,
Though unborn yet in Theseus' age,
Were pictured there in howling rage.
Their deaths were written in the stars.
Nor theirs alone, but also ours.
Mars knows, as do the stars above,
Who will be slain or die for love.
A thousand tales show this is true—
By far too many to pursue.   580
    Mars' statue stood upon a cart,
Malignant, armed with cunning art.
Above his head two figures shown,
Star-like signs and widely known,
One called Puella and one Rubeus.   *"The Girl" and "Briars," two symbols used*
The god of arms was figured thus: *in a method of divination*
A gaunt wolf crouched before his feet,
Glutting itself on human meat.
Mars' awful might was shown with skill,
To magnify his fame and will.   590
    Regarding the temple of Diana,
Let me adopt a briefer manner.
On every wall, it may suffice,
Chaste hunting was the prime device.
I saw Callisto blushing there.   *nymph raped by Jove*
Diana changed her to a bear
On finding she was got with child.
Now she's the lodestar, undefiled.   *North Star*
Her tale was spread before my sight,
Each figure neatly etched and bright,   600
She and her son sharp stars to see.   *Arcas, also transformed*
Next came young Daphne as a tree;   *She was transformed into a laurel*
I mean the nymph who fled for shame,   *to escape Apollo.*
The goddess bears the selfsame name.

Then Actaeon sprang along a path.
He spied Diana at her bath,
And, as a stag, was hunted down,
And ragged to death by his own hounds.
Atalanta glimmered by a door.
She brought to bay Diana's boar   610
With Meleager and his friends.
The goddess dogged them to their ends.   *for killing her boar*
Each wall told stories of this kind,
Far more than I can call to mind.

   A stag was bright Diana's seat,
With little dogs around her feet.
Beneath her sailed a growing moon,   *Diana's sign*
One nearly full, but waning soon.
Her gown was green as any leaf,
With bow, and arrows in a sheaf.   620
Her eyes looked down at Pluto's realm,[5]
Where dark dismay and sorrows whelm.
A birthing woman gasped before her,
Called her Lucina and adored her.   *Diana as goddess of childbirth*
The child held back; she wildly prayed,
Cried for Diana's help and aid.
The art was lively, finely wrought.
The pigments must have cost a lot.

*Now the lists are ready, and what a showy group of knights Palamon and Arcite
assembled! If only England could see the like! Each man armed himself as he
thought best. Arriving with Palamon was Lycurgus, the king of Thrace, wearing
a bearskin and riding in a golden chariot drawn by bulls. Arcite was backed by
Emetrius, monarch of India, a freckled man of twenty-five in a jewelled outfit.
Each king provided a hundred knights and fighting animals: Emetrius, lions and
leopards, and Lycurgus, hunting dogs the size of cattle.*

   *On the morning of the tourney, Palamon, Emily, and Arcite petition the
proper gods, and each one's prayer is granted, but not as they hoped. Palamon goes
to the temple of Venus, where he prays to obtain Emily, nothing else:*

---

5. Chaucer seems to confuse Diana (Artemis) with Persephone, the queen of Hades in
Greek myth, where Artemis and Persephone are rarely associated.

"I don't ask to vanquish false Arcite,
My lady, by some famous feat,   630
Or garner everybody's praise,
But I would have, for all my days,
Fair Emily, and die in love.
You choose the method from above.
I leave to you who wins this fight;
Name whom you wish the better knight,
But give me Emily to hold,
For although Mars is rough and bold,
Your power is greater in this kind.
Proclaim it so, and she is mine.   640
You'll have the love of Palamon
And on your altar from now on
I'll sacrifice and kindle fires.
But if you won't grant my desires,
I pray Arcite may run me through.
Prompt death would be a gift from you.
I'll hardly care, out of this life,
If Arcite takes my love to wife.
Yet here's the substance of my plea:
Dear Venus, grant the girl to me!"   650

*A signal from the statue of Venus assures Palamon he'll have his wish. Meanwhile,
Emily visits Diana's temple, hoping to be delivered from marriage entirely. If
that's too much to ask, she prays the goddess to give her the suitor who desires her
most:*

"Goddess, guard your claim to me,
A virgin wed to venery   *hunting*
And unchecked freedom of the wild.
I wouldn't be a wife with child,
Nor suffer any man's address.
Alleviate my great distress.
Bring aid for me in any shape.   *as Diana, Lucina, or queen of the underworld*
But grant that Palamon escape.
Arcite as well, who loves me so.
Avert this battle and bestow   660
A kindly peace between the two,
And all their love for me subdue.

Quench their hot, extreme desires,
Their quaking fits and smoking fires,
Or turn them to another place.
But if you won't provide this grace
Or if my fate's already set,
So I must wed, though with regret,
Give me the man who loves me most."

*Diana appears to Emily. Alas, the girl must marry one of the cousins, though the
goddess won't say which. Meanwhile, Arcite prays to Mars, recalling among other
things the time Mars was found in bed with Venus and caught in an iron net:*

"Great Lord, I'm inexperienced,   670
And yet love-tossed and sinned against
As any creature's ever been
For she I'm struggling to win
Cares nothing if I swim or sink.
She'll never welcome love, I think.
No, I must win her heart by force.
Attend me, Lord, and guide my course.
Help me win the coming fight.
As love's hot fire burned you at night,
Once on a time, and now burns me,   680
Oh grant me, Lord, the victory!"

*The armor on Mars' statue jingles, and a low voice murmurs, "Victory!" telling
Arcite that Mars will help him defeat Palamon. But the three gods' promises—
Palamon will gain Emily, Emily will have the man who wants her most, and
Arcite will win the victory—seem contradictory and lead in proper epic fashion
to a consult in heaven. Only Saturn, grandfather to Mars and Venus, offers a
practical solution. This is to be expected, says Chaucer, because age brings wis-
dom: "You may outrun old people, but you can't outwit them," he says.*
    As Part Four opens, Athens is abuzz on the morning of the tournament.

As soon as day began to spring,
Loud clanks and harness clattering
Rang out from every hostelry,
As armored men of each degree,
The lords and all their retinues,
Came forth to hear the latest news

And eye each other's arms and gear,
Prime harness drawn from far and near.
The fittings all seemed fine enough—   690
Chased gold and steel, embroidered stuff,
Bright shields and sumptuous horses' traps,
Gold helmets, hauberks, gleaming straps,   *coats of mail*
As lords rode out in lavish gowns
To lead their knights upon their rounds.
Spears were readied, helms secured,
Shield straps fastened, thongs procured.
Each need was met with hands and wits,
As horses champed their golden bits,
And armorers bustled, as at fairs,   700
With tools, while making last repairs.
Yeomen on foot and common men
Washed this way first and back again.
Sharp bugles blasted, drummers drummed—
The streets and walls and palace hummed.

*Theseus wants this tournament carried out with as little loss of life as possible.
No one may shoot arrows or use a poleax or short thrusting knife. Combatants
may run at each other one time with sharp spears, but then they must fight with
broadswords and maces—bludgeon-like weapons that stun more than cut. Cap-
tives must not be killed but led to a stake to remain there on their honor. Fight-
ing stops the moment either Palamon or Arcite is killed or captured.*

*Arcite and his hundred knights enter the lists from the west, beneath the tem-
ple of Mars, and Palamon from the east, through the gate dedicated to Venus.
The parties pause for a brief inspection and then lay on with vigor.*

Strong shafts splintered with each hit.
One knight was skewered, breast bone split.
Sprung spears flew high into the air;
Then in each hand the bright brands flare,
As silver sword hacked armored head,   710
And bloody injuries spattered red
Beneath bone-cracking battery.
One man charged a crush with glee
And threw down knights and kicking horses.
One rolled balled up beneath both forces.
One swung a broken shaft around

To trip a horse and bring it down.
One man wounded through the thick
Was dragged to the stake, ashamed and sick;
There, as agreed, he must abide,   720
With captives from the other side.

*Palamon and Arcite survive many ferocious encounters, though not without
wounds. No tigress whose cub has been stolen is more fierce than Arcite. No lion
lusts after blood as insanely as Palamon wants to kill his rival.*

*But nothing lasts forever. That evening, after a full day of even combat, King
Emetrius and twenty knights overcome Palamon as he is fighting with Arcite and
drag him to the captives' stake. This ends the battle, and Theseus, as arranged,
awards Emily to Arcite, the victor.*

What now can Venus do above?
She felt the slight as Queen of Love
And wept so fast because of this
Her streaming tears fell on the lists,
"Alas," she said, "humiliation."

"My dear, forego your indignation,"
Said Saturn. "Though Arcite and Mars
May triumph now, you'll win your cause."

Then trumpets and the standers-by   730
And heralds in full tongue and cry
Praised the winner's victory.
But leave their noise and hark to me—
A wonder promptly stilled their fun.

For Arcite had his helm undone,
And, curveting to show his face,
He galloped up and down the place,
Gazing up at Emily.
The girl looked back as lovingly—
For women, for the greater part,   740
Follow fortune with their heart—
Her smiling soothed his lover's thirst.

Lo, from the ground a fury burst
That Pluto sent at Saturn's wish.
The horse shied with a startled swish,
Leapt aside, and landed wrong.
Before Arcite could reason long,

He tumbled headfirst on the ground.
His frightened horse was also downed;
Its saddle crushed the young knight's breast.   750
His blood was thickened and compressed
And left him black as any crow.
Alack! It seemed a fatal blow.

*But Arcite lives. He's carried to the palace, where most think he will recover. In
fact, their mood is jubilant, for it appears no one was killed in the tournament—
not even the man pierced through the breastbone. Theseus makes peace between
the two forces and praises Palamon, who was hardly disgraced by being overcome
by twenty knights.*

*Unfortunately, though, Arcite worsens. Not even surgery, emetics, and laxa-
tives help. If neither medicine nor nature works, says Chaucer, "Farewell physic!
Carry the man to the church!"*

Arcite calls for Emily and bids her goodbye, saying,

"Not all the spirit in my breast
Can show one part of my distress
To you, my dear, whom I love most.
Accept the service of my ghost
To guard you here and hold you fast—
My life as well, but that can't last.
Alas, the woe! Alas the wrong,   760
That I have felt for you so long!
Alas my death, dear Emily!
Alas for your sweet company!
Alas, my queen! Alas, my wife,
My lady, lodestar of my life!
What is the world? What do men crave?
Now deep in love; now in the grave,
Alone without a voice or plea.
Farewell, my sweetest Emily!

*Arcite lives long enough to commend Palamon to Emily, but then death takes
him.*

From feet to breast he felt arise   770
The chill of death to seal his eyes.
Blank numbness hollowed every member.

His life grew dim, a chilling ember.
Only his mind held on at last,
Deep entrenched but failing fast
As his sick heart encountered death.
His eyes grew dark; he drew a breath.
He looked for her but couldn't see.
His last words? "Mercy, Emily!"
His spirit went I know not where.   780
Someplace, but I was never there.
I won't explain, for I'm no priest.
My source just says that he deceased.
No, I won't speculate or natter.
Let others write upon this matter.

*All Athens mourns for Arcite, no one more than Emily and Palamon. His body
is burnt with elaborate ceremony on a pyre forty yards long. Chaucer says he will
not tell the names of the trees used for the pyre, but of course he does: oak, fir,
birch, aspen, alder, holm oak, poplar, willow, elm, plane, ash, box, chestnut, lin-
den, laurel, maple, hawthorn, beech, hazel, yew, and dogwood! As the fire burns,
mourners throw in jewels and armor along with cups of wine and milk and
blood. Emily is led away, and the event concludes with funeral games.*

*Years later, when feelings are cooler, the Athenian parliament is discussing
Thebes. Theseus takes the opportunity to summon Palamon and deliver a round-
about address touching several points of medieval philosophy: God rules the world
with love and care. Love unites earth, air, fire, and water in the physical uni-
verse. God's purpose is evident in the overall design of things, for instance, the
limits placed on mortal lifetimes. As the whole divided world derives from and
illustrates a greater unity, so do individual lives unite to make up species, a mor-
tal creature's sole hedge against time. All lesser things must pass away:*

"Think of the oak, so long a sprig,
An acorn first and then a twig,
Then for an age a spreading tree.
It dies at last as we may see.
    "Consider even stubborn stone.   790
Beneath our feet it wears unknown
And wastes as we go walking by.
A river can at times go dry.
Great towns as well must wax and wane.

Time gnaws at everything mundane.
    "Men and women die as well,
The time is all that's left to tell,
Whether in youth, that is, or age.
Great kings expire like any page,
Some in their beds, some at sea,   800
Some in the field by fate's decree.
There is no help; nowhere to fly:
Each thing on earth at last must die.
    "What causes this? Great Jupiter,
The fount of all, unless I err,
Returning each thing to its source,
The well of being, life, and force.
This is the law; no living creature
Can change its terms or smallest feature.
    "It's simple wisdom, in my view,   810
To make necessity our virtue,
Accept what's given us at birth
And live, as creatures must, on earth.
Only a fool would seek to hide,
Rebel against the world's chief guide.
A man is blessed to have his hour
And perish at his fullest flower.
For then his fame will not diminish,
Defined for all time at his finish.
Indeed, his truest friends rejoice.   820
He died just when he would by choice,
Not when his hard-won honor's faded,
Achievements tarnished, admirers jaded.
Oh no indeed, it's best to perish
While one still has a name to cherish!
    "No honest man will disagree.
Why grouch and mourn incessantly
That good Arcite, a proven hero,
Left just when he was meant to go—
Escaped the prison of this life?   830
Why should his cousin and his wife
Begrudge the timing of his fall?
Think! Would he thank them? Not at all!
They spite themselves and spite their friends

With sorrows that can never end.
  "Hear my conclusion, then I'll rest:
All woe must yield to happiness
And praise to Jove for all his grace.
So now, before we quit this place,
Let's shape our pain for Arcite dead   840
Into new joy. Come, look ahead,
And where there was the greatest grief,
Let's soothe that ache and bring relief.
  "Sister," he said, "have my assent,
Subscribed to by my parliament,
To make good Palamon your knight.
He serves you with both heart and might,
And has since he first saw you here.
Now cherish him and hold him dear.
Accept him as your wedded lord.   850
Your hand, to show we're in accord.
Dear, show the man your tenderness.
He is royal enough, as I protest,
But if he were a simple knight,
He's served you well. It's only right
To recognize his constancy.
That's no small gift, all men agree,
And mercy ought to outweigh right."
  And then he turned to face the knight:
"Sir Palamon, let me persuade you,   860
Accept the offer that I've made you.
Come, take your lady by the hand."
  Between the two they forged that band
That we call wedded life or marriage
Before the high duke's baronage.
And thus with bliss and melody
Palamon married Emily.
Dear God, who made this world we know,
Confirm their love and make it grow.
Let Palamon enjoy his wealth,   870
Alive in bliss, secure in health.
Emily loves him equally
And he serves her, content and free.

No jealous word or other woe
Could part those two, united so.
So farewell, Palamon and Emily.
And God save all the company!
Amen.

Heere is ended the Knyghtes Tale.

The Miller

The Miller's Prologue

No sooner was the knight's tale ended
Than each of us proclaimed it splendid.
We called it memorable and moving,
Declared its noble thoughts improving,
Especially those who ranked as gentry.
Our Host was just as complimentary.
"The pouch is open now," he cried.
"Let's see what else we find inside.
No one could wish a better start.
Now let this Monk display his art,   10
And tell a tale to top the Knight!"
The Miller, full of drink and fight,
Where he sat reeling in his saddle,
Would not be ruled without a battle.
He waved the Host's commands away
And roared like Pilate in a play: *standard dramatic villain*
"By God's arms and blood and bones,
I'll tell *my* noble tale at once,
And it shall quit the good Knight's tale."
Our Host saw he was drunk with ale   20
And said, "No, Robin, that's not right,
Our betters should succeed the Knight.
Pipe down now. Observe propriety!"
   "By God's great soul and my sobriety,"
The Miller said, "I won't obey.
I'll tell my tale or go my way."
"Well, tell it then," our Host replied,
"Since you're too drunk to be denied."
   "Listen," this Miller shouted round,
"I'm drunk. I know it by my sound.   30
If I misspeak or miss my mark,

Blame it on the ale of Southwark.
Now hear a story drawn from life
About a carpenter and wife
And how a clerk set both their caps!"
    Up shot the Reeve with "Shut your trap!
Hold back your drunken harlotry.
You sin against the bourgeoisie
To slander honest men in game,
And undermine a wife's good name.
Give over. Choose another tale."   40
    The Miller roared back like a gale:
"Ah, my blessed brother Oswald,
No wifeless man can be a cuckold.
But I don't say that you are one.
There are good wives beneath the sun.
For each one mucky, thousands glitter—
Or have you reason to be bitter?
Why sputter venom like a shrew?
I have a wife as well as you.   50
A cuckold! Not to save my ox
Would I put myself in that box,
Just for fear that I was one.
No! I'll believe that I am none.
No man should pry throughout his life
To learn God's secrets, or his wife's.
If you enjoy her *quelque chose*,   *French: "something"*
Why grudge the rest, wherever it goes?"
    That illustrates this Miller's mood—
Drunken, mean, combative, lewd.   60
His story's more licentious yet.
But I'm committed to rehearse it.
Now, gentle reader, I implore you,
When I put his tale before you,
Don't think me lecherous or shameless.
Most of my stories are quite blameless,
But I must tell the bad ones too,
Or shirk what I set out to do.
Turn the page and choose another;
My tamer tales would suit your mother.   70
They praise good morals and embody

The opposite of all things bawdy.
Just don't blame me for what you choose.
The Miller was far gone in booze,
A hopeless churl. So was the Reeve.
What else could men like these conceive
But sluttishness? I'm innocent.
So take these stories as they're meant.

THE MILLER'S TALE

Once upon a time in Oxford
A tradesman offered room and board   80
To guests, a thriving carpenter.
A needy scholar living there,
Having mastered basic arts,
Took astrology to heart,
And learned, by sundry calculations,
To answer men's interrogations.
He knew on given dates and hours
If they would suffer droughts or showers,
And other things that would befall—
No one could ever name them all.   90
    This clerk, called handy Nicholas,
Relished love and lovers' bliss,
But slyly worked to hide his weakness
And seem a blushing maid for meekness.
He had a chamber of his own,
Where he retired to be alone.
He hung fresh herbs in this retreat,
Chewed spices too, to smell more sweet.
Of mint or ginger root he savored
As on his *Almagest* he labored   *astronomy text*
Beside his astrolabe and books.
His auguring stones lay in a nook   *for predicting the future*
Above the headboard of his bed.
His cupboard bore a scarf of red
And a hollow, jangling psaltery   *stringed instrument*
Which filled the nights with melody

So sweetly that his chamber rang
As *Angelus ad Virginem* he sang.   *a Latin hymn*
Each time he piped the song "King's Note,"
His housemates blessed his tuneful throat.   110
In such pursuits his time was spent,
With friends to help him pay the rent.

    The carpenter had wed a wife,
And valued her above his life.
This girl was eighteen years of age,
And he kept her in a narrow cage,
For being old and full of phlegm,
He went in fear she'd cuckold him.
He'd not read Cato (his wit was rude),
Who said, "Wed your similitude.   120
Marry your own generation
Or live in constant trepidation."
So now his head was in the snare,
And he watched the girl with jealous care.

    The wife was fair, as I've determined,
As sleek and slender as an ermine.
She wore a belt with stripes of silk
Above an apron white as milk,
Arranged in pleats across her thighs.
Her smock was white. What drew all eyes   130
Was her white collar, neatly chased
In coal-black stitching, interlaced
To match the ribbons of her cap,
A studied fashion, no mishap.
Her broad silk headband sat on high.
"Come hither" twinkled in her eye.
Her brows were neatly plucked and narrow,
Bent like bows to launch an arrow.
She was a finer sight to see
Than a slender, blooming pear tree,   140
And softer than the wool of wethers;   *neutered rams*
At her waist, a purse of leather
With silken fringe and gleaming beads.
No matter where your wandering leads,
You'll never find another such,
So pert a doll, so sweet to touch.

I swear her skin gave off a glint
As bright as coins fresh from the mint.
Her singing was as clear and able
As any swallow's on a gable.   150
She skipped as lightly as a lamb
That frisked and gamboled by his dam.
Her mouth was sweet as mead's bouquet
Or a hoard of apples stored in hay.
Skittish as a tender colt,
Long as a mast, straight as a bolt.
She wore a brooch upon her breast
Broad as a shield-boss or a crest.   *round ornament on a shield*
She laced her shoes up tight and high.
She was a primrose, a sweet pig's eye,   *flowers*
Fit for a lord to roll in bed
Or any lesser man to wed.
    Now then, sirs, this was the case:
One day our handy Nicholas
Approached the wife to flirt and play.
(Her husband was at Osenay.)   *an abbey near Oxford*
As clerks are subtle beyond measure,
He briskly grabbed her nether treasure
And said, "For love of you I cry.
Surrender, dear, or I must die!"   170
And grappled her around the hips
And groaned, "Now let me kiss your lips,
Or I will perish by your face."
The girl sprang like a colt in trace.
She wrenched away her head with speed
And said, "What? Never by my creed!
You must unhand me Nicholas,
Or I will shout out 'Help! Alas!'
You mustn't grope me in this way."
    But Nicholas moaned "Welladay!"   180
And spoke so sweetly and so fast
That she relented at the last
And swore by holy martyred Thomas
She'd comfort him. She'd keep the promise
When she saw an open field.
"My husband's jealous eye is peeled,"

She said, "Take care! Tiptoe with dread;
If we're discovered, sweet, I'm dead!
You must be stealthy in this case."
        "Of course I will," said Nicholas.   190
"A clerk has but himself to blame
If he can't win a thinking game
Against a woodwright." So they agreed
To wait their chance to do the deed.

    Once Nicholas knew that she'd be kind,
He ran his hands up her behind
And kissed her well and took his psaltery
And strummed a thunderous melody.

    One day Alison went to church
To pray and do Christ's holy work   200
Upon a solemn holiday.
Her forehead gleamed as clear as day
Where she had washed it after work.
The parish had a brisk young clerk,
A handsome lad named Absolom.
His golden hair was curled and shone,
Glistening and arranged with art,
On either side beside his part.
Red cheeks, eyes of a grayish hue,
Rose windows carved on either shoe,   *pierced work resembling church windows*
He minced his way down all life's paths
In tight red hose that showed his calves,
And a pale blue tunic like the sky,
With fancy lacing to catch the eye.
Then too he wore a fine crisp surplice,
As white as blossoms in a mist.
He was a merry lad, I swear,
And he could shave, let blood, clip hair,
Or execute a deed or quitclaim.
His dancing brought him yet more fame,   220
For he could trip with nods and smiles
In twenty different Oxford styles
And saw upon a dainty fiddle
And sing falsetto, high and brittle,
Or finger tunes on his guitar.
There was no tavern, brewhouse, bar

Where any pretty waitress was
He did not vie for her applause.
But still his speech was too fastidious,
And he considered farting hideous.   230
    This Absolom, so blithe and gay,
Carried the censer on holidays,   *incense pot*
Censing the girls and young wives first
With killing looks that he'd rehearsed,
And most of all the woodwright's wife,
Just now the focus of his life.
She was so sweet and lecherous,
If only she could be a mouse,
And he a cat, she'd be his dinner.
He set his heart and soul to win her.   240
She dazzled him. Ah, he was suffering.
From no wife would he take an offering.
He claimed his courtesy forbid it.
    That night was fine; a bright moon lit it.
Absolom took his guitar abroad.
He couldn't sleep; love's urgent prod
Pricked up his pulse. His heart was swelling.
He made his way to Alison's dwelling,
About the time the cocks had crowed
And stood before his mother lode,   250
Outside a little shuttered window.
There he sang out soft and low:
"Ah now, dear apple of my eye,
Pity me, or I must die,"
With tremolos upon the strings.
The carpenter waked and heard him sing,
And turned to face his wife in bed.
"What is this, Alison?" he said.
"Absolom out calling by our wall?"
"Yes, John, I heard him caterwaul,"   260
She answered. "What a shameful mess!"
Well, this went on, as you might guess.
For days to come young Absolom
Could think of only Alison.
Awake all night, blear-eyed all day,
He combed his locks and made them gay,

Wooing her with emissaries
And following her to fetch and carry.
He warbled like a nightingale.
He bought her sweetened wine and ale. 270
He sent her hot cakes every day.
Since she was town-bred, he offered pay.
(With some girls tender words will jibe,
While others hold out for a bribe.)
　Once, to show his depth of soul,
He appeared onstage in Herod's role,
But nothing served his case, alas,
For she loved only Nicholas.
Absolom might as well flip sand;
He'd never bring this bird to hand. 280
Instead, she laughed at him and scoffed:
His pains were slight; his wits were soft.
It's very true, as all men say,
The nearby sly one wins the day,
While the far-off lover loses.
Let Absolom do just as he chooses;
As he was seldom in her sight,
Our Nicholas eclipsed his light.
Rejoice, you lucky Nicholas;
Let Absolom sing out "Alas!" 290
　It happened on a Saturday,
When John was gone to Osenay,
That Nicholas and Alison
Met to plan their liaison.
Young Nicholas would use his wile
To trap the husband with his guile
And then, if all their plans went right,
He'd lie in her smooth arms all night.
(She clearly wished as much as he did
To see her jealous husband cheated.) 300
The lad was one who never tarried.
He slyly to his chamber carried
Meat and drink to last two days.
Then he told Alison to say,
When John should ask her where he was,
She'd no idea at all, because

She hadn't seen him, quick or still.
Indeed, she feared that he was ill.
No cry of hers or servants stirred him.
If not some sickness, what deterred him?   310
   The day passed uneventfully
With Nicholas waiting quietly,
Dozing and eating at his desk,
Till, Sunday evening just at dusk,
John wondered where the lad had got to.
What sort of pass had he been brought to?
"I am afraid, by holy Thomas,
There's something wrong with Nicholas.
God grant that he's not sick or dead!
The world is fickle now," he said.   320
"Today I saw a corpse in church,
And Monday last I saw him work.
Go up, Robin" (to his knave),
"Call him out with voice or stave.
Let me know what you discover."
   The lad went forth to rouse our lover.
Outside the room that Nicholas rented
He knocked and called like one demented:
"What? How! Master Nicholay!
Say, do you mean to sleep all day?"   330
   He paused to listen. Not a word!
He found a hole, low in a board,
The house cat's passage to the room,
And peeped inside despite the gloom.
At length he made out Nicholas
Gaping like a man possessed,
Or someone addled by the moon!
He dashed downstairs again and soon
Explained that Nicholas seemed enchanted.
   The carpenter roused himself and ranted: 340
"Help us, dear Saint Frideswide!   *known for her healing power*
You never know what will betide!
The man has softened his psychology
By his long study of astrology!
I knew he would, the silly sod!
No one can learn the mind of God!

Blessed is a man indeed,
Knowing nothing but his creed.
Another seeking hidden lore
Roamed looking upward evermore   350
Into the stars. Ha! As was fit,
He tumbled in an open pit.   *Plato tells this of Thales.*
He hadn't seen it! By Saint Thomas,
I pity handy Nicholas.
I'll cure him of his studying;
I'll find a way, by Heaven's King!
Here, let me pry against the floor,
While, Robin, you heave up the door.
We'll roust him from his queer fit yet."
He pulled up on the staff and let   360
His lad, who relished smashing things,
Heave the door from its fastenings.
It fell in with a thunderous sound,
But Nicholas never moved or frowned.
He kept on goggling up in air,
A picture of abject despair.
John shook him sharply by the arm
And called to him in great alarm:
"What! Nicholay! Why, look down here!
Think of Christ, whom we revere!   370
I cross you against all elves and feys!"
He said a night spell several ways—
Toward each quarter of the floor
And by the threshold of the door.
"Christ Jesus and Saint Benedictus
Let no unholy thing afflict us.
I call upon white *paternoster*
And every saint from here to Gloucester!"   *silly conjurations*
    Finally, handy Nicholas
Began to stir and sigh, "Alas!   380
Must all the world be lost again?"
    "What?" said John. "Are you insane?
Think on God like working men."
But Nicholas called for drink and then
Said they must counsel privately.
"My vision touches you and me;

So pack the others off to bed."
His news was secret, so he said.
    The carpenter went to play his part,
Returning with a brimming quart   390
Of mighty ale for them to share.
Nicholas shut the door with care.
    He said, "Now, John, beloved host,
"Swear on your blessed father's ghost
That you won't pass on what I tell you.
I call on Jesus to compel you.
Betray me and your soul is lost!
And while you live, to your great cost,
You shall be mad. I swear it's true."
"Why, you don't think I'd babble, do you?"   400
Said the silly carpenter.
"Christ's blood forbid that I should err
By talking loosely. In God's name,
I'll spill no word to child or dame."
    "John," said Nicholas, "I will not lie.
I've found by my astrology,
Looking in the moon's clear light,
Near one AM tomorrow night
A rain will fall, with hail and mud,
To more than double Noah's flood.   410
In just an hour our world and we
Shall all be drenched beneath the sea.
Each one of us shall lose his life."
    John answered, "Oh, alas, my wife!
What? Must she drown? My Alison!"
His anguish left him quite undone.
"Is there no help for this?" he asked.
    "Of course there is," said Nicholas,
"If you will do just as I say.
You mustn't try some other way,   420
For Solomon's advice was good:
'Do what men tell you, as you should.'
If you obey, and do not fail,
I'll save us without mast or sail,
The three of us, that is, for look
How God saved Noah in the Book   *Gen. 6–9*

By warning him, to his great wonder,
How floods would wash the whole world under."
   "I've heard the tale of this," said John.
   "And have you heard how, later on,   430
Noah argued and implored
Before he got his wife aboard?"   *popular scene in mystery plays*
Said Nicholas. "She made him wish
That he had fed her to the fish!
Or that he'd built the stubborn crone
A ship that she could sail alone!
Now here's my plan. It calls for haste.
We have no further time to waste.
   "Go out at once and carry off
A brewing tub or kneading trough   440
For each of us. They must be large—
Enough to float in like a barge.
Provision each with drink and food.
A single day's worth will be good.
The flood will slack and drain away
The morning of the second day.
No other soul must give you aid;
We can't save Robin or your maid.
Don't ask me why, for I won't tell,
But know this too is great God's will.   450
Content yourself, unless you're mad
To have the grace that Noah had.
I'll rescue Alison, by my salvation.
But not without this preparation.
   "Here's more to do. You must agree,
When you have tubs for just us three,
To hang them high among the beams,
But no one else must know our schemes.
Next, when you've done as I have said,
Supply each craft with beer and bread   460
And an ax apiece, to cut the lashings.
When the water rises, splashing,
We'll chop a passage through the gable,
Garden-ward, above the stable,
So we can float, secure, elated,
Although the world is inundated.

You'll bob along, I undertake,
Just like a duck behind her drake.
I'll call, 'Alison, John, what cheer?
The flood is passing, never fear!'   470
And you will say, 'Ah, Nicholay!
Your plan has worked. We're well aweigh.'
Then we will rule the world for life,
Great lords, like Noah and his wife.
    "One thing could still spoil our delight:
We must be sure on that same night
When we have got ourselves onboard,
Not one of us shall speak a word
Or cry out, even in a prayer,
That's God's command in this affair.   480
    "If noise is bad, why, sin is worse.
You and Alison must have no commerce,
Not in looking nor in deed.
Hang far apart. And now, Godspeed!
Tomorrow when the world's asleep,
Into our kneading tubs we'll creep,
And wait there as God wills we should.
Get to it. Show you've understood.
I will not offer more direction.
Men say, 'Wise agents are perfection.'   490
It takes no clerk to hang a trough.
So save us wisely. Now, be off!"
    The silly woodwright went his way,
Often sighing, "Welladay,"
And told his wife what you have heard.
Of course she knew it, every word,
And knew what lay behind it too,
But clutched her heart and changed her hue
And said, "Alas! Defend us John!
Save us or we are undone!   500
I am your true and wedded wife.
Look to me now. Preserve my life!"
    Ah, the power of affection!
Men can die of false dejection,
So deeply can impressions root.
John is gaping, stricken mute:

His mind's eye sees, with no more urging,
Noah's flood rampaging, surging,
To drown young Alison, his dear.
He quakes and wails with sorry cheer. 510
His throat constricts, he starts to cough.
He runs to fetch a kneading trough,
A mighty brew tub, and a cistern,
And haul each to his house in turn,
And hang them up beneath the rafters.
He made three ladders shortly after,
Bored the uprights, set each rung,
To climb up where the vessels hung.
Then he provisioned every tub
With ale and cheese and other grub— 520
Sufficient for a day afloat.
Before he finished with each boat,
He made up errands to employ
His maid in London with the boy.
As it grew dark on Monday night,
Without so much as candle light,
In silence and great secrecy,
Into their tubs they climbed, all three.
    They settled in as each preferred,
And Nicholas hissed: "Now, mum's the word!" 530
"Mum," said Alison; "Mum" said John,
But he began to pray anon,
Softly whispering each refrain,
With both ears cocked to hear the rain.
    John was tired. His fears were deep.
He slipped into a labored sleep
About the time the last light glimmered.
His troubled spirit seethed and simmered.
Then too, he snored. His head mislay.
Down from his tub sneaked Nicholay. 540
Down Alison as softly sped.
Without a word they went to bed—
John's bed, that is, where they delighted,
Leaving the carpenter benighted.
There Alison and Nicholas
Did all they'd dreamed they would at last

Until the bell for lauds was ringing   *about 3 AM*
And clerics filled the church with singing.
   Our other wooer, Absolom,
The lad that love so worked upon,   550
That week had gone to Osenay,
Among a group on holiday.
He asked a passing cloisterer
For news of John the carpenter
As they stood there beside the church.
The monk had not seen John at work
All week, he said. "I understood,
We sent him out to cut some wood,
Just as he must often do,
And sleep abroad a night or two.   560
Or maybe he's at home today.
He might be there. I couldn't say."
   Young Absolom heard this with delight,
And thought: "Lord, will I prowl tonight!
I surely haven't seen the man
About his house since day began.
   "When the first cock crow is uttered
I'll knock where Alison's room is shuttered,
The lowest window, close at hand.
By God, I'll make her understand   570
My love and longing. I can't miss.
I know I'll get at least a kiss.
At last some comfort for my pay!
My mouth has itched the livelong day.
That must mean kissing at the least.
Last night I dreamed a richer feast!
I'll lie down for an hour or two,
And then may all my dreams come true!"
   At length, the first cock's crowing done,
Up rose this jolly Absolom,   580
Donned his best clothes, bright and rich,
Chewed cardamom and licorice
To smell more sweet. He dressed his hair,
And underneath his tongue, with care,
He placed a sprig of herb-of-Paris—   *perhaps* Paris quadrifolia
A charm that would debauch an heiress—

And hastened to the woodwright's house
To catch the wife without her spouse.
Sidling up outside her window,
About waist-high, it sat so low,   590
He coughed once with a modest sound
And said, "My sweetest Alison,
My honeycomb, my cinnamon,
Awake, my dear, or I'm undone.
You never think about my woe,
How hot I burn wherever I go.
I hunger for you, I admit,
Like a lamb kept from the tit.
My only longing is for you.
A turtledove would seem untrue   600
Compared to me. Ah, dear, be swayed."
    "Clear off, Jack Fool," she said.
"So help me God, I will not kiss you.
I love another—he's my bliss, too,
As you are not. Christ, Absolom,
Get out or I will throw a stone.
Now let me sleep, by twenty devils!"
    "Alas," said Absolom, "how evil,
That true love should be spurned this way,
But kiss me, dear; ease my dismay,   610
For love of Jesus and of me."
    "And will you go at once?" asked she.
    "Yes, darling," said this Absolom.
    "Make ready, then, I come anon."
"Hush," she hissed to Nicholas,
"And you shall laugh your fill at last."
    Young Absolom sank to his knees
And said, "I'm lord of all I see.
Surely this is just the start!
Darling! Your grace! Sweet Bird! Your heart!"   620
    The window opened with a click.
"Come here," she said, "and kiss me quick,
Before our nosey neighbors see!"
    Absolom wiped his mouth with glee.
The night was dark as pitch or coal,
And out the window she put her hole.

Absolom fared no better or worse,
But with his mouth he kissed her arse,
And savored it, before he guessed
And gagged and spit in rare distress,   630
For he knew women have no beard.
He'd felt a thing all roughly haired.
"Ack," he said, "alas, ugh, phutt."
    "Tee-hee-hee!" she said, and shut
The window in the young clerk's face.
    "A beard! A beard!" roared Nicholas,
"By God's dear body, what a skit!"
Poor Absolom heard him, every bit,
And paused just long enough to hiss:
"I swear, by God, you'll pay for this!"   640
    Who's rubbing now and scrubs his lips
With dust and sand and straw and chips,
But Absolom? "I'll give my soul,"
He said, "to fry on Satan's coals,
If I now swerve aside or rest
Till I avenge this pretty jest.
O God, if I had only flinched!"
His eager love was wholly quenched,
For from the time he kissed her anus
All thought of paramours was heinous.   650
Indeed, his lust was dissipated.
He found all women vile and hated
Their gender so he almost wept.
But luckily the town still slept.
He went to see the smith Gervaise,
At work before the cattle grazed,
Sharpening coulters and welding plows.   *a blade that goes before a plowshare*
His knock was just enough to rouse
The smith from work and make him come.
    "Who's there?" he said.
    "It's Absolom!"   660
"What, Absolom, by Christ's sweet cross!
Up so early? Are you lost?
Some saucy girl, I swear it's true,
Has got her grappling hooks in you.
Saint Note above knows what I mean."   *Saint Neot, a Cornish hermit*

Absolom didn't care a bean
For jokes like these. He found them thin.
He had a lot more wool to spin
Than Gervaise knew. He said, "Dear friend,   670
This coulter heated white to mend,
Is what I need. Please let me take it.
You'll get it back. No fear I'll break it."
   Gervaise agreed. "If it were gold
Or bag of precious coins untold,
I'd give it to you; that's no lie,
But, by the Devil, tell me why."
   "Let that," said Absolom, "be as it may.
I'll tell you later, when it's day."
He caught the iron where it was cool   680
And went at once to wield the tool.
Back at the window in a trice,
He coughed discreetly, knocking twice,
Just as he had done before.
Pert Alison answered him once more:
"Who can this be? A thief, I swear."
"Oh, no," he said, "it's me, my dear.
Your Absolom, my chicken wing,
And I have brought a golden ring,
My mother's ring. It's well engraved,   690
The finest gold, or I'm not saved.
And you shall have it for a kiss."
   Now Nicholas was up to piss
And thought he could improve the joke.
He'd have *his* ass kissed by the bloke.
He opened up the window wide
And thrust his derriere outside,
Beyond the buttocks to the waist.
Absolom strained to see the place:
"Speak," he said, "my bird, my heart."   700
   This Nicholas let fly a fart
Greater than a thunder stroke.
It almost made our lover choke.
But he swung his iron into the farce
And smote young Nicholas on the arse.
   Nicholas' hind end popped and fried,

Around the iron a hand's breadth wide,
And thinking he would surely die,
The lad began to bawl and cry:
"Water! Water! By God's heart!"   710
    The carpenter woke up with a start,
Heard someone shouting, "Water! God!"
And thought: "Ah! This is Noah's flood!"
He sat straight up without a word
And swung his ax to cut the cord.
His tub fell with a fearsome crash.
He had no time to stir his hash,
But lay upon the floorboards, stunned.
    Then Nicholas and Alison
Called, "Help! Awake! Alack! Alas!"   720
Their clamor couldn't be surpassed,
As neighbors rushed to gawk at John
Where he lay still and pale and wan.
His arm was broken in the fall.
He woke up wincing, but that's not all;
Each word he said was shouted down,
By Nicholas and Alison.
They told the neighbors he'd gone mad
With fear of Noah's flood and had,
Because his silly wits were soft,   730
Brought home three mighty kneading troughs,
And hung them up beneath the roof
And made them sit with him for proof
That they believed his fears were just.
    The neighbors laughed, as people must,
At such a tale. They peered and poked
About the place, retold the joke,
And howled whenever John protested.
They guessed, of course, how he'd been bested,
But none would credit his contentions.   740
They held him mad without dissention.
Nicholas was backed by all the clerks,
Condemning John's distempered quirks.
The whole town laughed to see John humbled
And know his pretty wife was tumbled.
Though Absolom thought that he would die,

All knew he'd kissed her nether eye,
And Nicholas was scalded on the bum.
That's it. God save us, all and some!

Heere endeth the Millere his tale.

THE REEVE

THE REEVE'S PROLOGUE

We laughed out loud, I must confess
At Absolom and Nicholas.
Then different folks said differently,
But everyone at length agreed
We liked the tale and weren't aggrieved.
Our one dissenter was the Reeve.
Because he was himself a woodwright,
He took John's downfall as a slight;
And stared around and looked perverse.
"By God," he said, "I could rehearse   10
The blacking of a miller's eye,
But I'm too old for ribaldry.
My grass-time's gone, I must eat hay.
An old man mustn't talk that way.
This white top shows my age and cares;
My lusts should freeze to match my hairs,
Unless I'm like an open-arse,   *a medlar, an apple-like fruit*
That fruit that just keeps getting worse
Till tossed out on a garbage pile.[1]
Old men go bad in medlar style.   20
Unless we're rotten, we're not ripe,
But dance like fools to any pipe.
We hope, as sure as men drink ale,
For a white top and a green tail.

---

1. Medlar fruits have an anatomical-looking opening at the blossom end and lend themselves to scatological references (See *Romeo and Juliet*, 2.1.37–8). They are also best eaten when they've softened to the consistency of apple butter. As Chaucer demonstrates, the Reeve can never get his metaphors straight. He may be saying that that unless he controls his passions in age, he will go on rotting like a medlar. Or he may mean that, like a medlar, he will never be worth anything until his flesh is fully rotten. The medlar's crude common name also shows the Reeve is *not* too old for ribaldry.

But we're not leeks. Our wares hang down
Despite our will to cat around.
Though we can't use it, lust's not dead.
Its fires are only banked instead.
   "Four other coals match lust indeed—
Boasting, anger, lying, greed. 30
These never lose their glow with age.
Though limbs grow creaky by that stage,
The will's still spry, and that's the truth.
I boil with lust like any youth.
My life has ebbed, and death's approached
Quite near since my life's cask was broached.
When I was born, too long ago,
Death tapped that keg and let it flow;
Since then my busy spigot's run.
The emptying is nearly done. 40
The stream of life runs almost dry,
And though my tongue keeps up its cry
Of misery, that too has passed.
Dotage is all we're left at last."
   Our Host despised this sermonizing
And shouted like an angry king:
"Why plague us with your dismal wit?
We might as well read Holy Writ!
We'll have no preaching from a reeve
Till cobblers captain ships and weave! 50
Tell us your tale, and mind the time.
Here's Deptford, and we're half through prime!   *It's about 7:30 AM; they're five*
Greenwich next, the home of shrews,   *miles on their way.*
Your tale, and briefly, if you choose!"
   "Then hear it," said this Reeve, Oswald,
"But promise you won't be appalled.
My tale must dabble in the mire,
If I'm to counter fire with fire.
   "The Miller told, God curse his spite,
How Alison beguiled a woodwright, 60
I felt his scorn, for I'm one too,
So here's what I intend to do.
I'll pay him back in his own terms.
My tale will prick him till he squirms.

He sees a dust mote in my eye,   *Matt. 7:3; Luke 6:41–2*
I'll show the beam in his, or try."

THE REEVE'S TALE

At Trumpington, just outside Cambridge,
A brook runs down beneath a bridge,
And standing by this pleasant rill,
In all God's truth, there is a mill.   70
The jolly miller dwelling there
Was peacock-proud and free of care.
For he could pipe or catch a fish
Or shoot an arrow where he wished,
Play drinking games or wrestle hard;
And at his belt he wore a sword,
A dagger too, well ground and slim.
No prudent man would rankle him.
A Sheffield blade tucked in his hose,
A full round face with flattened nose,   80
And ape-hair matted on his skull
Proclaimed the man a savage bull.
Few neighbors ever dared to anger
This vile and vengeful noggin-banger.
Then too he pilfered grain and meal,
A sly deceiver, born to steal.
Insolent Simkin was his name.
His wife was of some local fame.
The parson had begotten her,
And paid her dowry, I infer,   90
To join the miller to his blood.
Nuns tended to the little bud,
For Simkin wanted to be sure
The girl was gently raised and pure,
And fit to be a yeoman's wife.
She grew up spoiled for common life.
On holidays, no one could see
A vainer pair of their degree,
He, with his hood wound round his head,

She, tripping in a gown of red,   *Working people weren't supposed to wear red.*
His fiery hose dyed just the same.
Everybody called her "dame."
No man dared seduce this wife,
For Simkin would cut short his life—
Corner him and go to work
With cutlass, bodkin, knife, and dirk.
Such men are hot as boiling tar
(Or want the town to think they are).
As she was born beneath a cloud,
She made it up by being proud,   110
And went about with nose in air.
She thought no lady living there
Could match her blood or noble carriage
The nuns taught her before her marriage.
   They had a daughter, you should know,
A girl of twenty years or so,
And a jolly infant less than one,
A little boy, their only son.
The girl was large—she grew up fast—
A pushed-in nose, eyes gray as glass,   120
A big, broad bum, and pillowy breast,
But her hair was striking, I attest.
   At least the parson thought her fair.
He meant to make the girl his heir:
She'd have his goods and household stuff,
And more, if she wed well enough.
He hoped she'd win a noble match,
The grandest suitor she could catch.
Since holy church goods must go wholly
To churchmen and their families solely,   130
He'd make her rich, her and her lord,
By skimming from the Church's hoard.
   Our miller had exclusive rights
To grind for all surrounding sites,
Especially one Cambridge college,
King's Hall, a noble fount of knowledge.   *later merged into Trinity college*
He ground the scholars' wheat and malt.
   It happened once, through no one's fault,
Their manciple became unwell,   *business agent*

Confined entirely to his cell.   140
If Simkin robbed their flour of old,
He stepped it up a hundredfold.
Where once he stole a little bit
He now filched all that he could get.
Let the warden rage and curse.   *master of the college*
That only made his losses worse,
While Simkin sulked and acted hurt.

   Two ragged scholars, bright and pert,
Were living in this same King's Hall,
Apt lads for any prank or brawl.   150
Each thought he spied a chance for fun,
And begged the warden, two on one,
To let them journey as they willed
To see a load of dry grain milled.
They'd foil the miller, by their neck.
He couldn't short them half a peck.
Just let him try! Of course they'd know.
At length the warden let them go.
One was John, Allan the other,
Both from a little town called Strother,   160
Far to the north. I don't know where.

   They chose a horse for this affair,
Brought out the grain and strapped it on,
And set out jingling, just at dawn,
With swords and bucklers by their side.
John knew the way without a guide.
At the mill they dumped the grain,
With "Fresh work, Simkin, in your vein!
How are your daughter and your wife?"

   "Welcome," said Simkin, "by my life.   170
Allan and John, what brings you here?"

   "Ach, friend," said John, "need has no peer.
Without a servant one can't shirk;
As need determines, he must work.
Our manciple is nearly dead,
To hear the teeth clash in his head,
So I have come, and Allan too,
To bring our unmilled grain to you.
Perhaps you'll grind the load today?"

"Done," said Simkin, "right away!   180
What will you do while it is milling?"
     "Stand by the hopper, if you're willing,"
Said John, "and watch the grain go in.
I never saw, by all my kin,
How hoppers shuttle to and fro."
     Then Allen said, "And I will go
Below the millstone, by my crown,
And watch the flour tumble down
Into the trough, a pleasant sport,
For, John, I'm one of your own sort,   190
A novice miller, as you say."
     "Ah," Simkin thought, "my lucky day.
How can they think I'm not aware
They mean to hold me to my share?
Let's see them match my roguery
For all of their philosophy!
The more smart tricks they try to play,
The more I mean to steal today.
In place of flour, I'll give them bran!
Your scholar's not the wisest man,   200
Or so the wolf heard from the mare.[2]
So let them watch. As if I care!"
     He stepped outside beyond their sight,
And when he saw the time was right
He made a circuit of the mill
And found their horse well hitched and still,
In a little arbor's shade.
The miller slipped into the glade,
Removed the bridle, set it free.
The horse let out a glad "Weehee!"   210
Toward a swamp where wild mares ran
And made off as the miller planned.
     Saying nothing of the horse,
The man left things to run their course
Until the flour was fairly ground,
Neatly sacked, securely bound.

2. The mare told the learned wolf the price of her foal was written on the bottom of her
hind hoof. When he looked, she kicked him.

Then John found out the nag was gone
And called out, "Allan, we're undone!
The horse has bolted, by God's trumpet!
Stir yourself! Come on, man, hump it!　　　　220
The warden's sure to have us brained!"
Allan forgot his meal and grain.
All those cares evaporated.
He stared about him addlepated.

   The wife came squawking like a hen:
"Alas, your horse is in the fen!
Those mares will lead him far away!
Curse the hand that let him stray;
He should have been much better tied!
You've lost him now for sure," she cried.　　　　230

   "Allan," said John, "put off your sword.
And I'll do likewise. On my word,
I can outrun any buck.
We'll catch him with a little luck.
You should have put him in a stall.
My God, have you no sense at all?"

   The clerks stripped down to run a course
Against their foe, Bayard, the horse.

    Meanwhile, the miller seized his hour,
And half a bushel of their flour.　　　　240
He gave it to his wife to take
And knead into a mighty cake.
He said, "Just watch those scholars work!
A miller's too much for a clerk.
Their learned arts get in their way.
But, Lord, they're nimble! Watch them play!
The horse is faster, by my crown."

   The silly clerks ran up and down,
With "Whoa!" and "Stop!" and "Watch out there!"
"I'll head the beast! He's gone! Now where?"　　　　250
But it was far into the night
Before the horse gave up the fight.
Splashing in mud as black as pitch,
They got him bridled in a ditch.

   Then worn and wet as beasts in rain
They led him to the mill again.

"Alas," said John, "that I was born!
All we've achieved is shame and scorn.
The grain is gone, and we're two fools.
Unfit to play by grown men's rules.
Whatever will the warden say?"   260
    And so John grieved along the way,
Leading Bayard through the mire.
They found the miller by his fire.
Now it was late and they were caught.
They wrung their hands and humbly sought
A lodging there. They said they'd pay.
    Sly Simkin answered, "Welladay!
Such as I own, you'll have a part.
The house is small, but can't your art,   270
By argument, stretch any place—
A mile from twenty feet of space?
See if my room will suit you each,
Or make it bigger with a speech."
    "Simkin," said John, "by Cuthbert's ghost,   *Saint Cuthbert, c. 635–87*
Indeed you make a merry host.
I've heard men say, 'Have one of two:
What's there or what you brought with you.'
If you provide us meat and beer,
Allan and I will hold you dear,   280
And we shall pay. Don't think we'll balk.
No empty hand can catch a hawk.
Look now, here's silver, by my head."
    The girl was sent for beer and bread
While smiling Simkin broiled a goose,
Secured Bayard from getting loose,
And made a bed in his own room,
Spread sheets and blankets in the gloom,
Close to where the couple slept
And where his daughter's bed was kept—   290
Three beds together, side-by-side,
Because, for all the miller's pride,
There was no other room to use.
The scholars supped and traded news,
And felt the brew go to their heads,
Till midnight came, and time for bed.

The miller's brain was turned by ale,
Sheer drunkenness had left him pale.
He burped and snorted through his nose
And babbled hoarsely in his throes.   300
He climbed in bed beside his wife
And found her keen as any knife,
For she had wet her whistle too.
The baby's crib, as such things do,
Sat by the footboard of her bed.
Now that the crock of ale was dead,
The girl retired with little noise,
And so did both the college boys.
They didn't need a sleeping draught.
The miller had drunk himself so daft   310
He let out horse-snores in his sleep
And thunderous farts both long and deep.
His wife sang tenor to his bass.
The walls shook in that little space.
The girl snored too, for company.
    When Allan heard this melody,
He shook his friend and said, "Asleep?
I swear their snoring makes me weep.
God, how they sing their midnight hymns!
May wild fire burn their heads and limbs!   320
Their snores have set me wondering:
How to repay such thundering?
I'll never get a bit of rest;
Still, . . . that may turn out for the best.
Ha! John, as I'm a proper bloke,
I'll give that girl a manly poke.
Some compensation's owed to us,
For, John, I swear the law reads thus:
'If in one thing you're aggrieved,
Choose another to be relieved.'   330
Our wheat is stolen, John, I say,
And we've been badly used today.
Well, since I've had no quid pro quo,
I'll pay myself before I go.
By God, I'll have that girl indeed!"
    "But, brother," said his friend, "take heed!

The miller plays for heavy stakes.
Suppose she squeals and he awakes.
He'll do us grievous injury!"
    Allan said, "Just wait and see."   340
The room was steeped in darkest black.
He found the girl upon her back,
And got to work when he came nigh
So swiftly that she couldn't cry,
Not that she cared, once he was on.
Let Allan play; consider John.
    John lay still a little space,
Stark consternation on his face.
"Alas," he said, "a wicked jape!
Of all of us, I am the ape.   350
Allan has something for his harms,
To wit, the daughter in his arms.
He took a chance, and now he's sped,
While I lie like a chump in bed;
And when this joke is told one day,
I'll be the nitwit of the play!
Well, let me rise and try my luck.
No one succeeds without some pluck!"
He rose up then and felt around,
Seeking the cradle, which he found   360
And moved discreetly by his bed.
    The wife soon shook her muddled head,
And stumbled out to have a piss.
Then back. But soft now, what's amiss?
There was no cradle by her way!
"Alas," she said, "I've gone astray.
This must be the young clerks' bed.
God's providence great," she said.
She found the cradle with her hand,
And then the bed, just as she planned.   370
As nothing happened to recall her,
She snuggled down beside the scholar
And lay quite still and would have slept,
But John let out a snort and leapt,
And clasped the wife in such a way,
She knew what game he meant to play,

And let him delve for all his worth.
Ah, now both scholars swam in mirth,
Until the cock began to sing.
   Allan was running out of string,   380
The lad had worked beyond his strength.
"Farewell, Moll," he said at length,
"It's morning now; I mustn't wait.
But from this hour, I tell you straight,
This scholar will remember you."
   "Ah, love," she said, "I hope that's true!
But hear this, Allan; listen well:
As you go out by Father's mill,
Step in the door and look around.
You'll find a cake of fifteen pounds.   390
That cake was made of your own meal,
Fresh flour I helped my pa to steal.
Farewell," she said, and turned aside,
And with the word she almost cried.
   Allan thought: "Before it's dawn,
I'll creep back into bed with John."
He found the cradle with his toes.
"By God," he murmured, "that was close!
My head's so woozy from my work,
I've come the wrong way by some quirk.   400
This cradle marks the miller's bed.
Let's try the other one instead."
And so he crawled, the devil's prey,
Into the bed where Simkin lay.
He thought the miller there was John,
Climbed in beside him with a yawn,
And grabbed his neck and whispered low,
"Pig's head! Here's something you should know.
For Christ's sake hear a noble story,
For by Saint James in all his glory,   410
Three times so far in this short night,
I've swived the girl with great delight,
While you lay quailing in your bed!"
   "Muck!" said the miller, "I'll have your head!
Traitor! Scholar! Where's my knife?
By God, you'll pay me with your life!

What? Would you ruin and degrade
My daughter, such a well-born maid?"
He gripped the scholar's Adam's apple
And held him down to knee and grapple   420
And smote him roundly on the nose.
Hot blood shot out as from a hose.
The miller freshened his attack.
They writhed like two pigs in a sack.
Never was a fight more stark,
Till Simkin stumbled in the dark,
And fell down backward on his wife.
Now she knew nothing of their strife,
For she was sleeping like the dead,
Worn out by serving John in bed.   430
She started up, called out in fright:
"Great Cross of Bromeholm, give me light!   *a shrine in Norfolk*
In manus tuas! Set me free!   *"Into your hands" [Lord, I commend*
Alack! The devil's taken me!   *my spirit]—Luke 23:46*
My heart is shattered; I am dead;
He's crushed my womb and cracked my head!
Up, Simkin, for the scholars fight!"
    Next, John awoke without a light,
And groped about to find a staff.
The wife did too on her behalf.   440
She knew the layout brick by brick,
And by the wall she found a stick.
A sliver of the moon's bright light
Gleamed in the room, though it was slight.
Two shadows tussled to and fro,
But who was who, she couldn't know.
Just then she saw a whitish patch
Jounce up and down with great dispatch.
"Ah, that's the scholar's cap!" she thought.
Edging up to where they fought,   450
She swung the staff with all her might,
But missed the lad for want of light,
And cracked her husband's hairy skull.
That did for him. She heard him fall:
"Help!" he said. "I die today!"
The two clerks thrashed him where he lay,

Then gathered up their horse and traps
And took their flour, and more perhaps.
They found their cake inside the mill,
The full half-bushel by its feel.   460
    And thus the miller was lambasted,
And lost his flour and cake untasted,
And cooked his goose for free, by God,
For two who flayed him with a rod.
His wife's debauched, his daughter too,
To give the churlish knave his due.
He proved the saw, a bitter pill:
"The wicked man shall suffer ill."
A swindler swindled, you'll agree,
Suits God in his high majesty.   470
Christ save all pilgrims without fail!
And thus I've capped the Miller's tale!

Heere is ended the Reves Tale.

THE COOK

THE COOK'S TALE

The Cook's story starts out to be a rough and tumble narrative like the Miller's and the Reeve's, but it takes place among a lower sort of people, and in London—the Cook's hometown—not Oxford or Cambridge. The prologue begins with a good-natured quarrel, when Harry Bailey, the Host, accuses the Cook of unsavory practices—selling dried-out and warmed-over meat pies and roasted geese with spoiled stuffing. The Cook promises to retaliate with a tale against innkeepers, but not now. His present story will concern "a jest that happened in our city."

The tale, just a fragment, never gets off the ground. The Cook introduces Perkin Reveler, a grocer's apprentice marked for trouble. His life is full of loose living and short bouts of jail time. He can roll dice with suspicious facility and enjoys spending money, no doubt the reason his master often finds the strongbox empty. Upset by all this, the grocer discharges Perkin, who moves in with a fellow scamp. This fellow has a wife who pretends to keep a shop but really supports herself by whoring . . . and at this point the story breaks off. One manuscript contains the note, "Of this cokes tale maked Chaucer na moore."

The Man of Law

The Man of Law's Tale

The Introduction to "The Man of Law's Tale" is useful for setting the time of
The Canterbury Tales, *but everything else about it is perplexing. As the pro-*
logue opens, the Host notices that it is ten o'clock in the morning on April the
eighteenth and calls for another story. The Man of Law agrees, but says that
Chaucer, although he is inept at meters or rhyming, has beaten him to all the
good choices. He then goes on to list many of these preempted tales, mostly love
stories Chaucer included in The Legend of Good Women. *Nevertheless, the*
Man of Law says he can manage a story in prose. But when his tale arrives it is
written in rhyming stanzas!

Next comes a separate prologue about the evils of poverty, based on a 12th-
century treatise on human miseries by Pope Innocent III, good stuff in its way,
but not noticeably relevant to the tale that follows—a ramshackle potboiler about
Constance, daughter of the emperor of Rome, who is sent to marry the sultan of
Syria on condition he convert to Christianity.

Needless to say, there are complications. The sultan's wicked mother kills her
son and sets Constance aboard a rudderless boat to drift three years until she
comes to land in England, in Northumberland. Constance has no memory of
who she is, but she still manages to heal a blind man and convert the local con-
stable and his wife to Christianity. A knight falls in love with her, but she spurns
him. He kills Lady Hermingild, the constable's wife, and blames Constance for
the crime, denouncing her to Alla, king of Northumberland. Things look bad for
Constance until the false knight swears to her guilt on the Gospels and is struck
down by a ghostly hand. A voice confirms the knight's treachery, and Alla him-
self converts. He goes on to marry Constance, and in due course they have a lit-
tle son, Maurice.

It turns out, though, that Alla's mother is no better than the mother of the sul-
tan in Syria, and she causes Constance to be set adrift again, this time with her
baby. The king finds out what his mother has done and has her executed, but
Constance welters at sea for five more years, coming ashore only once, in a hea-
then country where she is nearly raped.

Meanwhile the Roman emperor is grieving for his daughter, who he assumes was lost at sea. He sends out an expedition to punish Syria, and on its return the senator in charge comes across Constance and her son in their boat, rescues them, and carries them to Rome to live with him and his wife—who is Constance's aunt, if she only knew.

King Alla? He decides he must go to Rome to ask forgiveness for killing his mother. As he sits at a feast there, Maurice comes to gaze at him. The boy looks so much like his mother that Alla goes to the senator's home, where he discovers Constance!

When the emperor himself comes to dinner with Alla, Constance announces she is his daughter (Chaucer never says how her memory returned), and the reunions are complete. Alla and his family sail to England, but within a year he dies, and Constance and Maurice return to Rome, where they live with Constance's father until he dies as well. Then, for a further wonder, Maurice becomes emperor.

The tale includes some interesting passages, including this comment on Alla and Constance's wedding night—a prudish take on human sexuality, which Chaucer explores with more zest elsewhere:

They went to bed, as reasonable and right,
For though men's wives are modest, holy things,
They need to lie there patiently at night
And bear such business as men's craving brings.
This duty comes to brides with wedding rings.
All wives must put their holiness aside
At certain times—that cannot be denied.

The Epilogue to "The Man of Law's Tale" provides more evidence that Chaucer's final plans for The Canterbury Tales *were radically unsettled. It seems to introduce "The Shipman's Tale," but various manuscripts identify the person who offers to tell the next story as the Summoner or the Squire instead. Another school of thought has it that the pilgrim in the Epilogue that follows who objects to sermons was originally the Wife of Bath, who was supposed to tell what is now "The Shipman's Tale" before her present tale was assigned to her.*

At any event, the Epilogue adds another note to Chaucer's presentation of the religious issues of his day.

EPILOGUE TO THE MAN OF LAW'S TALE

Up spoke the Host with this tale done,
"Good men, listen, every one!
This was a thrifty story and no loss.
Sir Parson, now, by Jesus' cross,
Where's the tale you pledged before?
Wise men like you, well steeped in lore,
Can do us good, by God's simplicity!"

    The Parson answered, "*Benedicity!*   *bless us*
What makes him swear so sinfully?"
"Ah," said the Host, "a saint, is he?   10
I smell a Lollard in the wind.[1]
Now listen,"—here the fellow grinned—
"Hear me, gentles, it's determined,
We'll now enjoy a wholesome sermon.
This Lollard here will preach somewhat!"

    "No, by my father, he shall not!"
The Shipman said, "nor will he teach,
Or gloss God's word with lying speech.
We all believe in Christ," said he,
"Why stir us up to disagree,   20
And sow sharp thistles in our corn?
No, Host, as sure as I was born,
I myself will tell a tale,
A merry story without fail,
A tale to wake this company,
And one without philosophy!
No quiddities or terms of law.
There's little Latin in my maw!"

---

1. A general term for early puritans who condemned worldliness in or out of the church and objected to nonbiblical practices, like pilgrimages.

THE WIFE OF BATH

THE WIFE OF BATH'S PROLOGUE

My life gives me authority,
Enough and more, it seems to me,
To speak of all the woe in marriage,
For since I was twelve years of age,
By God, who's evermore alive,
Of wedded husbands, I've had five
(If they were all legitimate),
And each a man of worth and weight.
But someone said, upon that heading,
As Christ attended just one wedding—   10
At Cana, it was, in Galilee—   *John 2.1*
That fact alone should prove to me
That I should marry only once.
Then there's that text where Christ confronts
Beside a well, as God and man,   *John 4.6–26*
A neighborly Samaritan:
"You've married five," he said, "but stay.
I say the man with you today
Is not your husband." So he said,
But who knows what went through his head?   20
No one can explain his grounds
For placing five men out of bounds.
How many husbands might she marry?
Now I don't wish to be contrary,
But no one has defined that number.
Priests may reproach, condemn, encumber,
But I know well, without a lie,
God bade us wax and multiply.   *Gen. 1.28*
That gentle text I understand!
This too: that when I take a man,   30
Sirs, *I* become his chief concern   *Matt. 19.5*

107

Not his relations, though they burn.
These rules define the wedded state,
And not how many men you mate.
Bigamy, octogamy—
To me such terms are value free.
    How many wives had Solomon?
Why, hundreds when the count was done.
I wish it were permitted me
To taste love half as oft as he!   40
Ah, what a gift he had for wives!
No living man could match his drives.
God knows, and why should we forget,
That king had many a merry fit
With each of them while yet alive!
So I praise God I've had my five.
Then too, I always picked the best
For manly wares and all the rest.
As many schools improve a clerk,
And widespread practice in his work   50
Corrects a craftsman, all agree,
Five husbands have perfected me.
Welcome the sixth when he appears!
I won't live chaste through all my years,
But when my spouse is dead and gone,
I'll wed another man anon.
Saint Paul himself says I am free
To wed a man who pleases me.
He sanctions marriage, though he's stern.
Far better that we wed than burn!   *1 Cor. 7–9*
Though folks may call it villainy,
Lamech invented bigamy.   *Gen. 4.19*
Abraham was a holy man,
And Jacob too, I understand,
Yet each of them had several wives
Like other men of holy lives.
Who has ever heard or read
That God forbid mankind to wed?[1]

---

1. The Wife silently shifts the subject from multiple marriages to virginity, a much easier
topic to discuss from her point of view.

Why, no one, or it's news to me.
Did he require virginity? 70
Of course he never did, nor could.
Where Paul discusses maidenhood,
He says it is a blessed state *1 Cor. 7.25*
When women live without a mate.
That's all he says, and though it's true,
It's not a law—a good thing too.
Say God commanded chastity:
No one could wed by his decree.
With no seeds sown in marriage then,
He'd lose all virgins—and all men! 80
Paul couldn't bar, despite his bent,
What God ordained. No, he was sent
To make the virgin life a goal
For those already chaste of soul.
　　But that's not all of us, you know.
God designates. And rightly so.
Saint Paul himself was always chaste,
Abstemious in every taste.
He wished the same for every man *1 Cor. 7.7*
But never issued that command. 90
Thus I have leave to wed again.
No single man should think it sin
Or bigamy, once my mate's dead,
To take me up and share my bed.
Though Paul held women bad to touch, *1 Cor. 7.1*
Reclining on a couch or such
(That put the fire to the flax,
And you've seen how that mixture acts!),
He only termed virginity
A better choice than frailty; 100
He calls us merely frail, you see,
Who moderate our chastity.
　　I grant his point. Virginity
Surpasses sexuality.
Virgins are clean, body and soul;
We wives must play a lesser role.
But even in a lord's household
Not every dish is made of gold.

Some are wood, and yet they serve.
God calls us just as we deserve.　　　　　　　　　　110
Each person has a gift, we're told:　　　　　　　*1 Cor. 7.7*
Some formed to give and some, withhold.
　　Virginity's a great perfection.
A life is crowned by that election,
But Christ, who is perfection's fount,
Knew well not everyone would want
To sell his all and feed the poor,　　　　　　　*Matt. 19.21*
Though he himself did that and more.
Only the best of us should try.
Only the best, my lords, not I.　　　　　　　　120
No, I'll bestow my flowers in life
On husbands, as befits a wife.
　　Just tell me your interpretation
Of members shaped for generation.
Why were the sexes made that way?
Sure, nature didn't go astray.
It's only half an explanation
To say they're simply for purgation,
Or to pretend that such details
Just set us females off from males.　　　　　　130
That's simpleminded as you know;
Our whole lives say it isn't so.
Though clerks may blame me, on my oath,
I say we have these tools for both:
For daily tasks and as a way
Of getting children, if we may.
Why else would this old saw be true,
"A man must pay his wife her due"?　　　　　　*1 Cor. 7.3*
By "man must pay" what could be meant
But serve her with his instrument?　　　　　　140
No, those parts have a dual causation—
For purging and for procreation.
　　Of course I don't say everyone
Must use his gear as I have done,
That is to say, engendering.
For chastity's a noble thing.
Christ was a maid shaped as a man,　　　　　　*virgin*
And ever since the world began,

Saints have lived in chastity.
I'll not decry virginity.   150
Virgins are bread of finest wheat,
Wives, barley bread, more coarse and sweet.
Yet barley loaves of God's creation,
Fed Jesus and his congregation.   *John 6.9*
So just as God's hand molded us
I'll live my life in open trust
And use my wifely instrument
Without restraint, as it was sent.
If I'm standoffish, give me sorrow!
My man shall have it night and morrow,   160
Whenever he comes to pay his debt.
My husband, sirs, must be my thrall,
A man to answer every call,
And tire his flesh, while I'm his wife.
For I have power throughout my life
To rule his body, and not he.
That's what Paul's teaching means to me.
He bid our husbands love us well.
Lords, I agree, as you can tell!   *Col. 3.19*

   Up spoke the Pardoner anon,   170
"Ach now, good lady, by Saint John,
You preach right nobly, on my life,
For I was set to take a wife.
But now you've made the cost so clear,
I vow that I'll not wed this year!"
   Be still! said she. I've just begun.
I'll make you taste, before I've done,
A drink that savors worse than ale!
And when you've heard to good avail
The martial trials of married life   180
(And I have been a warlike wife;
That is to say, I was the whip),
Then let me know if you will sip
The barrel I shall tap for you.
But hear my tale before you do.
I'll give examples of my wiles.
"Who will not learn from others' trials,
Must be the butt of others' tales."

Ptolemy knew what that entails;
Consult his *Almagest* and see.   190
　"Grant mercy, lady, pardon me,"
The Pardoner said. "As you began,
Please tell away and spare no man.
But teach us youths your strategies."
　I shall, she said; just as you please.
But first I ask the company:
If I seem overbold and free,
Don't be aggrieved at what I say.
I only mean to joke and play.
　Now, sirs, I will tell my tale.   200
As truly as I relish ale,
Of those five husbands that I had,
Three were good, and two were bad.
The three good men were rich and old
And scarcely able to uphold
The contract binding them to me—
You take my meaning, as I see.
I swear I'm laughing even yet
At how I made them heave and sweat.
Their antics gave me little pleasure   210
Once I controlled their land and treasure.
With that I ceased my diligence,
My wifely love and reverence.
They loved me so, by God above,
That I thought nothing of their love.
A woman's work is never done
To capture love when she has none.
But once I had them in my hand,
Their bodies, purses, and their land,
Why should I care if they were pleased?   220
I was the one to be appeased.
I made them sweat, placating me.
They toiled whole nights in agony,
Yet never won for all their woe
The bacon prize set up at Dunmow.[2]

2. At Dunmow in Essex a side of bacon was presented to any couple who avoided quarrels
for a year and a day.

I governed them with such dispatch
That they were happy just to catch
My smile with gay things from the fair.
But my compliant moods were rare,
For I could sting them piteously.   230
    Now listen close and follow me,
All wives who want to understand
The fittest way to treat a man.
Men can't rival, though they try,
A woman's gift to swear and lie.
(Of course I don't mean proper wives,
But those perniciously advised.)
An able wife who knows her good
Can make men trust her as they should,
Believe her maid and not the town.   240
Here's what I said to beat them down:
    "Sir, only dotards talk that way.
Why is our neighbor's wife so gay?
She's honored over all the rest.
I sit at home and poorly dressed.
What are you up to over there?
Are you so fond? Is she so fair?
What do you whisper to our maid?
A common lecher and his jade!
But let me have a passing friend   250
In innocence, why you contend
I've lost my virtue at his house.
You drag home drunken as a mouse,
And preach to me upon your bench!
'A man just digs an endless trench,'
You say, 'to wed a needy wife.
And if she's rich, of gentle life,
Why, she repays his loving folly
By being proud or melancholy.
And if she's fair, then he must dread   260
Some gigolo will turn her head.'
You say our virtue's soon untied
When it's assailed from every side.
    "You say some men admire our wealth.
Or else our shape, good looks, or health.

Perhaps they watch us sing or dance,
Or love our style of dalliance,
Or praise our hands or slender arms,
Or woo us for our other charms.
'No man can hold a wall,' you say,   270
'When it's assaulted night and day.'

    "Nor is an ugly wife secure.
You say her spaniel looks ensure
She'll wag her tail for any man
Until she finds one she can land.
'There's not a goose but soon or late,'
You say, 'she'll find herself a mate.'
A husband's helpless, doomed, you hold.
No living wife can be controlled.
I've even heard you preach in bed.   280
You say no man's required to wed,
Nor should he, if he'd save his soul.
May lightning blasts consume you whole!
Go break your scrawny neck and choke!

    "You say that falling walls and smoke
And chiding wives cause men to fly
From their own houses. What a lie!
What makes old dotards drivel so?

    "You say wives let their vices show
Once they are wed and feel secure: 290
A fitting proverb for a boor!

    "You say a hound or ox or horse
Is bought on trial by common course,
Like bowls and washpots that one tries,
Spoons and stools and such supplies,
Or basins, clothes, and knives and files,
But wives aren't subject to such trials
Till they are wedded—dotard, shrew!—
It's only then our faults come through.

    "You say that now your daily duty,   290
Is coining tributes to my beauty.
You say I make you scan my face
And call me fair and praise my grace,
And make a feast to mark my birthday,
And work to keep me fresh and gay,

And give my old nurse help and aid,
And cultivate my chambermaid,
And kowtow to my father's kin—
Ach, what a sink of lies and sin!
   "Yet Jenkin drives you to despair, 310
The apprentice with the golden hair—
Shining, crisped, upon his crown—
Because he squires me up and down.
I'd spurn him if you died tomorrow!
But tell me why, to my great sorrow,
You hide your treasure chest and key,
When half your goods belong to me.
Would you hoard money from your wife?
No, you shall not, upon my life!
You can't contrive by force or stealth 320
To rule my body and my wealth.
One will elude you, curse your eyes,
For all your prying and your spies.
You'll never lock *me* in your chest!
Just say, 'Dear, do as you think best.
I'll not attend to tales or malice;
I love and trust you, dearest Alice!'
No woman will be kept in charge.
We must be free and roam at large.
   "A man as learned as men may be, 330
The astrologer Don Ptolemy,
Put this down in his *Almagest:*
'Of all wise men, that one is best,
Who doesn't care who rules the world.'
Ptolemy's saying, when uncurled,
Means 'Have enough, and never care
However well your friends may fare.'
That is, old fool, for all your spite,
You get your fill of me each night.
Only a miser blind to shame 340
Would grudge to share his lantern's flame.
No sharing hurts his light, indeed.
Enough is plenty. More is greed.
   "And then you carp, if wives are gay
With clothes and gauds and fine array,

Those goods can harm our chastity.
Because you know I disagree,
You cite these words in Saint Paul's name:
'Chaste array and modest shame,'
Paul said, 'These are a woman's rules,   350
And not curled hair and precious jewels,
Or pearls or gold or costly gowns.'   *1 Tim. 2.9*
Faugh! I reject both text and grounds.
They move me no more than a gnat.

　"And then you say I'm like a cat:
To keep a preening cat inside,
You spoil her looks. You singe her hide,
For if her coat is sleek and gay,
She won't stay by you half a day.
She'll escape and go a-calling,   360
Stretching, purring, caterwauling.
If I'm well dressed, to hear you rant,
I only mean to gallivant.

　"Peer as you like and set your spies.
Call Argus with his hundred eyes,   *sent by Hera*
To guard me as no other could.   *to guard Io*
I'd hoodwink Argus, if I would.
I could set his cap, I know.

　"You say that three bad things work so   *Prov. 30.21 ff.*
To plague men and destroy their mirth,   370
That no one can endure a fourth.[3]
I pray that Jesus blunt your knife!
You tell me that a hateful wife
Is one of these supreme mischances.
Say, are there never other answers
To your foul riddles, on my life,
Than those that denigrate a wife?

　"You say a woman's love is hell,
A desert land without a well,
An unrestrained and raging fire   380
That burns its fuel and then desires
To spread as far as one can see.

---

3. The four bad things: a servant in charge, a fool who eats well, an odious wife, and a
handmaid who inherits from her mistress.

You say as worms consume a tree
So does a wife consume a man—
A truth all husbands understand. . . ."
   Friends, that's the way I dealt with strife,
I made those old men rue their life.
I damned their drinking and caprice.
I called on Jenkin and my niece,
To swear their charges were untrue.   390
Ah, Lord, the grief I put them through!
All innocent, as God is kind,
But, like a horse, I bit and whined.
Though guilty, I got off by squawking.
I cowed them with torrential talking.
The first in line is first to grind.   *i.e., at a mill*
I started first and nagged them blind.
They'd confess (I'd growl and glower!)
Offenses quite beyond their power.
I'd damn their lust—and plump their egos—   400
When illness made them rasp and doze.
   (How they managed to suppose
That I was jealous, heaven knows.)
I swore I only walked at night
To keep their fancy girls in sight.
That pretext won me hours of mirth.
We wives are fitted out at birth
For such deceiving. God supplies
Us arts to make men doubt their eyes.
Why, even now it makes me proud: 410
I beat them all, as I've allowed,
With tricks or force or loud complaints,
Or murmurs that would try a saint.
Their luck was even worse in bed.
I scolded so, they went in dread.
I'd leave the bed itself in pride
If they so much as touched my side
Before they had rewarded me.
Then I'd endure their nicety.
No doubt you understand this tale.   420
Prepare to pay; it's all for sale.
No empty hand can lure a hawk;

For money, though, I'd never balk.
I'd even feign an appetite,
Though bacon's far from my delight.   *dried, old flesh*
And thus, my lords, I'd scold and mope,
For though they sat beside the pope
They'd get no peace at their own board.
In short, I paid them word for word.
I swear by God omnipotent,   430
I'll say in my last testament,
I gave back every word I owed.
I made my tongue so sharp a goad
They had to yield—I'd never cease—
Or give up any hope of peace.
They snapped and snarled, you understand,
But knew I had the upper hand.
     Then I would say, "Dear, don't be silly,
Do what I say like our sheep, Willy.
Come, husband, let me kiss your cheek.   440
A good man should be mild and meek,
Wrapped in patience like a robe.
I've heard you say you honor Job;
So bear with us, the ones you preach to.
If not, depend on me to teach you
How sweet peace is compared to strife.
Now, you or I must rule our life.
As men are mild, disposed to thought,
Give way to me, dear, as you ought.
Why must you always grouch and groan?   450
Perhaps you want my crotch alone?
Have it! Take it! Every bit!
By God, I'm glad you relish it;
If I should sell my sweet *belle chose*   *pretty thing*
I'd walk as fresh as any rose.
But, no, I keep it for your tooth.
Your fears are groundless. That's the truth."
     Three husbands sank beneath such lore;
Now let me speak of number four:
     Ah, that one was a reveler;   460
That is to say, he had a paramour—
And I was young and ripe for play,

Bold and stubborn as a jay.
How I could dance! I wasn't frail.
I'd outsing any nightingale
When I had drunk a draught of wine.
Metellius, the Roman swine,
Beat his poor wife to death for toping.
Ha! I'd have cured his interloping!
He never could bar *me* from wine!
Still, drinking leads to Venus' shrine,   470
For just as sure as cold breeds hail,
A liquorish mouth has a lecherous tail.
A drunken woman has no defense—
Ask lechers their experience!
    But, Christ, when I look back and see
My youth and strength and jollity,
It tickles me, and well it should.
Even now it does me good.
I had the world once in my time.
But age dims everything with grime.   480
I've lost my beauty and my pith.
So what? The Devil go therewith!
The flour is gone now, sad to tell,
But I still have the bran to sell.
I'll still be genial and jocund.
Now let me speak of my fourth husband.
    Although it gave me great despite,
Some strumpet was his chief delight.
But I got even, to his cost.
I hung him on the selfsame cross,   490
Not by adultery as such,
But making people think as much.
I fried the man in his own grease.
His fancies seldom gave him peace.
God sent me for his purgatory,
For which I hope his soul's in glory.
He sang for woe and hung his jaw.
I was the shoe that rubbed him raw.
God alone knows how I wrung him,
Thwarted him, deceived him, stung him!   500
When I'd been to Jerusalem,

He died, and so I buried him
Beneath the rood screen in our church—[4]
No Persian tomb. I didn't search
For some Appelles' sepulture.   *Appelles designed the lavish tomb of Darius.*
Why spend a fortune to immure
A man like him? Why be so brave?
His coffin suits him in his grave.
   Now of the fifth one let me tell.   510
I pray his soul is not in hell!
He was the sharpest one, God knows!
Why, even now I feel his blows
And will until my dying day,
But in our bed he was so gay,
And wheedled with so fine a grace
To pleasure me in his embrace
That though he beat on every bone,
He held my heart, and he alone.
I loved him best of all, for he   520
Withheld his love to punish me.
We women harbor, I'll not lie,
A strange and wayward fantasy:
Whatever we can't have at will,
We clamor for it, good or ill.
Forbid a thing, and we pursue it.
Approve of it, and we won't do it.
Some men act scornful to entice us
And thus inflate their asking prices.
Too cheap a conquest lacks appeal.   530
At least that's how most women feel.
   My fifth man, then, God bless his spirit,
Was not a tycoon—nowhere near it.
No, he was once a clerk at Oxford,
And later he returned to board
With my best friend in all our town—
God save her soul!—my Alison.
She knew my heart and secrets too
Far better than our priest could do.

---

4. A screen, usually ornate, between the nave, or congregation's part of a church, and the choir, or chancel.

I'd tell her anything at all.   540
If my poor man pissed on a wall
Or did a thing that meant his life,
To her (and to one other wife,
And to my niece, whom I loved then)
I'd detail where and how and when.
I blabbed so often, by my head,
My husband's face was always red.
He knew no man of average sense
Would trust me with his confidence.
   It happened that one time in Lent—   550
A season I as much as spent
With Alison to flirt and play
And gad abroad from March to May—
That Jenkin, Alison, and I
Walked out into the fields nearby.
My husband was in town that spring,
Which left me free as any king,
To see the people and be seen.
How could I live out what was fated,
Unless I went where it awaited?
So I embarked without discretion   560
On churchly vigils and processions
And pilgrim jaunts and Bible plays,
And sermons and gay wedding days,
And always in my scarlet gown.
No moth or worm in all our town
Could gnaw a hole in that array.
And why? I wore it every day!
   Across the fields we tripped along,
Caught up in foolish play and song.
We blushed and mooned and flirted so   570
That I at last let Jenkin know
He was the man, and only he,
I'd wed if I were ever free.
For I'm the sort, sirs, understand,
Who's never caught without a plan
In love or in my other interests.
There's no heart in a mouse's breast
That has but one poor hole to hide him.

He's dead if that one hole's denied him.
   I claimed he had enchanted me
(My mother's brand of subtlety)
And said I dreamed of him all night—
He slew me as I lay upright
And all the bedclothes swam in blood,
But I took comfort in that flood,
For blood betokens gold, I thought.
A pack of lies, for I dreamed naught,
But spoke as Mother said I should.
Her love advice was always good.   590
     But tell me, sirs, . . . what was I saying?
It's here, by God. My tale again!
   When Husband Four was on his bier,
I moaned and groaned with sorry cheer,
As good wives must, for that's our place.
Yet I took care to hide my face.
Because I'd found another man,
My tears held back, as dry as sand.
   Men bore the corpse to church next day
With neighbors sighing "Welladay!"   600
Jenkin himself was in the crowd
Behind the bier, and I allowed,
I'd never seen another pair
Of legs and feet so clean and fair.
I gave him all my heart to hold.
Now he was twenty winters old,
And I was forty; that's the truth.
I always had a young colt's tooth.   *youthful desires*
I had gap teeth, and that was fine.
Who else should wear Dame Venus' sign?[5]   610
By God, I was a lusty one,
Fair and rich, excelled by none,
And truly all my husbands said
My *queynt* was fit for any bed.   *"dainty part"*
From birth the working of my stars
Was ruled by Venus and by Mars.
As Venus made me lecherous,

5. Gaps between the teeth showed a lecherous disposition.

Mars made me bold and treacherous.
Born in the Bull when Mars was there,   *the constellation Taurus*
Supplied with love and pluck to spare,   620
I followed every inclination
Thrust on me by my constellation.
That's why I never could withhold
My Venus box when well cajoled.
Yet I have Mars' mark on my face   *this mark is unidentified*
And in another secret place.
As God may witness my confession,
I never used the least discretion,
But chose my men by appetite.
Short or tall or dark or light,   630
I never cared, if someone loved me,
How poor he was, or what degree.
    What can I say? A few weeks later,
This pretty Jenkin, no one greater,
Married me with pomp and pleasure.
I gave him all my land and treasure,
All the gains I'd won before,
And afterward repented sore.
I'd ask for things. He wouldn't hear.
He cuffed me so upon the ear   640
(I ripped a leaf out of his book),
My ear went dead where I was struck.
But I was cross-grained as a cat
And talked him down in every spat.
I vowed I'd roam just as before,
No matter how he scowled and swore.
He paid me back, for he would quarry
His book for every hurtful story—
How Simplicius Gallus left his wife
And stayed away throughout his life.   650
He saw her bare head, nothing more,
When she was peering out his door.
    Another Roman, much the same,   *Sempronius Sophus*
Because his wife went to some game
Without his leave, he cast her off.
He'd also cite his favorite scoff
From sour Ecclesiasticus,   *25.25*

A proverb dripping with distrust
Of wives who roam and gad about.[6]
And next he'd trot old verses out: 660
"Who builds a house of willow switches,
Rides a blind horse through dikes and ditches,
And trusts his wife with other bitches,
Should surely hang and lose his riches!"
Such maxims aren't worth a haw.   *hawthorn-apple*
Not this, nor all his other saws,
Could ever make me feel corrected.
I hate to have my faults detected,
And so do other wives as well.
He'd gnash his teeth when I'd rebel,   670
But I'd not give an inch, I promise.

   Now let me tell, by holy Thomas,
The reason I ripped out the page,
For which he struck me in his rage.
He had some works that night and day
He'd read aloud to my dismay:
Valerius and Theophrastus   *ancient authors*
(Both hated women and harassed us);
Another clerk of ancient Rome,
That cardinal now called Saint Jerome,   680
Who wrote a tract against Jovinian;
Crisippus and Tertulian;
Trotula, too; and Heloise   *Heloise had a famous affair with the*
(Yes, she affronted Church decrees);   *priest Peter Abelard.*
The Parables of Solomon;
And Ovid's *Art*—no more, I'm done.   *The Art of Love*
All these were bound in one great book,[7]
And all the time he could he took,
Each time he had the least vacation
From other worldly occupation,   690
To read to me of wicked wives.
For he knew more bad women's lives

---

   6. Ecclesiasticus actually tells husbands to curb their wives' speech.

   7. Jenkin's collection of antifeminist writings is unique, though manuscript books like it
are known. Crissipus may have been only a name to Chaucer. Trotula was a woman physician
and not an antifeminist, though Chaucer may not have known that.

Than there are names in Holy Writ.
No clerk will willingly admit
That any good is found in wives,
Except in some saints' pious lives.
They slander us. You know they do.
Who paints the lion, tell me, who?[8]
By God, if women wrote these tales,
As clerks do, or some other males,   700
We'd hear more of men's wickedness
Than all their gender could redress.
Scholars are ruled by Mercury.
That god and Venus don't agree.
He favors scholarship and reason.
She loves excess in any season.
That's why his star sign hovers low
When hers puts on its greatest show.
Thus Mercury is on the lees
When Venus rules the sky in Pisces,[9]   710
And Venus falls as he is raised,
And women leave most clerks unfazed.
When clerks are old and cannot do
Dame Venus' labor worth a shoe,
They all endeavor to disparage
The female sex along with marriage.
    But, as I said, it was my luck
To lose my hearing for a book!
Once Jenkin sat beside his fire
Reading like a country squire,   720
Of Eve, who for her appetite
Caused all of us to share the blight
For which the Son of God was slain
And bought us with his blood again.
Of course, it was a she who thus
Loosed sin and death on all of us.
    And then he read of Samson's hairs.

---

8. A man in a fable shows a lion a picture of a man killing a lion. "Ah," says the lion, "who painted that, a man or a lion?"

9. Venus is dominant in Pisces, and the influence of Mercury is at its lowest then. In Virgo the positions are reversed.

His lover mowed them with her shears,
And that cost Samson both his eyes.
    And next he read me, if you please,   730
Of Deianira and Hercules.
She made him beg for death's release.[10]
    Then he declaimed another piece
About the wife of Socrates.
Xanthippe drenched his head with piss.
He scarcely knew what was amiss
But said, as he wiped off the stain,
"She thunders yet, but here's the rain."
    Pasiphaë the Queen of Crete   *She made love to a bull.*
Was one of Jenkin's favorite treats.   740
Eugh! That was a grisly story—
The crown of all his oratory!
    Clytemnestra's lechery
And how she killed her spouse with glee   *Agamemnon*
Got our Jenkin's full attention.
    Then too, he rarely failed to mention
Amphiaraus, who lost his life
Through the actions of his wife,
Eriphyle. A clasp of gold
Was all it took, and he was sold.   750
She told his foemen where he was.
They killed him, but she was the cause.
Livia and Lucilla next;
Each one cost her man his neck—
One for love and one for hate.
Livia despised her mate,   *Drusus*
And poisoned him, his mortal foe.
Lucilla loved her husband, though.   *the poet Lucretius*
To hold him fast, she took a notion:
To make him drink a true-love potion.   760
He was dead before the morrow.
Thus all wives bring their husbands sorrow.
    He told me how Latumius
Complained to his friend Arrius

---

10. By accident. Nessus, a dying centaur, tricked her into smearing a robe with his blood.
When Hercules put it on, the robe clung to his skin and set him afire.

That in his garden on one tree
His wives had hung themselves, all three,
Each one with a broken heart.
"Hoo!" said Arrius, "For my part,
Give me a slip of that same tree
To see if it will work for me."   770
   Concerning later wives, he read
How some had killed their men in bed
And frolicked with a paramour,
Their husbands dead upon the floor.
Some drove nails through their men's brains
And watched the blood drip from their veins,
Or else put poison in their drink.
He spoke more harm than you can think.
And then he'd start rehearsing proverbs.
They sprang up in his head like herbs.   780
"You'd be," he said, "far less at risk
With lions or a basilisk,   *deadly serpent of myth*
Than with a woman prone to chide."   *Ecclus. 15.16*
"Climb up on the roof and hide,"
He said, "from angry wives below.
They're always fractious, as you know.
They hate whatever their men love."   *Prov. 21.9*
And "A woman's shame is like a glove:
It slides right off her with her smock."
And "A fair face in the Devil's flock   790
Is a golden ring in a old sow's nose."   *Prov. 11.22*
I swear to you no nonwife knows
How my rage grew with each new libel.
   I saw he'd never quit his bible,
His bale of lies, his book of sages,
So I reached out and snatched three pages
Clean from the book, beneath his nose.
I hit him too, you may suppose,
So he fell backward in the fire.
Up he jumped—his rage was dire—   800
And punched me roundly in the head.
Lord! I collapsed and acted dead.
Now when he saw how still I lay,
He made as if to run away,

But I began to stir instead.
"You've killed me now, false thief," I said,
"Robbed and murdered, what a crime!
But come and kiss me one last time."

    He ventured near and knelt beside me,
And said, "No matter what betides me,   810
I'll never buffet you again.
You pushed till I was half insane.
Forgive me, dear, that's all I seek."
By God, I clubbed him on the cheek!
And said, "There, thief, accept your pay!
I'm dead. I have no more to say."
But, still, at length with care and tact
We found our roles and made a pact.
He put the bridle in my hand,
The government of house and land,   820
And of his tongue and his behavior.
We burnt his book, as God's my savior.
And when I gathered in to me
All the rule and sovereignty,
And when he said, "My own true wife,
Do as you will throughout your life:
Preserve your name and my possessions"—
We had no more head-knocking sessions.
As God's my hope, I was as kind
As any wife you'll ever find,   830
And true to him, and he to me.
I pray great God in majesty
May bathe his soul in heaven's glory.
And now, sirs, I will tell my story.

WORDS BETWEEN THE SUMMONER AND THE FRIAR

    The Friar laughed to hear all this.
"Good Dame," he said, "upon my bliss,
A long preamble to a tale!"
The Summoner broke in like a gale:
"Lo," he said, "for all God's care,

A friar jumps in anywhere.   840
A fly and a friar, if you wish,
Will try their luck in any dish.
What do you know of preambulation?
Trot, shut up, or go sit down!
Don't thrust your nose in others' sport."
   The Friar had a hot retort:
"Faith," he said, "before I go,
I'll tell a comic tale or so
To make us laugh at your disgrace."
   The Summoner said, "Well, damn your face,   850
And damn your gall, and God damn me,
If I don't venture two or three
Of friars before Sittingbourne,   *forty miles from London*
Each guaranteed to make you mourn.
I see that you can't take a joke."
   "Peace!" said the Host, "or may you choke!
Now let this woman tell her tale.
You speak like farm hands drunk on ale.
Dame, tell your story, for the best."
"I will," said she, "at your behest,   860
If I have license of this Friar."
"Tell on," he said, "that's my desire."

THE WIFE OF BATH'S TALE

 Once in good King Arthur's days,
Which Britons now revere and praise,
Fairies filled our pleasant land.
The elf-queen and her gay command
Danced on many a vernal mead—
Or most men think they did, indeed—
Many hundred years ago.
But now they're gone, as all men know.   870
For now the great deserts and prayers
Of mendicants and other friars
Who wander all the fields and streams
Like motes that swarm in bright sunbeams,

Blessing chambers, halls, and bowers,
Cities, boroughs, castles, towers,
Towns and barns, stables, dairies,
Have routed out those ancient fairies.
For everywhere there was an elf,
You look and, lo, the friar himself!   880
Going about, he prays and sings
His matins and his holy things
On his way to beg and bless.
But women now are safe, I guess.
Behind each bush and every tree,
There is no incubus but he,   *seductive sprite*
And he will just subvert our virtue.
    This Arthur I alluded to
Retained a lusty bachelor
Who went one day along a shore   890
And happened, riding on his own,
To meet a maid, like him, alone.
He threw her down, with little said,
And robbed her of her maidenhead.
This villain's work raised such a pother
That soon it reached the court and Arthur,
Who damned the boorish knight to die.
His head must roll—nowhere to fly!
Perhaps that's what the statutes said.
The queen had other plans instead   900
And asked her husband for the knight,
To punish him as she thought right.
The courteous king gave up the man
To live or die at her command.
She thanked the king for what he gave,
Then pondered how to treat the knave.
"See here," she told him, "how your tricks,
Have put you in this wretched fix.
Your life is forfeit, sir; it's mine.
I send you on a quest to find   910
What one thing women most desire.
Fail me, and your fate is dire.
I won't demand your answer now.
No, I'll have mercy and allow

The coming year for you to try
To find the single best reply.
Come swear to this, and vow to be
Back here in time to answer me."
　The man was in a sorry plight.
His queen was well within her right.　　　　　920
He had no reason to protest,
And so he undertook the quest.
He prayed that God would save his neck,
But feared he'd have a pointless trek.
　He left the court and took his way
In hope someone he met might say
What every woman most preferred.
But nothing that he ever heard
Convinced him that his trial was passed.
Each one he asked belied the last.　　　　　930
Some said that women lived for wealth.
Some said honor; some said health.
Some lust in bed; some, clothes and goods;
Some said frequent widowhoods.
Some said that our hearts are eased
When we are humored, praised, and pleased.
That's close to true, it seems to me,
For women thrive on flattery.
A sycophant who comes on call
Delights most women, great or small.　　　　940
　Some said we never rest until
We're free to do just as we will,
And no man dares dispraise our habits,
But says we live like pious abbots.
That covers most of us indeed,
For when men pay unseemly heed
To our shortcomings, we will bite.
Try if you will. You'll find I'm right.
For be what women may within,
We won't admit the smallest sin.　　　　　950
　Still others said our favorite treat
Is being held to be discreet,
Trustworthy in affairs as well,
Aware of things we'll never tell.

Sirs, that thought's hardly worth a flea.
No woman honors privacy.
Midas' story proves that's so.

    The tales of Ovid plainly show
That Midas had, beneath his hair,
Two ass's ears—an ugly pair   960
Of defects that he sought to hide
To keep his place and save his pride.[11]
Only his wife had seen his ears.
He trusted her for all his fears
And placed her in his confidence.
(This showed his basic lack of sense.)

    She swore, "No! Not for all of Greece,
Would I destroy my husband's peace
And undercut his kingly name!
Besides, I'd have to share the shame."   970
But nonetheless she almost died
Keeping this piece of news inside.
The secret swelled and pressed her heart
Till she must tell at least a part;
And since she couldn't tell a man,
Away into a marsh she ran.
Her breast burned so it seemed on fire,
And, as a bittern dabs in mire,   *wading bird*
Down to the water went her lips.
"Don't tell a soul or let this slip,"   980
She said. "Make certain no one hears:
My husband has two ass's ears!"
If she'd not let her secret out,
It would have stifled her, no doubt.
You see, we women might delay,
But all we know comes out someday.
For what became of Midas' ears,
Read Ovid, where the tale appears.   Metamorphoses, *xi*

    Back now to our oafish knight.
For all his wandering day and night,   990

---

11. Midas was given these ears for preferring Pan's music to Apollo's. In Ovid, however, Midas is betrayed not by his wife, but by a slave. His slave whispers the secret in a hole and covers it up, but reeds grow from the place and announce it to the world.

He couldn't find what women wanted.
Conflicting answers had him daunted.
He must go home; the time was nigh.
The queen awaited his reply.
But on the way he chanced to ride
Beside a forest where he spied
About two dozen lovely maids
Dancing in the woodland glades.
He made toward the girls to ask
If they could help him with his task.   1000
But when they saw him riding there,
They vanished lightly into air,
And on the green, sirs, by my life,
There sat an ancient, loathsome wife.
A fouler sight you'll never see.
She scrambled up beside his knee
And cackled, "Sir, there's no path here.
But what explains your sorry cheer?
Tell me, young man, what you need.
Old heads like mine are wise indeed."   1010

      "Dearest mother," said the knight,
"I have to learn before tonight
What women want. I need advice.
If you can say, just name your price."
"Ah, that I could," she said, "but shan't
Unless you swear to me you'll grant
The next request I send your way,
And you will hear it, lad, today."

      "Done, mother," said the knight, "I swear."
      "Then," she said, "You're in my care.   1020
Your life is safe, as you will see.
The queen herself must side with me.
The proudest wife who wears a gown
Cannot deny my answer's sound.
They can't dispute what I will say.
Let's go and face the court today.
She whispered something in his ear,
And said, "That's all it is, my dear."

      They rode to court, not far away,
The knight relieved to keep his day.   1030

He had his answer pat, he said.
Full many a wife and many a maid,
Full many a widow (for they're wise)
Sat with the queen in her assize.
They gathered there for his response,
While he affected nonchalance.
    It soon grew quiet in the court.
The knight stood by with his retort—
The thing that women love the best—
Observing silence like the rest.   1040
The high queen beckoned, and he spoke,
Standing stoutly, like an oak.
    "My lady, most of all," said he,
"You women value sovereignty:
To rule your husband or your love
To do your will. By God above,
That's your wish, although you kill me.
I'm at your mercy, as you see."
In all the court, no wife or maid
Could disapprove of what he said.   1050
They all agreed he'd won his life,
And on that cue up spoke the wife
Whom he had met upon the green.
"Mercy," she said, "My lady! Queen!
Before you leave, grant me my right.
I taught that answer to this knight,
And in return at my behest
He said he'd grant my next request.
He vowed to do it if he could.
And now, sir, make your promise good: 1060
Take me to you as your wife.
For as you know, I saved your life.
Is that not so? What do you say?"
    But all he said was "Welladay!
I know as well as you I promised,
But, for God's love, change your request.
Take all my goods, but let me go!"
    "I won't," she said, "by Scorpio,
For though I'm old and foul and poor,
Not for all the gold and ore   1070

Beneath the earth or here above
Will I forbear to be your love."
   "My love!" he said. "No, my damnation!
No other man of my relations
Has ever tasted such disgrace!"
But nothing worked. This was his case:
He was well caught; now he must wed
And take that old wife to his bed.

   Well, some might think it mean of me
That I neglect, as you will see,   1080
To tell the joy and rich array
That dignified their feast that day.
But here's my answer, short and plain:
There was no joy that day, just pain
And heaviness and gnawing sorrow.
They wed in secret on the morrow.
The knight hid all day like an owl.
His life was ruined. She was so foul.

   Still greater woe welled in his head
That night when she was in his bed.   1090
He writhed and wallowed to and fro.
His wife lay sweetly smiling though,
And said, "Now, benedicity,
Is this the way a knight should be?   *bless us*
Is this the law of Arthur's house?
Are his knights so fastidious?
I am your own, your loving wife,
The lady, sir, who saved your life.
I'm sure I never did you wrong.
So, sweetheart, why hold back so long?   1100
You're like a man who's lost his wit.
If I'm to blame, why, out with it,
And I'll amend things right away."
   "Amend?" he said, "and how, I pray?
By God, I'll never be consoled,
You are so loathly and so old!
You're low born, too. No family.
What else could you expect from me?
The heart will burst within my breast!"
   "And this," she said, "prompts your unrest?"   1110

"It does," he said, "and so it should."

"Well," she said, "my dear, I could
Correct all this within three days
If you adopted kinder ways.

"But do you think that gentleness
Is just old money, more or less,
And that's what makes you gentlemen?
Bah! That conceit's not worth a hen!
The virtuous man who works each day,
In town, alone, in every way,   1120
To do what gentle deeds he can,
Sir, he's the world's true gentleman.
A Christian's goodness comes from Christ,
And not rich elders, duly priced.
Though they may leave their wealth and fees,
And old, deep-rooted family trees,
They can't pass on their virtuous lives,
The reason that their fame survives,
And their true value, if we know it.

"Just listen to the princely poet,   1130
Dante, who has this to say,   *Purgatorio 7:121–3*
At least his thinking runs this way:
'Men seldom rise by human virtue;
Success falls under God's purview.
To him we owe our gentleness.
And all true men will say no less.'
Goods, sir, are all that we inherit,
And goods may work against our merit.

"You shouldn't have to learn from me
If virtue flourished naturally   1140
In families, right down the line,
You'd never see a large decline
From goodness and true gentleness.
Each child would match his parents' best.

"Take fire into the darkest house
From England to the Caucasus,
And shut the door and go away.
The fire will burn on anyway,
As bright as if a thousand watched,

For fire is fire and won't be scotched—   1150
No, *can't* be scotched until it dies.
  "True gentleness is not a guise,
Nor does it come with wealth and lands;
Rich men may shirk its stern demands.
It's not a fire that always burns.
No, every generation learns
A lord's son may do villainy.
A man who claims nobility
Because he's from a noble house,
Whose forebears honored all their vows,   1160
And yet won't do a gentle deed
Or pay his own best models heed,
Why, he's not gentle, duke or earl—
He's just a rich but common churl.
Think of this: the glowing fame
Of your august and ancient name,
Owes not a blessed thing to you.
Now, God may make you gentle too,
But that rides on his will and grace.
It's not a perquisite of place.   1170
  "You'll find a noble in Valerius,
A countryman called Tullius,   *third king of Rome*
Who scarcely owed his clan a thing,
Yet rose from herdsman to be king.
Read Seneca, Boethius,
The doctrine they bequeathed to us
Is 'Gentle is as gentle does.'
A lowborn wife's no curse because
High God may grant, as birth can't do,
That she may be both good and true.   1180
A woman's only gentle when
She lives in virtue, not in sin.
  "You charge me next with poverty.
Well, Christ, who ransomed you and me,
Chose to live among the poor;
And every Christian heretofore
Has known that Jesus, Heaven's king,
Would hardly choose a vicious thing.

Of course, glad poverty is best,
As men like Seneca attest.   1190
A serf content in poverty
Is rich, though some might disagree.
The man who covets things is poor,
For wants spring up around his door.
But one with neither things nor wants
Is rich for all your lordship's taunts.
Welcome poverty is gay.
Juvenal has this to say:
'Poor men are always free to sing;
As safe from thieves as any king.'   1200
Poverty is harsh but good;
It makes men work as few things could
And offers priceless education
To those who master resignation.
And though it can depress and daunt,
A gift that no one else would want,
Poverty can be the prod
That makes man know himself and God.
Then too it is a looking glass
Through which you see false friends, alas.   1210
You're right. I'm poor. That much is true.
But, sir, I'm quite as good as you.
    "Then too, you jeer because I'm old.
The soundest books and thinkers hold
That old age should be reverenced—
Certainly not gibed against.
Old folks deserve one's veneration.
This holds for every time or nation.
    "You say I'm foul. My lord, that's true.
Why then, don't fear I'll cuckold you,   1220
For wrinkles and senility
Are sovereign guards to chastity.
Yet I'll take pity on your plight
And cater to your appetite.
    "Sir, you may have me as you please:
Foul and old at all degrees,
But yet a true and humble wife,

A trusted stay throughout your life;
Or young and fair and doubtless wild,
So you must fear you'll be beguiled,   1230
And likely will be when I roam
Or when you think I'm safe at home.
Now which arrangement suits you best?"
      The knight looked harried and oppressed.
Consternation made him say:
"You tell me, lady; I'll obey.
I'll gladly follow your direction.
Choose yourself upon reflection
What's advantageous for us both.
I won't object, upon my oath.   1240
What you think best will do for me."
      "Ah," she said, "full mastery!
I hold the reins, no second guessing?"
      "Indeed," he said, "and with my blessing."
      "Kiss me," she said, "and don't be loath,
For from today I will be both—
That is to say, both good and fair.
For may I die in black despair
If I don't stay as good and true
As any wife you ever knew.   1250
And if I'm not as fair of feature
This selfsame night as any creature
Between the farthest east and west,
Why, kill me, dear, at my behest.
Draw the curtain, now, and see."
      He looked at her, and verily
She was so young and beauteous,
He clasped her in a glad caress.
He seemed to hear the heavens chime,
He kissed her face a thousand times,   1260
And she complied with every measure
That might increase his joy and pleasure.
      They lived in joy throughout their lives.
Now, sirs, may Jesus send all wives
Meek husbands who are fresh in bed
And strength to rule them when we wed.

And may Our Lord cut off men's lives
Who won't be governed by their wives.
And old and angry married skinflints . . .
God curse them all with boils and squints!   1270

Heere endeth the Wyves Tale of Bathe.

The Friar

The Friar's Prologue

Our worthy Friar seized his chance.
He fired the Summoner a glance,
Yet, mindful of our fellowship,
He let no open insult slip
But turned instead toward the Wife.
"Dame," he said, "God bless your life!
Defining spouses' roles is hard—
Enough to put a clerk on guard—
And though I value all you say,
It hardly suits the game we play.   10
The tales told here should entertain.
Your learned sources tire the brain.
Leave preaching to the clergy, do.
Now, friends, *I've* got a tale for you:
To show how summoners behave!
A summoner? The name means *knave.*
What's lower than a summoner?
Nothing at all unless I err.
Summoners snoop. They never rest
Till they have sniffed out bawdiness
And been whipped out of every town."   20
  "Here, Friar," said the Host, "slow down.
Control yourself. Don't jar and grate.
We won't take sides in your debate.
Tell on, but let the Summoner be!"
  The Summoner said, "Don't speak for me!
I promise when I get a turn,
This jumped-up Friar's ears will burn.
I'll show him up, confound his eyes:
A suck-up beggar oozing lies,
With twenty other friars' crimes   30

We've all observed at sundry times.
I'll paint him as he really is."
    "Peace," said the Host, "no more of this!"
And then he beckoned to the Friar:
"Sir, tell your tale as you desire."

THE FRIAR'S TALE

    Once there lived, not far from me,
A holy man of high degree,
A bold, redoubtable archdeacon,
Exposing vices like a beacon.   40
Defamers, fornicators, bawds,
Witches, adulterers, cheats, and frauds,
Church pillagers and perjurers,
Impious men and usurers,
Lechers and simoniacs   *sellers of church offices*
All felt the sting of his attacks.
He made them blubber and lament.
Those tithing less than ten percent,
If any parson turned them in,
Were sure to suffer for their sin.   50
Short tithes and scanted contributions
Called down his sharpest prosecutions.
Before you felt the bishop's crook
Your name was in this cleric's book.
All sinners in his jurisdiction
Were treated to a quick conviction.
He had a summoner at hand,
The smoothest rogue in all that land,
A man who set out many spies
For each abuse that should arise.   60
He'd treat a lecher like his brother
To get the goods on twenty others.
Now, though this knave was virulent,
I'll lay him bare. I won't relent.
For friars don't fear summoners.
They can't touch us for all their slurs.

We've always been outside their scope.
   "And so are whores in stews, I hope,"   *Prostitutes were licensed.*
The Summoner said. "Coincidence?"
   "Peace!" said the Host, "Now show some sense,   70
And let the Friar tell his tale.
Speak on, dear Friar, let him rail.
Roast him. Make him feel the fire!"
   Well, this false summoner, said the Friar,
Kept willing bawds across the land
As falconers keep hawks at hand.
They told him everything they knew
Or they themselves would feel the screw.
He battened off these secret spies.
He couldn't prosper otherwise.   80
His earnest master hardly guessed
How much he made to *not* arrest.
For he could wave a sheaf of writs
And simple men would lose their wits
And cosset him and buy him meals
Or offer bribes and special deals.
As Judas picked his fellows' purses,   *John 12.6*
So did this knave, despite their curses;
His master got but half his due.
He was, as well—I swear it's true—   90
A thief, a pimp, a common bawd,
Employing wenches in his fraud.
For when Sir Robert or Sir John   *probably priests' names*
Or Ralph or Jack or anyone
Lay with these girls, they let him know.
And why? To gain a quid pro quo.
For he would counterfeit a writ
And summon both to answer it.
He'd skin the man and pay the girl,
Then say, "I'm not a hateful churl.   100
I'll strike this matter from my book.
Don't worry now, you're off the hook."
Free, that is, but not for free,
For his true craft was bribery.
He knew that job. No tracking hound
Could tell a hurt deer from a sound

Better than he knew a whore,
Adulterer, or paramour.
Their carnal doings paid his rent,
So he was always on their scent.   110
    And so it happened on a day
This summoner was seeking prey
And rode to daunt an ancient widow
And squeeze some pittance from her woe.
Lo, as he went to do no good,
He met a yeoman in the wood.
This fellow's gear was bright and clean,
His jacket dyed a leafy green,
Beneath a broad hat fringed in black.
"Sir," said our man, "God shield your back!"   120
"Indeed," said the yeoman, "and bring you good,
But what's your errand in this wood?
And are you riding far today?"
"No, friend, just a little way,"
The summoner said, "for I've been sent
To gather in a scrap of rent."
"Ah," said the man he met, "I see.
So you're a bailiff?" "Yes," said he,
For even the wretch himself was shamed
To hear his true profession named.   130
"Well met," the yeoman said, "*mon dieu,*   French: *"my god"*
My friend, for I'm a bailiff too,
Though one who's quite a stranger here.
So, colleague, let me give you cheer
And offer you my brotherhood.
If I can ever do you good,
Say you visit in my shire,
I'll treat you just as you desire!"
    "Done," said the summoner, "as I'm a man!"
They took each other by the hand   140
And swore true brotherhood for life,
Then rode along with little strife.
    The summoner marked every word,
As bright-eyed as a butcher-bird,
And questioned his new friend as well.
He slyly asked, "Where do you dwell?

I'll have to know if I come calling."
The yeoman answered him by stalling.
"Far north," he told him, "by the sea.
I hope in time you'll visit me.   150
I'll tell you more before we part.
The road's not hard to learn by heart."
  "Now," said the summoner, "I pray,
Teach me as we ride today,
As you're my friend and brother bailiff,
Some stratagem or subtle shift
To make our hard profession pay.
Illegal? Tell me anyway.
Now what are your best bailiffs' tricks?"
  "Beloved brother, by the Styx,"   160
The man declared, "I'll tell you all.
My pay's a trickle, always small.
My lord is flinty and conceited.
The work is hard, and I'm mistreated.
So I confess it's been my portion
To live on kickbacks and extortion.
I threaten blows or legal action
To bleed men to my satisfaction.
That's how I live. I will not lie."
  "Friend," said the summoner, "so do I!   170
I'll take what anyone has got,
If it's not too heavy or too hot.
What I can steal with secrecy
Has never shamed or troubled me.
My trade's coercion, I confess,
But I won't change it nonetheless.
My stomach and my will are strong,
Though pious ninnies say I'm wrong.
And so, well met now, by Saint James!
But tell me, brother, what's your name?"   180
With that, they rode a little while,
The yeoman with a private smile.
  "All right," he said. "Perhaps I'll tell.
I am a fiend. I live in Hell
And ride on Earth to get my pay.
I gather what men give away.

Such gifts are all that comes to me.
But, brother, you're the same, I see.
You profit, and you don't care how.
We're much alike. I'd ride, right now,   190
On to the world's end for my prey."
    "Ach!" said the summoner, "Welladay!
I took you for a man indeed.
You're shaped like one of human seed.
When you're at home, that is, in Hell,
Have you a yeoman's form as well?"
    "No," said the fiend, "no form at all,
But guises come to me on call;
I can appear in any shape,
Once as a man, and then an ape,   200
Or like an angel, white as snow,
Nor is it strange this should be so:
A paltry juggler can deceive you.
Why be surprised that I can too?"
    "So," said the summoner, "you change
To any form as you arrange?"
    "Yes," said the fiend, "we find a way
To pacify our chosen prey."
    "And, pray tell, what's the point of this?"
    "All sorts of points, as you must guess,"   210
The fiend responded. "But, Lord, the time!
The day is short and it's past prime,
And I've not gained a thing today.
I'll rectify that if I may.
Nay, I must hold some secrets back!
Don't brood, my brother, for you lack
The wit to understand such lore.
You asked the meaning of my chore—
Well, sometimes we're the tools of God
To do his will and wield his rod   220
And punish or expose his creatures
In different shapes and sundry features.
Without him we can't stir at all.
If he opposes us, we fall.
Sometimes by his divine control
We tax the body, not the soul,

As we did Job, and nothing loath.
And sometimes we torment them both,
That is, we harm both soul and flesh.
At other times we just enmesh   230
The soul and let the body go.
When men reject our worst temptation
They win great honor and salvation,
But that is never what we hope.
We'd rather snag them in our rope.
Sometimes we follow men's behests,
Saint Dunstan worked us without rest.   *He controlled devils.*
Christ's apostles had me on call."
    "Yet what I asked, if you recall,"
The summoner said, "concerned your substance: 240
Say, is it made of elements?"
"No," said the fiend, "we only seem,
Or stir dead bodies, like a dream,
And make them walk and prophesy
Like Samuel, if Saul didn't lie.   *1 Sam. 5–19*
(I know some claim it wasn't he—
A fig for their philosophy!)
I say all this because you ask:
This shape I wear is just a mask.
But there's a place you'll shortly reach   250
Where you'll learn more than I can teach.
You'll know it all, no need to guess;
You'll take the lectern and profess
Infernal truths as well as Virgil.   *He guided Dante through Hell in the Inferno.*
Now, sir, ride faster, if you will.
I hope to keep you company
Till you decide to part from me."
    "Never," said the summoner.
"No, not if you were Lucifer.
My steadfastness is widely known,   260
I'd put my word against your own.
You have my oath that I'm your brother
And neither will betray the other.
So come, let's form a partnership
To share the proceeds of this trip.
You take what men may freely give;

I'll hope for things more substantive,
But if one wins more than the other,
Then I propose we share it, brother."
   "Done," said the devil, "by my creed."   270
They set their spurs, made better speed,
Riding toward a nearby town
Where the summoner meant to nose around.
They met a carter in the way,
Whose wagon groaned with new-mown hay.
The mud grew deep, the cart got stuck,
He flogged his nags and cursed his luck,
With, "Brock and Scot, now pull your weight,
Or may the Devil have you straight!
No lazier pair was ever foaled;   280
If I had sense, you'd both be sold.
The Devil take horse, cart, and hay!"
   "Hoo!" said the summoner, "So he may!"
He neared the fiend, all innocent,
And whispered fast to this intent:
"Listen, brother, by my head,
Attend to what this carter said!
Take everything he gave away:
His cart, his horses, and his hay!"
   "No," said the devil, "be content,   290
That wasn't really what he meant,
Ask him yourself if you doubt me,
Or wait a moment, and you'll see."
   The carter whacked his horses' rumps.
They hunkered as if pulling stumps
And moved the cart a little way.
"Jesus," he said, "bless you today.
Well pulled! Well pulled, my dappled boy!
Praise be to Christ and to Saint Loy!   *Saint Eloi, a French bishop*
My cart is moving now, by God!"   300
   "Ha!" said the devil with a nod,
"It's as I guessed, my eager brother,
He said one thing but meant another.
Let's ride in hope of better cheer.
There's nothing to be gotten here."
   When they arrived outside the town,

The summoner stopped and scrambled down.
"I know," he said, "a widowed wreck,
Who'd rather let you wring her neck
Than render up a single penny.   310
I'll have twelve pence from her, if any,
Or I will summon her to court,
Although there's nothing to report.
I know my trade, as you will see.
Perhaps you'll learn a bit from me."

    He banged upon the widow's gate.
"Come out," he said, "you reprobate!
I know you have a priest in there!"
"I don't," she said, "I don't, I swear!
God save you, sir, what is your will?"   320
"I have," he said, "a summons bill.
We'll excommunicate you yet
If you don't pay your holy debt
And tell the court of certain things."

    "Christ," she said, "dear King of Kings,
I know you'll think it's just a trick,
But I have been so weak and sick,
That I can't walk that far or ride.
The ribs are burning in my side!
Can you provide a legal writ?   330
I'll send a man to answer it,
No matter what it says I did."
"I won't," he answered, "God forbid!
But pay twelve pence and I'll acquit you.
It costs that much for me to do.
My master gets the cash, not I.
Come, cough it up and then goodbye.
Twelve pence is all. I mustn't tarry."

    "Twelve pence!" she said. "Dear Mother Mary,
Save me from this splitting care.   340
In all the world around, I swear,
I haven't got twelve pence to hold.
You know I'm poor and sick and old.
For God's sake, show a bit of soul!"

    "Not I. The Devil take me whole
If I excuse your rightful dues."

"I'm here," she said, "without two sous."

"Pay up," he said, "or by Saint Anne   *mother of the Blessed Virgin*
I'll carry off your cooking pan.
You owe that anyway, you know.   350
You fooled your husband long ago,
And I agreed to pay the fine."

"You lie!" she said, "you grasping swine!
I never was, as widow or wife,
Called to your court in all my life.
I was an honest wife and mate.
Go fry on Satan's hottest grate.
I give you to him with my pan!"

The foul fiend heard her curse the man
And smoothly said with soothing cheer: 360
"Now tell me, Mother Mabel, dear,
Do you mean every word you say?"

"May demons take the wretch today!
The pan too, if he won't relent!"

"Oh, no, old cow, I won't assent,"
The summoner said. "There's no release.
So stand and curse me as you please.
I'll have your smock, each scrap of cloth!"

The devil said, "Friend, don't be wroth.
The pan and you are mine by right.   370
I'll see you both in Hell tonight,
And you'll soon understand our works
Far better than the chief of clerks."
And with that word he snatched the man,
Body and soul at his command,
To where all summoners are born.
Now God, who gave mankind his form,
Guide and preserve us from all harm,
And lead us to our home again,
And let these summoners become good men!   380

Now, Lords, I could say what came next,
And would, indeed, were I not vexed,
Citing Christ and John and Paul,
The prelates and church doctors all,
To speak of Hell and grind your spirits,
Though nothing I could say comes near it,

Not if I spoke a thousand years
Of hellish pains and burning tears.
God keep us from that cursed place!
Sirs, pray to Jesus for his grace   390
To shelter us from Satan's snares.
Implore his mercy in your prayers.
"The lion lurks or prowls all day
To slay the faithful if he may."   *Ps. 10:8–9*
Arm your hearts against him, do,
For he'd be glad to capture you.
Christ will help you serve the right.
You won't be tested past your might.
And pray all summoners repent
Before their wicked lives are spent!   400

Heere endeth the Freres Tale.

THE SUMMONER

THE SUMMONER'S PROLOGUE

The Summoner rose up in his saddle
With glaring looks, prepared for battle,
And shaking like a leaf for ire.
    "My friends," he said, "hear my desire:
I think it's common courtesy,
That now this man has libeled me,
You let me tell my tale as well.
This Friar boasts of knowing Hell.
Well, if he does it's little wonder.   10
Friars and fiends aren't far asunder.
I'm sure you've all heard someone tell
How a friar dreamed himself in Hell,
And wandered freely up and down.
An angel led him all around
To see the souls racked in the fire,
But not once did he see a friar,
Though Hades seethed with other folk.
He touched the angel's gown and spoke:
    "Perhaps we friars have such grace,
Not one of us is in this place?"   20
    "Ha," said his guide, "more like a million!"
By Satan's innermost pavilion,
He pointed to the devil's tail,
Broader than a freighter's sail.
"Hold up your tail, you imp," he said.
"Now, friend, behold his arse with dread.
That's where you friars have your nest."
The fiend complied with his request,
And just as bees swarm from a hive,
That teeming asshole came alive   30
With twenty thousand buzzing friars,

Who skipped about amid the fires
And then returned the selfsame way,
Climbed up his bung, and there they stay.
Down clapped the tail. The fiend lay still.
By now the friar had his fill.
He'd seen the torments of the place,
So God revived his soul by grace;
His body started, came awake.
But all that he could do was quake.   40
That noisome hole stuck in his mind,
The heritage of all his kind.
God save you all, except the Friar.
Now let me prove that he's a liar!

THE SUMMONER'S TALE

There is, way up near Hull, I guess,
A swampy place called Holderness,
The territory of a friar
Who begged and preached throughout the shire.
Men often noted how this priest
Drove home one theme and never ceased.   50
He took it as his special mission
To make folk pray for sins' remission
And offer alms upon their knees
To build abundant friaries.
There God would find humility,
He said, and not scurrility
Or fat priests needing no support,
Who fed as well as any court
(Though he praised God they did.) He said
That thirty masses scarcely sped   60
A troubled soul to heaven's light.
Friars said mass from dawn to night,
While well-fed monks said one a day.
A soul would burn a month that way.
"Deliver them at once!" he'd shout.
"Just think of fleshhooks up your snout—

Hot awls and flames and fiery embers!
For Christ's sake, soothe their tortured members!"
And when at length he'd had his say,
He'd take their pence and go his way.   70
    Then, not content for all his gains,
He'd stalk about the streets and lanes
With pouch and staff and skirts tucked high.
At every house he'd poke and pry,
And beg for wheat or cheese or meal.
A fellow friar at his heel
Bore ivory plates of writing wax
And a stylus to record the facts.
If any gave, he'd use these tools
To write their names, the pious fools,   80
As if he planned to pray for them.
"Give us wheat," they'd say, "or ham,
A little cake or wedge of cheese
Or peck of rye or what you please.
A penny for a mass or alms,
A piece of pork to sing some psalms,
A strip of blanket, gentle dame,
Here, see my fellow write your name!
Bacon or beef or what you find."
    A sturdy servant came behind.   90
They'd picked him up outside their inn
To carry off what they might win.
Outside each house they made a game
Of rubbing off the giver's name
Where it was written in their tables.
They hoodwinked all with lies and fables.
    "A godless lie," the Friar roared.
"Peace," cried the Host, "keep our accord!
Now tell away as you began."
    Host, said the Summoner, that's my plan.   100
This friar entered one fine door
Where he had often been before—
They entertained him like a king—
And found a hush on everything.
The householder lay sick in bed.
"*Deus hic!*" the friar said.   *"God be here."*

"Thomas, friend, be safe from harm.
How many times I've rested warm
Upon your bench as I might wish
And eaten many a dainty dish." 110
He shooed away a sleeping cat
And put aside his stick and hat,
His pouch as well, and settled down.
His fellow went along to town,
Returned the knave, to his chagrin,
To his dull post outside the inn.
    "Dear master,"[1] said the ailing man,
"How have you done since March began?
I've missed you two whole weeks or more."
    "God knows, my son, I've labored sore, 120
And chiefly to assist your spirit.
I've said a thousand prayers or near it,
For you and other friends, alas.
Today I prayed for you at Mass
And preached to the top of my poor wit,
Embellishing on Holy Writ.
The Bible's hard, and for that cause,
I must teach simple men the gloss.   *interpreted meaning*
Such explication clears our way
For the letter kills, we clerics say. 130
I taught them to use charity,
That alms are true prosperity.
I saw your wife—where is she now?"
    "Out in the garden, I allow,"
Poor Thomas said. "She comes anon."
    "Ah," said the wife, "it's Father John!
How are you doing, if I may?"
    The friar rose up in her way,
And clipped her in a tight embrace,
While chirping with a sparrow's grace,   *a symbol of lechery*
And kissed her sweetly on the lips.
"I'm well, my dear, for all my trips,"
He said, "and may God bless your life!
I didn't see a sweeter wife

---

1. Master of Arts, a title required before going on for a special degree in theology.

Today in church, with due respect."
    "God knows," she said, "I have defects.
At any rate, we welcome you."
    "God save you, dear, you always do.
But now, my sweet, with your permission
I need to be about my mission,   150
And speak with Thomas if I may.
These parish priests, to our dismay,
Can't sound a conscience as we can
And properly confess a man.
I follow Peter and Saint Paul
In grappling for the souls of all
To yield Lord Jesus Christ his due,
And spread his Holy Gospel too."
    "Well then, sir," the woman said,
"Chide him till his face is red.   160
He wrangles like an angry pismire   *ant*
Although he gets his least desire.
And then in bed when he's not warm,
I cosset him with leg or arm,
But he groans like the old boar in our sty.
That's all I get from him. I try,
But I can't please him, as you see."
    "O Thomas! Thomas! *Je vous dis,*   *"I tell you"*
The Devil's in you," said the friar.
"This goes against Our Lord's desire.   170
Wrath's a mortal sin, I say!"
    The woman said, "I'll take my way;
I have your meal to see about."
    The friar said, "My dear, *sans doute,*   *"no doubt"*
I'll have a sautéed capon's liver,
Your soft white bread, but just a sliver,
A pig's head, then, if you agree.
I'd have no creature killed for me.
And that will be sufficient fare.
My needs are modest, you're aware.   180
The Bible's shaped my inmost soul.
My body plays a minor role.
Watchful prayer has ruined my stomach.
I wish it hadn't, for your sake.

I hope you don't mind hearing this;
I tell few others, by my bliss."
    "Father, one more word," she said,
"You haven't heard my child is dead.
He died against all expectation."
    "My dear, I had a revelation,"   190
Said Father John, "in my poor cell.
He died indeed, but I know well
His tender soul was borne to bliss.
My holy vision showed me this.
Our sexton now for fifty years,
He saw it too, as it appears.
He seems a saint on earth to me.
This year will mark his jubilee.   *50th anniversary as a friar*
I rose at once with all my peers,
Glad for all my streaming tears.   200
Although they knew no one would pay them,
They sang a solemn great *Te Deum*,   *a hymn of praise*
And I thanked Jesus Christ in prayer
For all that he had shown me there.
Morning, night, or any hour,
Our praying has a special power,
Revealing more of sacred things
Than laymen see, though dukes and kings.
Friars lead lives of abstinence
While other folk spare no expense   210
To drown themselves in meat and drink.
We know this world is but a sink.
Though Dives and Lazarus lived differently;[2]   *Luke 16:19–31*
Death switched their lots, as you may see.
A prayerful life is sparse and clean.
Your soul is fed, your body lean.
Saint Paul says any clothes or food
Are good enough, although not good.   *1 Tim. 6:8*
The modesty of our affairs
Ensures the Lord accepts our prayers.   220
    "Lo, Moses fasted forty days

---

2. Lazarus died begging crumbs at Dives' gate, but he was welcomed into the bosom of
Abraham. Dives went to Hell.

Before the Lord received his praise
And spoke to him on Sinai's top.
He waited with an empty crop
To take the laws God's finger wrote.   *Exod. 34:28*
Elijah tasted not a groat
Approaching Horeb in God's name.   *1 Kings 19:8*
God smoothed his journey all the same,
And met him on the mountainside.
Aaron, the high priest till he died,   230
He and all the other priests
Who offered sacred rites or feasts
Or flights of prayers in Yahweh's shrine,
Would never touch a drop of wine
Or anything inebriating.
No, they abstained while they were waiting,
On pain of death. Take heed, I say!
Priests must be sober when they pray,
Or else. . . . But now, no more of that!
    "Our Lord himself was never fat.   240
He lived in fasting and in prayer,
And that's why friars everywhere
Welcome want and poverty,
With humbleness and charity
And fortitude and abstinence,
And weeping, mercy, continence.
So our petitions and desires—
I speak of mendicants and friars—
May be received with better cheer
Than yours, with all your meat and beer.   250
Gluttony, no other vice,
Expelled mankind from Paradise.
Till then, humanity was chaste.
    "We mendicants earn special grace.
No text directly says that's so,
But all who read the glosses know
A friar's life's to be construed
In this, the first beatitude:
'Blessed are the poor in spirit.'   *Matt. 5:3*
The truth is plain to those who hear it.   260
Say, do the gospels favor friars,

Or wealthy men and other liars?
Fie on their pomp and gluttony!
Their sinfulness is plain to see.
   "I think they're like Jovinian,   *heretic monk attacked by Saint Jerome*
Whale-fat and waddling like a swan,
And oozing like a cask of wine.
They scoff at everything divine:
Reading out the psalms of David,
They belch, *'Cor meum eructavit!'*   *"My heart speaks out," Ps. 45:1*
We honor Our Lord's witness more
Subsisting humbly, chaste and poor.
We live God's word; we don't just hear it.
Just as a hawk of fiery spirit
Springs in the air, a friar's prayers
Fly up and quickly outstrip theirs,
And make their way to Our Lord's ears.
You're proof, dear Thomas. Jesus hears!
Now thank Saint Ives that you're alive.   *patron saint of Brittany*
Without our prayers you'd never thrive!   280
Our whole house prays both day and night
That God will send you health and might
And let you move more easily!"
   "That's not a scrap of help to me,"
The sick man said. "These last few years,
I've squandered money, it appears,
Supporting friars to no end.
I've nearly spent it all, my friend.
Goodbye, gold, for it's all gone!"
   The friar answered, "By Saint John,   290
What would you want with other friars?
A man who has what he desires
Should never seek to better it.
The fault's in your inconstant wit.
Do you think I and all my brothers
Are so weak, then, that you need others?
You'll hardly prosper through such stuff.
You've never given me enough.
Aye, give that house a quart of oats,
And give another twenty groats!   300
Toss John a penny; let him go!

Ach, Thomas, that won't do, you know.
What good's a farthing split in twelfths?
A thing's true value is itself.
Divide it; watch the value scatter.
No, I won't palliate this matter:
You want our prayers but you won't pay.
God knows that nothing works that way.
The workman's worthy of his hire.   *Luke 10:7*
I'd toss your money in the fire,   310
But that won't suit my friends in Christ.
Their efforts can't be underpriced.
They strive to build up Mother Church,
The purest sort of holy work.
Read of your name-saint in the East:
He won a million souls at least.[3]
Yet you lie here beset with ire;
The Devil set your heart on fire.
You chide the ones whose help you seek—
Your wife and me, because we're meek.   320
Well, Thomas, hear this much at least:
Don't anger her, as I'm your priest,
But take this saying to your heart;
The teaching's wise, if somewhat tart:
'Don't be a lion to your household,
Don't lay the scourge to young or old,
Or cause acquaintances to flee.'   *Ecclus. 4:35*
Let me repeat my former plea:
Beware of wrath that eats your heart.
That serpent crawls with subtle art   330
Beneath the grass to blight your peace.
Beware, my son, and wrath will cease.
Great shoals of men have lost their lives
Contending with their loves or wives.
You have a buxom, humble wife,
So why repine and stir up strife?
Suppose you felt a poison snake
Beneath your foot. Who wouldn't quake?

---

3. "Doubting Thomas." After the Ascension, it was said, he went to India and converted multitudes.

An angry woman's worse by far;
She follows vengeance like a star.   340
And wrath is also deadly sin,
Insufferable to God and men.
This anger will consume you whole.
Homicide? A wrathful soul
Won't stick at that, as parsons know.
A proud, hard heart makes anger grow.
Tales of anger and its sorrow
Could hold us here until tomorrow.
I pray to God, both night and day,
All Christian men turn wrath away.   350
The greatest danger one can see
Is irate men of high degree.
   "In Seneca, a potentate,   *De ira, 1:18*
A wrathful man, was holding state
When two knights ventured from his town.
Their guiding stars or fortune frowned,
And one came home without the other.
The ruler asked him for his brother,
Then cried, 'You killed him! Save your breath.
I hereby sentence you to death!'   360
A man then led the wretch away
To lose his head that very day.
In vain he wrangled and disputed.
His guard must see him executed.
But, lo, just then the missing knight
Came riding up in open sight.
They went back to the lord again
And said, 'Look, Sire, he isn't slain!
He's standing in your court instead.'
The ruler cried, 'He should be dead!   370
You all should—one and two and three!
The first knight made a fool of me.
I damned him, and I'll see him dead.
This newest one must lose his head
Because he made his fellow die.
And you, my own knight standing by,
Condemned yourself resisting me.'
And so he killed the lot, all three.

"Hot Cambises overdrank,   *ancient Persian king*
And wrath made him famous crank.   380
One day a knight who served this tyrant,
An honest councilor-aspirant,
Said to the king in confidence:
  'A lord is lost without good sense.
Drink will wreck a common man,
Much more a king with troops and land.
Many an eye and many an ear
Mark all his doings, never fear.
For God's love, moderate your drinking,
Or soon you'll find your prowess shrinking,   390
Through shaking hands and addled head.'
  "The king thought otherwise and said,
'I'll prove, as you will see and hear,
Drink won't affect me as you fear.
No wine can rob me of my might
Or steady hand or piercing sight.'
To make his point, he drank much more—
Huge bumpers—than he had before,
And when the cruel wretch was done,
He had men fetch the knight's young son.   400
They led him in and made him stand.
Cambises took his bow in hand,
And pulled the string back to his ear,
And killed the poor lad then and there.
'Now can I draw a bow?' he said.
'Have all my strength and purpose fled?
Has drinking wine destroyed my sight?'
What's left to say about the knight?
He lost his son—in other words,
Be careful how you speak to lords.   410
Say *'Placebo'* and 'Yes, I can.'   *"I will please."*
Though you may tell a simple man
His every fault and vice as well,
Don't stand between great lords and Hell.
  "Lo, bilious Cyrus, the Medes' lawgiver,   *Cambises' father*
Wrought execution on a river!
It drowned the horse he rode upon
While waging war on Babylon.

He changed its channel, dried its course,
Just to avenge a favored horse!   420
So keep King Solomon's command: *Prov. 22:24–5*
'Don't you befriend a wrathful man
Or take up madmen on your way,
Or you'll repent.' Take heed, I say.
    "In short, dear Thomas, quit your care;
All my advice is true and square.
Don't hold a knife to your own heart.
This anger rips your life apart.
Now let me offer you Confession."
    "No," Thomas said, "by my profession!   430
My parish priest was here today.
I told him all I had to say.
Why should I go through that again?
I've been absolved; what's left to gain?"
    "Then give me gold to build our cloisters,
We've lived too long on clams and oysters.
While others fatten and carouse,
We scrimp and fast to build our house,
Yet the foundation's scarcely done;
The paving's hardly been begun.   440
We've not a tile to shield our bones,
And we owe forty pounds for stones!
    "I beg you, help our fellowship,
Or we must sell our manuscripts.
Without our preaching, let me say,
Rank sin would flood the world today
And rob mankind of all we promise.
As you hope for salvation, Thomas,
You might as well shut off the sun.
For who can match what we have done?   450
We've served since great Elijah's time
Throughout the world in every clime.[4]
We're quite that old, as you have heard,
And quite that holy, praise the Lord!
Dear Thomas, show your charity!"

---

4. The Carmelites, a mendicant order, traced their history to Elijah, who discredited the prophets of Baal on Mount Carmel (1 Kings 18:19–40).

Now Father John was on one knee.
   The sick man lay half-crazed with ire
And wished the beggar in the fire
Along with his entire profession.
He said, "What's left in my possession   460
I'll give you, John, you and no other.
You say that I've been named your brother?"   *a lay member of Father John's order*
   "Yes," said the friar, "on my appeal.
Your wife has papers with our seal."
   "Well then, I've one gift left to give
To your foundation while I live.
I'll place it in your hand anon,
But here's what you must swear to, John:
It must be split with perfect art
So every friar gets his part.   470
Vow each will have an equal share.
The distribution must be fair."
   "I swear by Jesus, God and man,"
Said Father John, and took his hand.
"I promise you no one will lack."
   "Then slide your hand along my back,"
This Thomas said. "Grope well behind.
Beneath my buttocks. There you'll find
A thing I've held in privacy."
   "Ha!" thought the friar, "This goes with me!"   480
And down he reached into the cleft
To find what goods the man had left.
Now when this Thomas felt his hand
Draw near his bunghole, as he planned,
He blasted an enormous fart.
No horse that draws a market cart
Could detonate a louder blast.
   The friar tumbled back aghast.
"You churl!" he roared, "God's bones . . . I swear . . .
You prearranged this whole affair!   490
I'll make you suffer for that fart!"
   Now when they heard his raving start,
The serving men expelled the friar.
Behold! His very heart's on fire!
He found his colleague and his stores

With looks as wild as twenty boars.
He ground his teeth in unmixed fury,
And went for justice in a hurry.
He was confessor to the lord
Who ruled there by the town's accord,   500
An honored local magistrate.
The priest came raging to his gate
But found him eating at his board
And hardly dared to say a word.
At last he said, "You're well, I see."
The lord said, "Benedicity!   *"Bless us!"*
Now what's the matter, Father John?
What makes you look so put upon?
You bite your lip like one who grieves,
As if the woods were full of thieves.   510
Speak! I will help you if I can."
    The friar said, "A wicked man,
A villager of yours, I say,
Has used me shamefully today.
The poorest peddler would resent
The disrespect that scoffer meant.
What makes me even more irate,
This old, gray-headed profligate
Blasphemed our holy order too."
    "Now, Master, let me ask anew. . . ."   520
    "Not Master, sire, but servitor,
Though I earned that degree and more,
Don't call us *Rabbi,* please, or *Master*   *Matt. 23:8*
Or *Father* or *Your Excellence* or *Pastor.*"
    "I won't then, John, but why this grief?"
    "Sire," said the friar, "a gross mischief
Was done to both my house and me,
The Church as well, in each degree.
I pray to God we'll be avenged."
    "I'll see you are. Don't come unhinged!   530
Just say what this offense was worth.
You're my confessor here on earth;   *Matt. 5:13*
For God's sake, calm yourself, don't rail."
So John recounted all the tale,
The story you just heard me tell.

The lord's fair lady heard as well.
She weighed up every word and said,
"By Holy Mary's maidenhead!
And is this all you have to say?"
    "My lady, what do you think, I pray?"   540
    "The matter hardly needs a clerk.
A churl has done a churlish work.
Now God will punish him," she said.
"There's wool and wind inside his head.
I think he must be somewhat mad."
    "If so, my lady, that won't save him.
If he's not punished, I will shave him.
I'll flay the rascal everyplace.
I won't stand by and be derided.
You know a fart can't be divided!   550
And equal parts! Oh, what mischance!"
    The lord sat thinking, in a trance,
Revolving matters in his heart:
"Now what could give that rogue the art
To fashion such a clever scheme?
Sure, Satan sent it in a dream!
No stranger thing was ever known.
To measure farts once they've been blown!
And who could capture or devise
Fart-packages of equal size   560
So every man could have his part?
The sound and savor of a fart!
The scheming churl! Well, damn his face!"
"Lo sirs," he said, "a pretty case!
Who heard of such a thing ere now?
Each man alike? Pray tell me how.
Impossible! It cannot be.
Yet something in it interests me.
The hollow rumbling of a fart
Comes as the air is forced apart . . .   570
A clap, and then it wastes away.
Now how could anybody say
If it was served up equally?
A nice dilemma, you'll agree.
I'll think of this each time I'm shriven.

By God, the rogue was demon driven!
But eat up, for the man's insane.
So let the Devil rot his brain!"

How a Squire Solved the Problem of Dividing a Fart by Twelve

A squire was standing by the board.
He carved the meat and heard each word.   580
The friar's story and his plight
Infused him with a shrewd delight.
"Ahem," he said, "My lord, don't frown.
For cloth enough to make a gown,
I'll tell this priest, with your permission,
How he can fill that churl's commission."
      "Tell," said the lord. "Instruct the priest.
You'll have a gown fit for a feast."
      "Then, lord," he said, "when it is fair—
No trace of wind or moving air—   590
Obtain a cartwheel from your folks,
A heavy one, with all its spokes—
Twelve spokes in all, most commonly—
And bring those friars here to me.
Thirteen's a convent, as I've heard.
This holy father, on my word,
Will bring the number up to strength.
Then every priest must kneel at length.
To every spoke, as I propose,
A friar will apply his nose.   600
While Father John—and here's the nub—
Sniffs up from underneath the hub.
This Thomas must retain his gas
Until it's clamoring to pass.
Above the wheel he'll play his part,
And through the hub expel his fart.
My Lord, I trust this fine invention
Will justify my intervention:
The wheel will equally extend

The sound and stink to each spoke's end,   610
Except this worthy, Father John,
Because he's honoring his bond,
Shall have first fruits. That much is fair.
The use of friars everywhere
Is better men are better served.
John's special share is well deserved.
His sermon did us so much good,
He graced the pulpit where he stood,
And worked so well upon our hearts,
I'd give him first smell of three farts!   620
And so would all those in his cell;
He lives so piously and well."
     Now every man except the priest
Said Jenkin spoke as well at least
As Euclid did, or Ptolemy.
They praised his wit and subtlety,
The clever working of his brain.
He was no fool; he'd made that plain.
Thus Jenkin won a fine new gown.
My tale is done. And here's the town!   630

Heere endeth the Somonours Tale.

The Clerk

The Clerk's Prologue

"What ho, Sir Clerk," our brisk Host said,
"You sit your horse just like a maid,
Surveying her new husband's table.
Sir, you've said nothing, though you're able.
No doubt you sift some proposition,
But heed the Bible's admonition:
'Each thing has its time.' That's clear;   *Eccles. 3:1*
It's not your time to study here.
Now tell a tale, or be to blame.
For when you enter on a game,   10
Sir, you must play it by the rules.
No Lenten sermon fit for fools
To make us mourn our sins and weep,
Nor yet a tale to make us sleep!
 "No, tell a merry, rousing story.
Nip off your buds of oratory.
The higher style suits higher things,
As when you write to dukes or kings.
Speak plainly now, Sir Clerk, we pray
So we can follow what you say."   20
 The worthy Clerk, a humble man,
Said, "Host, I'm under your command.
We've all agreed you're ruler here,
And I will do your will, no fear,
In anything within good reason.
I know a tale fit for the season.
I had it from a pious clerk,
A man of holy words and work,
Though now he's dead, nailed in his chest.
(I pray that God will give him rest.)   30
It was great Petrarch, laureate,   *famous Italian poet*

His honeyed style and words of weight
Illumined all of Italy,
As others in philosophy
Or law enriched their other arts.
But nothing can resist Death's darts,
For in the twinkling of an eye   *1 Cor. 15:52*
Death slew the man, as all must die.
  A word or two about this poet,
Who told the story as I know it,   40
For at the entrance to his tale,
He let the muses fill his sail
And wrote a preface where we see
The wide expanse of Italy—
The Apennines against the sky,
The westward bounds of Lombardy,
And Monte Viso, home and source
From whence the Po pursues its course
Across to Venice and the sea,
Too long a narrative for me,   50
And speaking truly to my taste
Extraneous and quite misplaced,
Except to introduce his tale.
I'll tell it on a smaller scale.

THE CLERK'S TALE

Part One

The story begins with Walter, Marquis of Saluzzo, a Lombard town in north-western Italy. The city controls abundant lands, and Walter is a handsome and effective ruler, except in one thing: he has no heirs and seems indifferent to marriage. His people appoint a spokesman to call this to his attention.

"My lord," he said, "your people like you well,
So well, in fact, reviewing all your deeds,
That no one whom you govern here can tell
How anyone might better fit our needs.
To one thing, though, we pray you will accede:

Consent to take a wife, sir, that is best.   60
Secure our future; set our hearts at rest.

"Sir, bow your neck beneath that blissful yoke
Of sovereignty, not service as men say.
That state is best for you and for your folk.
And think, my lord, consider this, we pray;
Time can't be stopped. It slyly flits away.
For though we sleep or wake or stay or ride,
Time never rests. That cannot be denied.

"And while your mortal life yet flowers with youth,
That thief, old age, creeps in as still as stone,   70
And death can come at any time, in truth,
For anyone, companioned or alone.
We all must die, my lord, that much is known.
But no man knows just when his life will pass.
That hour, my lord, is hidden till the last.

"We ask this, lord, with dutiful intent.
You know we've never countervailed your good.
And know, my lord, if you will but assent
We'll choose for you as well as people could
A high-born wife to match you as she should—   80
A noble wife, of noble carriage too,
A credit to Saluzzo, God, and you.

"Guard us, sir, from accidents yet hid.
Dispose yourself, my lord, to take a wife.
For if it should befall, as God forbid,
Some unseen hazard robs us of your life,
And strangers rule your land, perhaps with strife,
Then woe to us and to your heritage!
So marry, lord, and save us from their rage."

The people's humble prayer and their bearing   90
Moved the marquis' heart toward consent.
"You know," he said, "my service is unsparing,
Yet marriage has been far from my intent.

No, single life has left me quite content.
Its unconstraint excels a husband's lot.
Today he's free; tomorrow he is not.

"But, nonetheless, I understand your bent,
And trust your wisdom as I've always done.
Lords, I'll reshape my life's course and assent,
And wed right quickly once I have begun.   100
Yet I'll brook no intrusions save this one.
In brief, I will not have you choose my wife.
I'll play that part myself, upon my life.

"No parent makes the child excel, that's plain.
For children must develop on their own.
Their virtue comes from God, not from the strain
From which they are engendered, blood and bone.
God loves Saluzzo, as he long has shown,
So now I trust our future and my life
To him alone. Let God give me a wife!"   110

Walter makes his people promise they will honor whatever wife he chooses, and
at their request he names a day for the wedding. He even starts preparations for
the marriage feast. But who will be the bride?

Part Two

Not far at all from Walter's splendid palace,
In which the marquis shaped his wedding plans,
A hamlet stood devoid of wealth or malice,
Where people toiled at all that life demands.
They raised up beasts for food and tilled their lands,
Resigned to daily labor for their keep:
To tend their herds and plow and sow and reap.

Among these plain, poor folk there dwelt a man
Whom those around thought poorest of them all,
Yet sometimes it may fit with Heaven's plan   120
To dignify the lowest ox's stall.
Janicula felt hunger's sting and gall,

But had a daughter praised in local fame—
A handsome maid, Griselda was her name.

To speak of gentle virtue, not just beauty,
She ranked with any girl beneath the sun.
Her low estate had seen to it that she
Knew less of vices than a cloistered nun.
The well supplied her drink, and not the tun.   *wine barrel*
She practiced virtue, hoping to please God,   130
And labored hard to turn away his rod.

This tender maiden scarcely was of age,
And yet the breast of her virginity
Enclosed a heart considerate and sage,
Well filled with love and saintly charity.
She kept her father well in their austerity
And watched their sheep and cooked and cleaned and spun
With little rest until the day was done.

Each day as she came homeward she was able
To gather cabbage, kale, and other greens   140
And boil or seethe or braise them for their table.
Her bed was hard. They lived within their means,
And yet she kept her father hale, if lean,
And served his needs with every diligence
That best befits a daughter's reverence.

Upon Griselda, earnestly at work,
The marquis often turned his restless eye—
While hunting or upon some other quirk,
Whenever he was near and passed her by.
His looks were not unprincipled or sly,   150
But thoughtful as he watched her at her duty.
He saw her inward light, not just her beauty.

He cherished in his heart her womanhood,
Her loving kindness, born of humble life.
He found Griselda fair, yet wise and good.
Let others put their minds and hearts at strife;
He knew this girl would make a sovereign wife.

He saw her value and resolved he would
Have her and wed no other if he could.

The wedding day approached, but no one knew   160
The name or the condition of the bride.
Among his people apprehension grew,
And many put their former hopes aside.
"Our lord," they said, "is stiff necked in his pride.
Will he not wed at all, despite our trust?
Will he revoke his word, beguiling us?"

But as they saw, the marquis sent abroad
For gems and lapis stones and other treasure,
For brooches, rings, and every sort of gaud,
And saw Griselda's gown sewn up with pleasure.   170
He used another girl to get her measure
And try the sumptuous clothes and ornaments
He thought a bride required for such events.

Ah, now the hoped-for time arrived at last,
The welcome morning of the wedding day!
The palace was inspected, and it passed:
Its halls and chambers waited, bright and gay;
Its storerooms swelled with food and rich array.
Each item was as fine as it might be—
The best that could be found in Italy.   180

The royal marquis in his regal clothes,
With lords and ladies crowding in his train,
The cream of all Saluzzo, Heaven knows,
And troupes of bright young men of his domain,
Amid loud music of a festive strain,
Down to Griselda's village made their way,
Where people stood amazed at their display.

The girl herself remained quite innocent.
She'd no idea what lay in store for her.
That morning to the local well she went   190
Then hurried home. The wedding was the spur,

For she had heard folk talk and felt the stir.
That day her lord the marquis would be wed.
She hoped to glimpse the party, so she said.

"I'll stand among the other girls," she thought.
"I know them all, my fellows and my friends.
I'll see his wife, if things go as they ought,
Yet I must do the chores that this day sends.
Be quick! I must work fast to reach my ends,
But then I'll see the lady, if I may.   200
I trust she'll pass our house along the way.

But as she went outside her little door,
The marquis rode into her yard to call.
She set her water bucket on the floor
Beside the threshold, in an ox's stall,
And fell down on her knees beside the wall.
With eyes cast low and serious and still,
She waited there to learn her great lord's will.

The thoughtful marquis looked down at the maid,
And soberly addressed her where she kneeled.   210
"I've come to see your father, girl," he said.
She made a proper answer, though she reeled:
"My lord, he's here at home, not in the field."
Then quick to show her reverence and obey,
She brought her father forth without delay.

*Walter asks the astonished Janicula for Griselda's hand and, when he agrees, in-
sists on asking Griselda as well. But first he imposes these conditions on the girl:*

"I say you must comply, and with good heart,
With all my wishes, and I freely may,
As I think best, cause you to laugh or smart,
And you must never grudge it, night or day.
When I say yea, you never shall say nay,   220
No, not by word or frown, or open strife.
Consent to this, and you shall be my wife."

Griselda agrees, and Walter carries her off, but not before his ladies discard her
peasant clothes, which they are reluctant even to touch. The humble girl is trans-
formed. The wedding is a grand success, and soon she and Walter have a daugh-
ter. The people love Griselda, who proves an able consort and ruler, with a spe-
cial ability to settle grievances. But well off as he is, Walter cannot rest content.

Part Three

It happened then, as sometimes is the case,
Before their daughter left her mother's breast,
The marquis had an impulse, dark and base,
To put Griselda's patience to the test.
The feeling grew until he was obsessed.
He felt an urge beyond all explanation,
To try his blameless lady's resignation.

Now he had tested her enough before,   230
And always found her gold. There was no need
To try her wifely virtue any more;
The craving in his heart was strange indeed.
And as for me, I say no man can speed
Who grossly tempts his wife without a reason
And pushes her to anguish by his treason.

Much like his urge, the marquis' plot was base.
He came alone, by night, to where she lay,
And showing her a stern and troubled face,
He said, "Griselda, think upon the way   240
Despite your sorry state and worse array,
I lifted you to wealth and nobleness.
You've not forgotten how it was, I guess?

"I trust, my dear, your present dignity,
Which flows from me alone, as you must know,
Has not yet sealed your eyes so you don't see
I raised you up from where you lay below,
To all the wealth and comfort life can show.
Now, listen, lady, hear each word I say.
I'll speak my mind while no one's in the way.   250

"You know how our strange union came to be,
How we were wed; it wasn't long ago.
And though, my wife, you still are dear to me,
The nobles of my court don't find you so.
They say it is Saluzzo's shame and woe
For gentlefolk like them to bow and grovel
To you, a common sheep girl from a hovel.

"And lately, lady, since your daughter's birth
Their grumbling has become still more pronounced.
It's one of my chief wishes here on earth   260
To live at peace among them, unrenounced.
Therefore, their wishes cannot be denounced,
And I must use your daughter for the best—
Not as I wish, but as my lords request.

"Now listen, wife, I hate what I must do,
And will not act without your free consent.
So help me now. Do what you promised to.
Surrender her, and say you won't resent
What I have ordered. Give me your assent.
Show perfect resignation, as you said,   270
And keep the vow you made the day we wed."

Griselda heard the marquis quite unmoved.
No word or gesture showed her inward feeling.
It seemed for all the world that she approved.
She said, "My lord, I must accept your dealing.
Do as you like with us. There's no appealing.
My child and I are yours to save or kill.
All yours, my lord. Do with us as you will."

*Walter sends a rough, forbidding man for his daughter, and Griselda yields her
up. She is certain the fellow means to kill the little girl, but asks only to kiss the
baby one last time and that he bury its body, not leave it for the birds and beasts.
Hearing this, the marquis almost relents, but he holds to his purpose. He sends
his daughter to Bologna, where his sister, the Countess of Panik, is to raise her
while keeping her identity secret, even from the girl herself. Meanwhile, though
Walter watches his wife closely for any sign of resentment, he sees none. Griselda
is as loving and compliant as ever. She never once mentions her daughter's name.*

Part Four

In just this way they lived for four years more
Before Griselda was with child again.   280
This time it was a little boy she bore,
A handsome lad, almost his sister's twin.
And when they told the marquis and his kin,
Not only they but all the country sang.
Throughout the land God's holy praises rang.

The boy was two and late weaned from the breast
Of his wet nurse when on a certain day
The marquis felt another urge to test
His marchioness, and in the former way.
Oh, wicked man to toy with her dismay!   290
But wedded men behave with no restraint—
Especially this one, married to a saint.

"Wife," he said, "I told you long ago,
My people rail at me for wedding you.
Your son has made their reprehension grow,
So they are now resentful through and through.
Perhaps I shouldn't listen, but I do.
Their grumbling and complaints have grown so tart,
I've come to fear their anger in my heart.

"Here's what they say: 'When our lord Walter's gone   300
The blood of this Janicula will rise.
Then we'll be ruled by that low peasant's spawn.'
They ask to be relieved from this surmise.
I'd close my ears, but I must not despise
My people's apprehensions and their plea,
Which they express to everyone but me.

"Now, I would live in peace if I still might;
And so I've come to tell you of my plan:
As I sent for your girl another night,
I'd have you give the boy now to my man.   310
I warn you, wife, to keep yourself in hand.

Don't let your heart give way to indignation,
But bear this as you should, with resignation."

"I've said," she answered, "and I ever will,
That I won't yearn or hold back or complain.
Do as you like. I'll never take it ill,
Although my son and daughter both are slain.
We're yours, my lord, and yours we shall remain.
My children have meant nothing on my part
But sickness first, and then a scalded heart.   320

"You are our lord and will be evermore.
You know your mind with no advice from me.
I left my clothing at my father's door
The day I married you, my lord," said she,
"And with it left my will and liberty.
You clothed me then, and now, good lord, I pray,
Say what you'd have me do, and I'll obey."

*Walter sends the same ugly ruffian for the baby, and though Griselda is convinced
the boy is going to his death, she gives him up. In fact, the man takes the little
boy to join his sister in Bologna, but Griselda knows nothing of this. The mar-
quis is amazed. How can Griselda surrender her beloved children so patiently?
But he still cannot leave well enough alone. As the Clerk says,*

Some hapless folk exhibit this condition:
That when they're wedded to a certain plan
They can't put off their settled disposition   330
But find themselves bound to it, foot and hand—
Doomed to play their parts as they began.
Just so, this troubled marquis' doubts persisted
She must be tried, his stony heart insisted.

*By now rumors of Walter's cruelty are widespread, but he goes on with his wicked
testing. The year his daughter turns twelve he forges papal bulls directing him to
marry her and divorce Griselda. He then sends for both children, specifying that
the girl must be dressed as if she were going to her wedding.*

Part Five

The man was still a slave to his strange quirk
And set himself to test his wife once more.
He'd sound her heart with his inhuman work,
To see if anger festered at her core
Or if she kept as steadfast as before.
He called to her out loud before the court,   340
Provoking words, and this was their import:

"It pleased me once, my lady, and would still,
To keep you as my consort, I must own—
Loved for your faith and for your pliant will,
Not wealth or any nobleness you've shown.
But now I see I cannot act alone.
The most exalted lords, as I can tell,
Are checked at every turn. They serve as well.

"I cannot do as every plowman does.
My people hound me daily, soon and late,   350
To find another wife. I hear them buzz.
Then too, the pope in Rome, who knows their hate,
Consents that I should take another mate.
And truly, lady, I have heard today,
Your lady, my new wife, is on the way.

"Be strong of heart; surrender her your place.
As for the dower that you brought to me,   *Of course there was no dowry.*
Why, take it back. I grant it with my grace.
Return now to your father's house," said he.
"Good luck can't last forever, as you see.   360
Now, wife, maintain a mild and even heart
Beneath the gifts of Fortune, or her smart."

Griselda answered with a patient mien:
"I knew, my lord, and know it yet today,
My birth, unlike your own, was low and mean.
I am no match for one like you, I say,
In rank or blood or opulent display.
I can't pretend to you, when all is weighed,
I'm fit to be your wife, or chambermaid.

Griselda bears the latest indignity with her usual patience. She returns Walter's
jewels and clothes, asking only for a smock to wear home, though she came to him
naked. Even the smock is for his sake. It would be disgraceful to let people see the
womb that carried their lord's children. Janicula meets Griselda with her old
coat, not surprised that the marriage didn't last. She goes back to her peasant's
life with no repining, as if her years at the palace had never been. The Clerk
praises Griselda and all long-suffering women:

No wonder, sirs, for in her greatest state   370
Her spirit kept its old humility.
She never let herself grow delicate
Or relished pomp or went like royalty,
But lived with patient, true gentility,
Discrete, not proud, and busy, strong, and able,
Meek to her lord and loving, wise, and stable.

We know of Job and how he bore his ills
Through clerks who praise his name in what they write.
Though he, of course, deserves their highest skills,
They don't extol good women as they might.   380
No man who suffers meekly shines as bright
As women often do for all to see,
Or if one does, my lords, it's news to me.

Part Six

From Bologna now the Earl of Panik came
To awe the people with his nobleness,
And all soon knew the advent and the aim
Of her he brought, their future marchioness.
He rode in such great pomp, as I profess,
That men imagined they would never see
A greater sight than this in Lombardy.   390

The marquis from his palace, high and great,
Before the earl arrived sent out a call
For poor Griselda, his rejected mate,
And she with humble heart, his lordship's thrall,
Appeared in court to offer him her all.
She came at once to greet him on her knees,
As if her highest thought was how to please.

"Griselda," said the marquis, "here's my will:
This tender maiden who shall marry me
Must be received in state and served with skill.   400
We offer her all honor, as you see.
And every person here, of each degree,
Must join the celebration, great and good,
And help Saluzzo greet her as we should.

"Alas, the women here will never serve
To decorate the palace in the style
A great feast like this marriage must deserve,
And so I'll put your housewifery on trial.
You know what I most like and most revile.
Although your own array is not the best,   410
I'd have you see my house is richly dressed."

"Not only," said Griselda, "am I pleased,
I'm honored too, to do your lordship's will.
I'll always do my best to see you eased,
I won't hold back, but work with all my skill.
Whatever comes to me for good or ill,
The heart within my breast will never cease
To love you and promote your joy and peace."

And with that word she started right away
To make the beds and set up every table.   420
She kept the servants moving through the day
And made them work as fast as they were able.
They swept and cleaned like spirits in a fable,
As she, the most industrious of all,
Decked out the marquis' chambers and his hall.

Midmorning the next day the earl arrived
And brought Griselda's children, all unknown.
The people ran to see them and contrived
To welcome them as if they were their own.
Above the others, though, the young girl shone.   430
"Our Walter is no fool," folks said. "My word,
It's plain this younger wife's to be preferred."

The girl outshone Griselda, and to boot,
They saw that she was young and gently raised.
A wife to give their marquis finer fruit,
Her bearing and her mien left them amazed.
Her noble brother, too, was roundly praised.
The people all were moved by these fair visions
To laud the marquis now for his decisions.

Oh, wretched folk, inconstant and untrue!   440
Unsettled as a spinning weather vane!
Unwisely drawn to anything that's new,
Just like the fickle moon, you wax and wane.
Your good opinion isn't worth a grain.
Your judgment's false; newfangledness, your rule.
No one would court your favor but a fool.

*Griselda is indispensable. In her tattered clothes she greets the guests and
arranges things so neatly she wins everyone's praise. When Walter asks how she
likes his new lady, she praises the girl but tells him she hopes he won't torment
this new wife. She might not be able to endure as much as a plainer woman
brought up in poverty. With this, her patience finally wins Walter over. At last
he fully relents.*

"This is enough, Griselda," Walter said.
"Don't be provoked or frightened any more.
I've tried your will and risked your love with dread.
No woman's heart was ever rubbed so sore   450
When you were wealthy here or home and poor.
But now I know, dear wife, your faith and grace."
He held her close and kissed her lips and face.

Griselda was too staggered to attend.
She didn't hear a word of what he said.
She seemed asleep. She couldn't comprehend,
Until she shook amazement from her head.
The marquis said, "My dear, by God who bled,
You are my wife and have been all along,
And I won't take another, right or wrong.   460

"See, here's your daughter, she whom you supposed
Would be my wife. The boy who came with her
Will be my heir and yours, as Heaven knows—
The lad you thought you lost is now secure,
Raised by this earl in state, you may be sure.
Now take them back, my dear, and never say
Your children have been harmed or filched away.

"And as for those who tax and slander me,
I warn them here that every act of mine
Came not from ill intentions, as they see.   470
I tried your wifely virtues by design.
I wouldn't harm my children, by Christ's shrine!
I kept them at Bologna, out of view,
Till I had wrung the utmost truth from you."

When she heard this, released from all her cares,
Griselda fainted there at Walter's feet.
Reviving, she was racked by sobs and prayers,
Then held her children fast, her joy complete.
She took them in her arms with kisses sweet.
Weeping in her bliss she held her dears   480
Until their faces all were bathed in tears.

Oh what a piteous thing it was to see
Her swooning, and her humble voice to hear.
"Ah, bless you, God, and thank you, Lord," said she,
"For you've returned my darlings to me here.
So now not death itself can make me fear.
My soul has found such favor in your eyes,
I don't care when or how my body dies.

"Oh tender dears, oh children, Heaven knows,
Your mother felt most certain in her heart   490
That you were dead and torn by dogs and crows,
But you were saved by God through his great art!
Then too your loving father, for his part,
Has kept you . . ." but that's all that she could say,
For with those words she fainted dead away.

Griselda is revived once more, and she and Walter preside over a great feast.
They later marry their daughter to a fine lord and bring old Janicula to the
palace, where he lives out his peaceful life. Later still, the son succeeds Walter,
though he is wise enough not to test his wife as Walter had Griselda. The Clerk
follows his story with account of its moral, which applies to men as well as
women.

This story wasn't told so other wives
Would match Griselda's great humility.
No, that would be to wish them monstrous lives.
Instead, it shows how men of each degree
Should bear up bravely in adversity.   500
And that's why Petrarch thought it worth his while
To draw the story out in highest style.

For since a woman bore so great a wrong
From mortal man, why, how much more should we
Take all the lashings God may send along.
For God must try his creatures, you'll agree.
But he won't make us sin. That's his decree.
The Gospel makes that point extremely clear: *James, 1:13*
You won't be tried unfairly, never fear.

God suffers us throughout our nights and days   510
With scourges of robust adversity
Full often to be beat in sundry ways—
But not to learn our worth, for certainly
Before our birth he knew our frailty—
Yet punishment can lead us to the good,
So let us bear our anguish as we should.

Now one more word, my lords, before I go:
I don't think you'd discover, nowadays,
A town on earth where new Griseldas grow,
For test our girls in such unsparing ways,   520
Their gold is so shot through with baser clays,
That though they may look fair until the end,
Like cheapened coins they'll break before they bend.

And last, because I love the Wife of Bath,
Whose life and all her gender God maintain
In perfect joy and shield them from his wrath,
I will with all my heart sing this refrain,
A song to please you all, but not profane.
So, sirs, now put aside my moral tale,
And listen to my song to good avail: 530

Lenvoy de Chaucer   *envoy or postscript*

Griselda died, her resignation too,
And both are fitly buried in Saluzzo.
And so, my lords, let's bid them both adieu.
Let no man turn his wife into his foe.
Try women's patience now, and you will find
That none of them endures oppression so.

And noble wives, use common wisdom, do.
Don't hold your tongues in meekness as you go.
And let no author make a show of you,
Recount a tale like this and shame you so.   540
Don't be Griseldas, timorous and kind,
Lest Chichevache[1] eat you head to toe.

Remember Echo, seizing every cue,   *a nymph in classical myth*
So quick to answer anyone's hallo.
Don't let your shyness rob you of your due,
But squawk and wrangle like a stubborn crow.
Absorb this lesson, fix it in your mind.
Women, match your husbands blow for blow.

All archwives, and your number isn't few,
Kick out like camels when your man says "Whoa!"   550
Use all your strength to beat him black and blue.
And bear up, skinny women, for you know,
A tiger uses claws and voice combined.
So rattle like a mill against the flow.

---

1. In Spanish legend, a skinny cow who eats nothing but patient wives.

Don't dread your husbands. Knock their hats askew,
For though they go in mail and draw a bow,
The arrows of reproach will come from you,
To pierce their necks and all the parts below.
Tame them, women! Bait them till they're blind;
You'll be amazed how quail-like they will grow.   560

If you are fair and men admire your hue,
Why, show yourself, and flitter to and fro.
If you are foul, spend freely, for it's true
All men are drawn in by a brilliant show.
Flit lightly like bright linden leaves entwined,
And make your husbands wail and nurse their woe!

Bihoold the murye words of the Hoost

Now that the worthy Clerk had told his tale
Our Host rose up and swore, "By God's white bones!
I'd rather than a barrel full of ale,
My wife had heard this legend, by my stones!   570
This is a gentle fable for the nonce!
You know, my lords, the virtues this might teach her.
But let it go; the tale will never reach her.

Heere endeth the Tale of the Clerk of Oxenford.

The Merchant

The Merchant's Prologue

"Weeping and wailing and other sorrow,
I know by evening and by morrow,"
The Merchant said. "Become a spouse,
And heartache moves into your house.
At least it fared that way with me.
My wife's as bad as she could be.
Let Satan take the bitch in hand,
She'll prove too much for him to stand.
Give examples? What's the use?
No greater shrew could shriek abuse.   10
What a gulf there is between
Griselda's patience and her spleen!
If I were free, I'd fly this snare,
The married state with all its care.
Test my words at will, I promise,
You'll find them true, by blessed Thomas,
Or true for most—I don't say all—
God grant that that will not befall!
    "Ah, good Host, I have been wed
These last two months, as I have said.   20
No wifeless man, though pierced with spears
Through heart and lungs could shed more tears
Than I have through that woman's spite!"
    "Now," said our Host, "God set you right.
You say your wife has caused you woe.
Tell us your story as we go."
    "I'll show," said the man, "how spouses war,
But of myself, I'll say no more."

The Merchant's Tale

In Pavia, in Lombardy,
There lived an old unwedded party,   30
A knight he was, of great prosperity,
Accounted sixty, though that was charity.
He'd long pursued with keen delight,
Each girl who sparked his appetite,
As fools do, who discount salvation.
But then he felt an aberration.
His stirring spirit or weakened wit
Gave rise to an obsessive fit:
Lo! He would be a married man!
All day and night he schemed and planned,   40
Anything to see him wed!
Praying to Our Lord, he said,
"Oh could I know the blissful life
Between a husband and his wife
And live within that holy state
That God decreed for man and mate!
No other life is worth a bean!
A wife's so lawful, willing, clean . . .
Yea, marriage is a paradise."
So said this knight. He was so wise.   50
    Still, sirs, as sure as God is king,
Wiving is a glorious thing,
Especially when a man is old.
Why, then, a wife is good as gold,
Especially one who's young and fair
And fit to give her lord an heir.
She'll comfort him with joy and solace,
While bachelors caterwaul "Alas!"
When love serves them adversity
And pricks their swollen vanity.   60
And truly, God arranged things so,
That bachelors pine and suffer woe.
They build on sand, and sand will slide.
They may find ease, but not a bride.
They live, indeed, like birds or beasts.

They do precisely as they please,
Whereas a husband and his wife
Pursue a fruitful, ordered life
Beneath the equal marriage yoke.
What joys the husband's state evokes!　　　　　　　　70
For who's so buxom as a wife?
Who's half so true and free of strife?
Who's so attentive to her mate,
Sick or well, soon or late?
She never falters in the least,
Though he's bedridden till deceased,
And yet some clerks will say "Not so."
Theophrastus stoops that low.　　　　*Greek writer, c. 370–287 BC*
Who cares if Theophrastus lies?
He wrote, "Live wifeless. I advise.　　　　　　　　80
That way you'll spare yourself expense.
A servant shows more diligence
For your estate than does a wife
With claim to half your goods in life.
And if you're sick, so God me save,
Your common friends or kitchen knave
Will better serve than one who ties
Her future wealth to your demise.
Each man who has a wife at home
May feel the pains of cuckoldom."　　　　　　　　90
All this and more his book bemoans,
May God disperse his wicked bones!
Although at times that clerk surpassed us,
Attend to me, not Theophrastus.
　　A wife's God's gift, approved and pure;
All other gifts are far less sure.
Lands or rent or other treasure,
Belong to you at Fortune's pleasure.
They pass like shadows on a wall.
Now, wives are not like that at all.　　　　　　　　100
They last though your affairs collapse—
Much longer than you wish, perhaps.
　　Then, marriage is a sacrament;
No wifeless man can rest content.
He's half a man; he's desolate.

(That is, if priesthood's not his fate.)
Wives merit every word I've said.
Women were men's helpmeets made.
Though Adam all the beasts surpassed,
He dwelt alone and naked-assed,
Until God pitied him and said, 110
"I'll make this man a helpful maid,
One like himself," and gave him Eve.
This proves my point, sirs, I believe.
A wife is man's sustaining consort,
His paradise, his wealth, his sport.
She is so willing and compliant,
She'll never grudge or act defiant.
One flesh God framed them both, and so
They share one heart in joy or woe. 120
  A wife! A saint! Oh blessed gift!
How can one weep or go adrift
Who has a wife? Sure, I can't say.
The peace that they enjoy each day,
No tongue can tell; no heart express:
If he is poor, she shares his stress,
Pinches pennies, shaves expenses,
Yet what he wishes, she dispenses.
She can't say "no" when he says "yes."
"Do this," says he. "It's done," she says. 130
Oh, count the joys of men who marry:
A healthful life, secure and merry,
A godly boon, approved, antique.
Each man on earth who's worth a leek,
Upon his knees throughout his life
Should thank great God he's got a wife
Or pray that fate will send him one
For comfort till his days are done.
Then his fortune is secure.
She'll not deceive him, that's for sure. 140
As long as he does what she tells him,
She'll be the fair wind that propels him.
Wives are so true, their words so wise,
A man should serve them till he dies.
We all should do what women say.

Look how Jacob, as clerks portray,
Followed his mother's word and knelt,
His smooth neck swathed in rough kid's pelt,   *Gen. 27:16*
To win his ancient father's blessing.
   Or Judith, if I'm not digressing,   150
To save God's people from distress,
Slew the sleeping Holofernes.   *Jdt., Apocrypha, 13:2–7*
   Then Abigail. Recall how she
Shielded Nabal from the king's decree,   *1 Sam. 25:1–35*
As not worth killing. Esther, too,
Did signal service to the Jews,
Preserving them with loving care as
They quailed in fear of Ahasuerus,
And advancing her uncle Mordecai,
Whom Haman had condemned to die.   *Esther 7:1–10*
There's nothing better in one's life,
As Seneca says, than a humble wife.
   Suffer her tongue, Cato advises,
Do what she will, whatever arises.
She'll grant you equal deference.
A wife's her household's best defense.
A single sick man sighs and moans;
Without a wife he's on his own.
If you are wise, you'll always work   170
To love your wife as Christ, his Church.
Esteem yourself esteeming her.
No man hates his flesh, that's sure,
But coddles it. Your wife is you,
So cherish her in all you do.
Husbands and wives, whatever men say,
Of secular folk live the surest way,
In unions that no trials can maim,
Or if they do, no wife's to blame.
All this Sir January, of whom I tell,
Pondered—and growing old, as well.   180
The lusty life, the lawful joys,
Long, honeyed days without annoys—
These made him summon all his friends,
Not to consult, but tell his plans.
   His face was longer than his story:

"Friends, I'm old," he said, "and hoary.
I've almost slipped into the pit.
My soul's bespattered, I admit.
My bodily powers are expended.
God grant that this can yet be mended.   190
Sirs, I will be a wedded man,
And soon, with all the haste I can!
I'll wed a maiden in her teens.
So help me find one fit and clean.
Don't make me wait, I mustn't tarry.
I too will seek the girl I'll marry,
One I can win with small delay.
But since you're many, I would say
You stand a better chance than I
To find the right girl, far or nigh.   200
    "There's one great point to keep in mind:
She can't be old. I'm not inclined
To take a wife who's more than twenty.
Ah, tender flesh! Though cognoscenti
Prefer grown pike to pickerel,
Old beef's too tough to rival veal.
A woman thirty years of age
Is parched and dry as winter sedge.
Besides, old widows know old tales
Of plots and schemes and lovers' ails.   210
God knows that their experience
Must frighten any man of sense.
Many schools make subtle students;
Thus wedding widows is imprudent.
A young thing, now, a man may guide,
Mold in his hands till he's satisfied.
And so, my friends, don't nominate
Some older woman for my mate.
Say I wed one and she displeased me,
With all her arts she couldn't ease me.   220
I'd slide into adultery,
And hell would have me when I die.
Nor bring me any girl with children!
I'd let wolves eat me in their den
Before my heritage should fall

In strangers' hands! I tell you all,
There are two reasons, as I've said,
That drive a normal man to wed.
You hear a lot of theorizing
On sundry causes, some surprising,   230
That lead a man to take a wife.
But say you can't live chaste through life;
Then wed some girl, in contemplation
Not just of sex, but procreation—
Children to honor God above—
Not just for lechery or love.
(Still, wives must serve their husbands' lust:
You say, 'Come here.' By God, she must!)
Or say you're ill and need a nurse.
She'll guard your body and your purse,   240
Tend your wants while living chaste.
But that's not me! Praise God, I'm graced
With vigor, health, and limbs unbent,
And I am stiff and puissant
In that which makes a man a man.
I know myself how straight I stand.
My hair is white, but like a tree
That blossoms with fertility
Before it fruits. I'm far from dead;
My only hoary part's my head.   250
My heart and all my limbs are green
As laurel all the year is seen.
Now that's my wish as I conceive it.
I pray you, help me to achieve it."
      His diverse friends regaled the knight
With anecdotes of wedded life.
Some men praised it; some disparaged
Everything to do with marriage.
But at length among the others
A strife arose between his brothers,   260
Brusque Justinus, smooth Placebo.
Their quarrels had started long ago.
      Placebo said, "Dear January,
You don't need our advice to marry.
Why worry what your friends may say?

You're wiser far, and anyway,
You yourself must make your choices
As wisdom bids you, not our voices.
I know you honor Solomon's saying:
'Seek advice without delaying.
You'll have nothing to repent,   270
Relying on your friends' consent.'
But though that was the king's behest,
My dearest brother, I protest,
As God may bring my soul to rest,
I hold your own deep wisdom best.
For, brother, I have seen the world.
A courtier, I've bobbed and whirled
Amid some great ones, in their wakes,
Playing at times for heavy stakes.
Among these lords of high estate   280
I never ventured to debate
Or contravene their fixed opinions.
Rich lords know so much more than minions.
Whatever one said, why, I'd agree,
An echo to his last decree.
It is a foolish counselor,
Consulting lords of wealth and store,
Who dares to say or intimate
Their wisdom may be second rate.
Rich men aren't fools! We know that's true.   290
Why, brother, only look at you!
Your words display such sterling wit,
That I applaud them, every bit—
Every premise, each conclusion.
I'll say it now, without collusion:
There's not a man in all this town—
All Italy!—whose thought's more sound.
Christ Himself approves your plan,
And truly not just any man
Who's reached your age would take a wife.   300
A young one too! By Father's leg,
Your heart hangs on a jolly peg!
Do whatever you propose.
Your judgment's best, sir, Heaven knows."

Justinus heard this, sitting by,
And rose up with a prompt reply:
"My lord," he said, "let me explain
Why you should count this counsel vain.
Seneca tells us, if we'll read him,   310
A man must settle who'll succeed him,
Who will be his earthly heir.
Since I must contemplate with care
Who gets my goods when I'm deceased,
I should be as discrete, at least,
Bestowing this, my earthly life,
Upon a co-proprietor, or wife.
Wife-choosing asks a deal of thought.
You must inquire—at least you ought—
Is she sober, or always drinking,   320
Or proud, or shrewish and unthinking?
A scold, or traitor to your trust?
Rich, or poor? Promiscuous?
I grant no man will ever find
A wife entirely to his mind—   *Obedience*
Or serving man or perfect horse—
But that's a poor excuse, of course,
Not to seek the best you can.
In general a wife suffices
If her good points outweigh her vices,   330
Though that can take some time to know.
By God, I've felt my share of woe,
As long as I have had a wife.
Praise who may the wedded life,
I find it irksome and expensive.
Its joys, trust me, are less extensive.
And yet the women round about
All praise my wife without a doubt.
They call her steadfast, true, and sure—
Humble, moderate, demure—   340
But I know how my own shoe pinches!
True, some men live like brainless finches,
But, brother, think—should a man like you
Pursue a state so many rue,
And with a girl who's young and winsome?

By him who made the world to come,
The youngest fellow in this rout
Is sorely taxed, I cannot doubt,
To keep his wife true to his bed:
Three years and she will want her head,   350
And spurn your love and your attention.
You'll fry in jealous apprehension,
Your joys will vanish like a dream."
    "Enough," said his brother, "on that theme.
Fie on your Seneca and proverbs!
I wouldn't give a sack of herbs
For those old saws. Far wiser men
Have heard me out and said 'Amen'!
Tell me, Placebo, is he right?"
    "You know yourself he's not, Sir Knight,"   360
Placebo said. "Truth's on your side."
With that the company all cried
Their patron January should
Be married where and when he would.
    Oh, what dreams, what fantasies,
Rose up now to haunt and tease
Old January! Night on night,
Sweet visions set his heart alight.
Girls' shapes and faces filled the air.
Just think that in a market square   370
You were a mirror, polished bright—
Soon pleasing girls would glut your sight.
In much this way old January
Could not decide which lass to marry.
His fancy ranged the neighborhood:
This girl was pretty, that one good.
As fast as he could pick a lover,
Another choice would rise above her.
For this one's pert, bewitching face,
The next was known throughout the place   380
For her great goodness or her bearing,
And such things made for hard comparing.
Some were rich but ill regarded.
At last his indecision parted,
And halfway as pleasant game,

He singled out one face and name
And chose her on his own advice.
Love may be blind, but it's precise.
That night when he stretched out in bed,
He shaped her image in his head,   390
Her beauty and her tender years,
Her arms, her waist, her pretty ears,
Her wise demeanor, gentle air,
Her earnest frown, like one at prayer.
Ah, soon his heart was firmly fettered.
His choice, he knew, could not be bettered.
He thought so much of his discretion,
He wouldn't grant the least concession
To other viewpoints if he heard them.
He knew his own thoughts and preferred them.   400
He sent for all his friends and neighbors
And told them to suspend their labors;
No longer need they search and ride.
Lo, he himself had found his bride.
    For Placebo and his other guests,
January had one more request:
That they would neither doubt nor question
How this girl merited selection.
She suited him, by God, he said—
By far the best wife he could wed.   410
    He named young May, a girl in town,
Whose beauty brought her great renown,
Although her family wasn't wealthy.
The maid herself was sleek and healthy.
He meant to take her for his wife,
To save his soul and ease his life.
He'd sample all her charms at leisure;
No other man would share that pleasure.
He sent his friends to broker this,
And see that nothing went amiss.   420
"Then," he said, "My soul can rest,
Secure I have attained the best.
There's just one doubt that troubles me.
I'd like to know if you agree.
    "I heard," he said, "once long ago,

No man could perfect pleasure know
On earth and still taste Heaven's bliss.
For though one never goes amiss
And fends off every sin in sight,
Yet married men win such delight,   430
Such cushioned ease, such spicy zest,
I swear my heart's sometimes oppressed
To think about the life I'll lead,
Such boundless joy in every deed,
For fear I'll have my heaven here.
I know men buy salvation dear
With grief and penance, guilt and pain;
How can my coddled soul obtain
Christ's blessing and eternal life,
If all my trial's a darling wife?   440
My brothers, please address this scruple.
You'll find me your most willing pupil."
     Justinus, who hated foolishness,
Was stung by this to bitter jests.
To make his scornful answer short
He used no source of any sort.
"My lord," he said, "If that's your worry,
God may resolve it in a hurry.
Perhaps before you're even wed
He'll send you cause to hang your head   450
And reassess the married life,
Which now you find so free of strife.
Perhaps the Lord will show you yet
More ample causes for regret
Than those that trouble single men!
Here's what I advise you then:
Sir, don't despair or go in fear;
Your purgatory may be near.
Perhaps she'll be God's lash in life
To purge your soul through earthly strife.   460
You'll shoot to heaven like an arrow!
Though your experience is narrow,
There's not enough felicity
In marriage, as you'll shortly see,
To threaten anyone's salvation.

A wife is part of God's Creation.
Just use her with due moderation.
Don't let her lead you to temptation
In luxury or other sins.
That's my advice. My wit is thin.   470
My lord, dismiss such morbid thoughts;
These fears of yours will come to naught.
The Wife of Bath, as you'll recall,
Equated marriage to a brawl.
Her comments were so sound and brief;
Consider them. God spare you grief!"
    Forthright Justinus took his way
From January's house that day,
But when they saw it must be so,
His other friends went to and fro   480
Arranging details, terms, and days
To bring his chosen girl, young May,
Home to January's bed,
To please the knight and see him wed.
It would take too long to sift
Through every bond and deed of gift
By which he settled land on her.
Soon she was dressed in jewels and fur
And fancy lace and rich array
Against the chosen wedding day,   490
When they met at the church and went
Together to the sacrament.
The priest came forward in his stole.
His chief concern was young May's soul.
Sarah's and Rebecca's lives,
He said, were models for all wives
In wedded truth and wifely spirit.
He spoke the Mass so all could hear it,
Then crossed, invoked, and prayed and blessed
To seal the pact with holiness.   500
    So they were wed the fittest way
And later, at the feast that day,
The hall rang out as they were toasted.
No palace of high princes boasted
Such dainty food or minstrelsy

The length and breadth of Italy,
And as the festive meal wore on
Not Orpheus or Amphion   *musicians in Greek myth*
Ever wove such melodies.
At every course they played a piece   510
More sonorous than Joab's horn   *2 Sam. 20:22*
Or Theodamas, who played to warn
Thebes City when the foe was near.
Bacchus poured sweet wine and clear,
And Venus smiled upon them all,
For January was her thrall:
Soon he'd employ his manly power,
As he desired, in love's soft bower.
Holding a torch aloft in pride,
The goddess danced before the bride.   520
The least that I can say is this:
That Hymen, god of marriages,
Never saw a merrier groom.
Let Martianus give me room.   *Martianus Capella, fifth-century*
Although he wrote at length concerning   *Roman writer*
Mercury's nuptials with Learning
And how the Muses sang out then,
I wouldn't call his tongue or pen
Fit to describe the signal day
When January married May,   530
Or stooping age wed tender youth.
Try it yourself. You'll see, in truth,
I don't exaggerate a hair.
    May looked so sweet upon her chair,
She filled each watcher with enchantment.
Not even Esther ever bent
So meek a look on Ahasuerus.   *Esther 7:5*
No mortal could describe her fairness,
But this is not too much to say:
She far outdid her namesake, May,   540
And all that month's sweet exhalations.
    The old knight swelled with exaltation
Each time he saw her. His new station
Pricked him with anticipation.
He'd strain her to him and enjoy

Her supple body, as at Troy
Paris clipped his white-armed Helen.
But even as this dream was swelling,
He thought, "Alas, so young and pure!
I pray to God you can endure   550
My puissance. It's sharp and keen!
I fear you can't; yet I don't mean
To let myself use all my might. . . .
Ah, God! If it were only night,
And such a night as lasts forever!
First, all these folk must leave, however."
He shooed the dawdlers from the place
As best he could while saving face,
Impatiently dismissed the party.
    No common guest, however hearty,   560
Had reason not to drink up fast
And scatter spices and leave at last.
Contentment went with every man,
Except a squire, one Damian,
Who carved at January's board.
He thought of May, whom he adored,
All through the feast, half crazed with pain.
He burned with love in every vein,
For Love had struck him with the brand
She bore, while dancing, in her hand.   570
At last he dragged himself to bed.
For now there's no more to be said.
I'll let him lurk there, weak and faint,
Till May herself hears his complaint.
    Oh, perilous fire that breeds in bedstraw!
Familiar foe that none foresaw,
Embodied lie in livery dressed,
Oh adder twining in the breast!
God shield us from your machinations!
January! Put off love's impatience.   580
See how this squire, this Damian,
Obliged to you, and your born man,
Intends to do you villainy.
God grant that you are standing by;
The worst foe's one who's always nigh.

  By now the sun's diurnal arc
Was run, and now it touched its mark,
The far horizon in the west.
And night, in his dark mantle dressed
Overspread the hemisphere,   590
And so the last guests left with cheer,
And hearty thanks on every side,
To undertake their homeward ride.
Soon after this, old January
Would go to bed, no longer tarry.
He tossed down warmed and sweetened wine
And seasoned drinks with spices fine,
Designed to aid his potency
With aphrodisiacs, two or three,
From secret recipes he'd gleaned   600
From that bad monk Dom Constantine   *Constantinus Afer, an 11th-century*
And his engaging book *De Coitu*.   *Carthaginian*
The knight quaffed every murky brew,
And then he asked his private friends
To leave him to pursue his ends
And quit the house for courtesy.
His purpose was not hard to see.
One drink, and they closed off the room
And brought the bride in, still as doom.
At last the priest had blessed the sheets   610
And led the friends into the streets,
And January held his bride,
His darling May, his paradise.
He kissed her lips; he stroked her hair;
And with his whiskers, unaware—
Like dogfish skin or briar thorns,
For he had shaved for her that morn—
He rubbed about her tender face,
And said, "Dear May, I must trespass,
On you, my spouse, don't be offended,   620
Love's stiff and stark till it's expended.
But just consider this," he said,
"No workman in a job or bed
Can work both well and hastily.
This lesson fits us perfectly.

It matters not how long we play,
As we were wedded fast today.
God has blessed the yoke we're in,
And now no act we do is sin.
A man can't sin with his own wife,   630
Or harm himself with his own knife.
Dear, we have leave to love at will."
With that he set to work until
The day broke with a growing light.
A claret-sop revived his sprite.   *bread soaked in wine*
Once more he started up with cheer
And bussed his wife and sang out clear,
All coltishness and raggery,
Chattering like a spotted pye.   *magpie*
The slack skin quivered on his throat   640
As he intoned his merry note.
God knows what went through young May's heart
To see him sitting in his shirt—
His nightcap and his neck so lean—
She held his love not worth a bean.
Now January began to fail;
"Ah, day has come and slacked my sail,"
He said, and laid his old head down.
Later, when folk stirred in the town,
January rose, but fresh young May   650
Kept to her room for three more days,
As new wives do, and for the best,
For every worker must have rest;
Otherwise, he can't endure.
Sirs, this applies to all, I'm sure,
Bird or beast as well as man.
      Now let me speak of Damian,
Who languished in the old knight's dwelling.
Lords, if I could, here's what I'd tell him:
"O ill-placed Damian, my lad,   660
Your luck is poor, the outlook bad.
How can you plead your case to May?
Speak out at once? She'll just gainsay
Your wishes and perhaps betray them
To your great cost. Sing 'Welladay' then!"

Poor Damian broiled in Venus' fire,
And thought he'd die from sheer desire,
Yet he resolved to risk one throw.
He must, or be consumed by woe.
He found a pen and ink to borrow   670
And wrote a manifest of sorrow,
A supplicant's complaint or lay,
Unto his darling Lady May,
Then pinned this poem, done up in silk,
Above his breast, as white as milk.
     The moon, that on the wedding day
Had been in Taurus, spread its rays
In Cancer when young May appeared
To all the house as midday neared.
By custom, noble brides back then   680
Withdrew from daily sight of men
For four full days, or three at least,
Before they came downstairs to feast.
Her fourth day done and High Mass ended,
May joined her husband and attended
A public meal in rich array,
As bright as any summer's day.
At that same meal old January
Thought of his squire. "Now by Saint Mary,"
He said, "Where is this Damian?   690
Is he no more my serving man?
Is he sick or just gone truant?"
The other squires were smooth and fluent:
The boy was taken ill, they said.
He moaned and groaned like one half dead.
No other cause could make him tarry.
     "I thought so," said old January.
"He is a gentle lad, in truth.
I pray that death won't take the youth,
For he's as trusty, wise, and frank   700
As any young knave of his rank.
He's manly, too, and quick to serve.
We'll see to him as he deserves.
When we have eaten—yes, today—
I'll visit him, and so will May.

We'll bring him any aid we can."
When they heard this, the others blessed him
For courtesy, and all professed him
The kindest master in the shire,
To bring such comfort to his squire.   710
"Good dame," he said to fresh young May,
"Call your ladies; make your way
To Damian, lying in his room.
I hope you'll cheer his weary gloom.
Tell him I will visit too,
But first I'll rest an hour or two.
Don't be long now, little bride.
I want you napping at my side."
With that he turned away to call
The squire who oversaw his hall   720
And give him certain things to do.
    May and her ladies took this cue,
And made their way to Damian.
The young wife sat beside the man
To comfort him and soothe his head.
The squire half-turned himself in bed,
And secretly, while acting faint,
He passed the girl his love complaint,
With all his words of love and more.
He groaned a bit and sighed full sore   730
And whispered confidentially:
"Mercy! Don't discover me!
If this is known, I'm dead at best!"
She slipped his missive down her dress,
Then went to January's room,
And sat beside him in the gloom.
He turned to her and caught her hand
And kissed her time and time again,
But rolled away to sleep at last.
May stood up quietly and cast   740
As if she had to ease herself.
She read the squire's pleas with stealth,
Then tore them up for both their sakes
And cast them swiftly in the jakes.   *privy*
    Who's thinking now but fair, fresh May,

As back beside the knight she lay?
He slept till wakened by his cough,
And then he wished her garments off.
His mind was moved by pleasant whims.
And all those clothes encumbered him.   750
She must obey the oaf a while,
But I'm afraid you'd think me vile
If I should tell you all his dealings
Or whether May found them appealing.
And so I let them labor there
Till bells rang out for evening prayer.
    Perhaps by destiny or chance
Of nature or the covert glance
Of constellations, Heaven stood,
In a way that boded good,   760
Through Venus, for a lover's plaints—
For all things work by such constraints.
In other words, the time was right
To move a lady's appetite.
At least it seems that was the case.
God knows that all things work by grace.
But this I'm certain, fresh young May
Felt such a surge that very day
Of pity for sick Damian,
She vowed she'd make him whole again,   770
No matter who should be displeased.
    "I mean," she said, "to see him eased.
Though it's forbidden, it shall be;
He shall enjoy the best of me,
Though he owns nothing but his shirt."
How pity wells in gentle hearts!
    Credit May with warmth and passion.
She hoped to save him in her fashion.
Some women live for pride alone
And nourish hearts as hard as stone.   780
These would let a young squire perish
Before they'd comfort him or cherish
Anything but evil pride;
They wouldn't stick at homicide!
    But May was made of sweeter stuff.

She wrote a letter soon enough
To grant young Damian her grace
If she could find a time and place
Where she could complete the task.
She swore she'd give him all he asked.　　　　　　790
At her next call she saw her chance,
Transfixed him with a melting glance,
And thrust the letter where he'd find it.
Dawning hope? The boy defined it!
May gripped his hand with fervent feeling,
But with an outward mien concealing
Her hopeful love—then went in beauty
To January and her duty.

　　Up rose brisk Damian next morrow,
No sign of sickness or of sorrow.　　　　　　800
He washed and combed and preened and dressed
In hope young May would be impressed,
And fawned before his lordship's feet
Like any dog that begs a treat.
He was so pleasant to the court
(For he had charms of every sort)
That all the men there praised his name,
And May was flushed with his acclaim.
Thus I leave this Damian,
And find my other thread again.　　　　　　810

　　Some clerks maintain felicity
Rests in delight, and certainly
Old January held the same.
For in all worldly things his aim
Was but to live deliciously.
He chose his goods judiciously
To suit his rank, as would a king.
High up among his choicest things,
He had a garden walled with stone,
Reserved for him and May alone.　　　　　　820
The scribe himself, as I suppose,
Who wrote *The Romance of the Rose*　　　　*Guillaume de Lorris, flourished c. 1230*
Could not have pictured such a place.
Priapus, who gives gardens grace,　　　　　　*phallic god*
Though he's a god, could never tell

The charms of this one, or its well
Beneath a laurel, shining green.
Pluto and his dainty queen,
Proserpina, with all their train,
Disported in this sweet domain   830
Among the shades about that font.
   This garden was the old knight's haunt.
No other man could have the key
Except himself, but he was free
To come and go just as he pleased
And toy with May among the trees.
In summer this sweet garden served
As trysting place, where unobserved
They did more than they could in bed.
The air went to the old man's head.   840
For many a pleasant summer day
He reveled there with fresh young May,
But worldly joys must sometime end
For foolish knights, as other men.
   Oh, sudden stroke! See fortune fly!
It's like a scorpion, cruel and sly,
A smiling face when it would kill,
With poisoned tail and evil will.
Oh brittle joy! Inveigling venom!
Oh monster painting joys to come!   850
You make us trust our expectations,
Then dash them without hesitation!
Why gull this old decrepit knight
With gilded hopes and hidden spite?
Ah, now you've robbed him of his eyes!
He weeps and wails and hopes he dies!
   Alas, this noble January,
Our pampered old voluptuary,
Was stricken blind all suddenly
And quaked with sorrows piteously.   860
Among the rest, hot jealousy
Quite overwhelmed his fantasy
With fears that his young wife would stray.
He wished death for himself and May,
Fearing if the girl survived him

She'd find another love to thrive in.
He'd have her die, or else be racked
With lifelong grief in widow's black.
Still, as another season passed,
His sorrow lessened, till at last   870
He saw things were as things would be
And shouldered his adversity—
Except in this: his jealousy
Increased, if such a thing could be.
His vile conjectures grew so bad,
Whatever freedom his wife had
Was eaten up by his suspicion.
Controlling her became his mission.
She couldn't stir on horse or foot
Unless he went with her and put   880
At least a hand upon her arm.
The girl grew grim for all her charm.
Her love for Damian flaring higher,
She thought she'd die of sharp desire.
Unless she somehow slaked this thirst,
It seemed her very heart would burst.
   Meanwhile Damian matched May's pain.
His life was torment, all hope vain.
Scheme as he might, he found no way
That he could speak to darling May   890
And bare his bleeding heart for her
Unless old January should hear.
He never let her out of reach.
Still, they could write in place of speech.
The lad soon knew the girl's desire,
And she, that she still charmed the squire.
   But say the knight were young and hale,
Could see as far as ships can sail—
Betrayal's no worse when you're blind,
Than if you see, as many find.   900
   Lo, Argus had a hundred eyes
To pierce through anyone's disguise,
Yet he was fooled and others too,
Including some who thought they knew
They'd never be. I'll say no more.

This May, whose tender heart was sore,
To circumvent the knight's repression
Contrived a cunning wax impression
Of January's garden key
And left it where the squire would see.   910
He knew where the key would fit,
And made a perfect cast of it.
A wonder rides upon this key.
Attend a while, and you will see.

  Oh noble Ovid, your word's true,
There's no deceit, well known or new,
That love won't find when it has need.
Who will of Piramus and Thisbe read   *Metamorphoses, iv*
Knows though a wall kept them apart,
A chink let them unpack their hearts   920
By whispers no one else could hear.

  Eight June days dawned now, mild and clear,
Before our knight, old January,
Egged on by May, pert as a berry,
Would romp with her in his parterre,
Unwatched inside his walled-off lair.
He called her when the day was new
And said, "My bird, my wife so true,
Now may we hear the turtledove;
The winter's gone; it's time for love!¹   930
Come forth, my sweetheart, fitly dressed,
With dove-like eyes and wine-sweet breasts.
The garden's walled all round about.
Come forth with me, and have no doubt
My heart is yours, my darling bud,
Dear spotless soul, so sweet and good.
Come forth, and let us use our leisure,
Just you and I, my wife and treasure."

  He thought these stupid words were fine.
To Damian, May tipped a sign   940
To take his key and go before them.
He entered fast and waited for them.
As no one saw him pass the gate,

---

1. January's language throughout this passage recalls The Song of Solomon.

Now all he has to do is wait
Beneath a little bush, alone.
   Old January, blind as stone,
Drew May inside and shut the gate,
And sauntered on toward his fate.
The garden burgeoned all around them,
Just trees and flowers and birds surround them.   950
   "Dear wife," he said, "now we're together,
I swear I love you, no one better.
For by the Lord that sits above,
I'd die before I'd hurt you, love.
Think how I chose you, dear, indeed.
I felt no money-lust or greed,
But love and longing filled my mind.
I know I'm old, and also blind,
But, dear, be true. I'll tell you why.
Three things will come to you thereby: 960
Christ's love will flow, your honor stand,
And you shall have my towers and lands.
I'll give them to you. You'll succeed
To all my wealth by written deed.
And now, God grant me all I lack,
Kiss me, wife, to seal this pact;
I may be jealous and obtuse,
But love for you is my excuse.
When I think of your great charm
And my old age, I grow alarmed.   970
I cannot for the life of me
Bear to lose your company.
I swear to this without a doubt.
Come kiss me now and roam about."
   Fresh May heard January kindly
And answered him, it seemed, benignly,
But first a sob caught in her throat.
"I have," she said, "a soul to note,
As well as you, and reputation,
And wifely honor and salvation.   980
I placed all this at your command
The day the priest gave you my hand.
So let me answer you this way:

I pray you'll never see the day
That I bring shame to womankind
Or damage this good name of mine
By being false. Should I grow slack,
I pray you tie me in a sack,
And drown me. Yea, and nothing more.
I am your lady, no one's whore.   990
You doubting men will break our trust,
And then it's we you charge with lust.
A thousand men use this approach
And heap us women with reproach."

  She turned and saw the eager squire,
Beneath his bush at her desire,
And made a signal to him there
To hasten up a fruiting pear.
Hand over hand young Damian went.
He understood her full intent,   1000
For May, to cheat her husband better,
Had told him in her latest letter
How they would sport among the pears
And laugh at all the old man's snares.
I leave the squire perched upon a limb
And May afire to come to him.

  High in the clear blue firmament,
Phoebus streamed with gold and sent
His rays to gladden every flower.
In Gemini he shone with power.   1010
Soon he'd begin his declination
To Cancer, and Jove's exaltation.
A short way off, the king of faerie
Walked in the garden, making merry
With maidens from his wide domain,
The girls of Queen Proserpina's train.
He'd raped his wife to suit his needs
From looming Aetna's flowery meads.
Claudian set the story down,   *in* The Rape of Proserpina
How the queen was snatched and bound.   1020
Now Pluto found a grassy perch
From which to further his research
In women's wiles. "Dear wife," said he,

"Each just observer must agree:
Experience shows us every day
The treasonous tricks that women play.
Ten hundred thousand known to me
Display your lust and frailty.
Oh, Solomon, the best of men
For thoughts beyond the common ken, 1030
We do well to recall your words,
As good a guide as life affords.
Your studies led you to conclude
One man among a multitude
Was virtuous, but not one wife.
No woman leads a decent life.
This holy king scorned all your pack.
Nor does Jesus, son to Sirach,[2]
Often treat you with respect.
So let consuming plague infect 1040
And wildfire burn your cheating flesh!
I'll tangle you in your own mesh.
See this old deserving knight?
Because he's been deprived of sight,
His serving man will cuckold him—
This Damian, so crisped and trim.
Behold the lecher in his tree!
Now I will use my majesty
To give them all a great surprise.
I'll grant the old knight back his eyes, 1050
Just as the wife begins to cheat.
He'll see her for a bitch in heat—
He'll know her then, I guarantee!"
    "Ah, would you?" said Proserpine.
"Lord, by my grandfather's soul, I swear
That I'll inspire her, even there,
To cause the man to doubt his eyes
By filling up his ears with lies.
And for her sake, from now, all women,
Though taken in the act by men, 1060
Shall be such fluent self-excusers

2. Often identified as the author of Ecclesiasticus.

They'll briskly bear down all accusers.
They'll all have answers when they want them.
Witnesses? Hot words will daunt them.
We'll weep and swear and act indignant,
Defy and spit, fierce and malignant.
You men will be perplexed as geese.
  "Quote other liars if you please.
I knew already Solomon
Searched for good women but found none.   1070
But what of that? Whole hosts of others
Revered and loved their wives and mothers,
And other women in their lives.
How many women who served Christ
Enriched the Church with saints and martyrs!
The Romans praised their wives and daughters
And many noble matrons too.
Don't think that I'm attacking you.
When Solomon says no woman's good,
Sir, read him as he hoped we would.   1080
He meant true virtue is divine.
No he or she caught up in time
Has any claim to that estate.
  "Besides, was Solomon so great?
His reign was rich and glorious;
He made a temple for God's house,
But he served heathen gods as well.
Is there a better route to Hell?
For all his fame, I must aver
He was a lecherous idolater,   1090
Who in his age forsook the truth.
If God had never blessed his youth
For love of David, the Bible tells,
He would have lost all Israel
Before he did. A butterfly
Weighs more with me than all these lies
That circulate against our sex.
I am a woman. When I'm vexed
I must speak out or break my heart.
We're jabberers for Solomon's part,   1100
Well I'll repay him all my days

By jabbering in his dispraise.
What, tax womankind with villainy!"
   "Peace, peace, dear dame, attend to me,"
King Pluto said, "now by my troth,
I yield. But I must keep my oath
To grant this wronged old man his sight.
My word must stand, that's only right.
I am a king. I cannot lie."
   "And I'm a queen," she said, "so I   1110
Will teach this young wife what to say.
Save wrangling for another day.
We'll jar no longer, my dear lord."
   Now think of January on the sward,
Strolling with his darling May,
And singing like a popinjay,
"You I love best, and other none."
They strolled and sang and felt the sun
Till they arrived beneath the pear
And brisk young Damian waiting there,   1120
Half-hidden in the shining leaves.
   Now charming May, like one who grieves,
Began to sigh and clutch her side.
"Ah, my noble lord," she cried,

they compromise

"If I don't have some fruit to taste
I'll faint with longing here and waste
For want of just a few green pears!
May Heaven's Queen dispel your cares,
You know a woman in my plight   *a hint she's pregnant*
May have a violent appetite   1130
And die if it's not satisfied."
   "Alas, alas," the old knight cried,
"There's no one here to climb the tree,
And I am blind. I cannot see!"
   "Be calm, my lord," said fresh young May.
"If you will help, I'll find a way.
Put your arms thus, around the tree—
I know how you discredit me—
And I will climb among the pears,
Once underway, like climbing stairs."   1140
   "Dear wife," he said, "you shall not lack.

Just set your foot upon my back."
He stooped, and young May seized her time,
Stepped lightly up, and up she climbed.
She scrambled to a sturdy limb—
Ladies, I pray you, don't be prim;
I am a rude, straight-spoken man—
Where all at once this Damian
Pulled up her smock, and in he thrust.
    When Pluto saw this show of lust,   1150
He unsealed both the old knight's eyes.
The garden appeared to his surprise;
Its green light told him he could see.
He peered around with dawning glee
And quickly thought of young, fresh May,
Looked up and saw her clear as day,
With Damian, in a gross position
No one must name without permission.
The knight let out a roaring cry,
As mothers do when babies die: 1160
"Out!" he cried. "Harrow, alas!
Oh, May, what's this you've brought to pass?"
    She answered, "Why, what ails you, lord?
Have patience, now your sight's restored.
I've brought back light to both your eyes,
My soul is damned if these are lies.
I learned if I would make you see
That I must struggle in a tree,
And hard, to counterpoise your sin."
"Struggle!" he said, "It went straight in!   1170
God grant you both a shameful fate.
Your guilt is plain, beyond debate.
He swived you there, I saw it clear,
Or else may I be hanged this year!"
    "Alas," she said, "the treatment failed,
For surely if it had availed
You wouldn't hurl such words at me.
Your eyes are dim and cannot see."
    "I see," he said, "as well as ever—
Let God be thanked now and forever—   1180
And I was sure he served you so."

"Your sight's confused," she said, "I know
I saved your eyes—then this attack.
If I knew how, I'd take them back!"
    "Now dear," he said, "Forget my words.
Come down, my love, forgive your lord.
If I said wrong, you've raked me raw,
But I could swear I thought I saw
Damian using you to his taste,
Your skirts hitched up above your waist."   1190
    "Yea, sir," she answered, "so you thought.
But then a man abruptly brought
Out of sleep cannot perceive
Things truly. Though he may believe
With all his heart in his mistakes,
His eyesight wavers till he wakes.
Just so, a man who's long been blind,
Restored to sight—he thinks—may find
His vision playing tricks, alack.
Until your sight is truly back,   1200
You may be fooled by what you see—
Misjudge, as you did here with me.
Beware, I pray, by Heaven's King,
For many think they've seen a thing
That's not at all what it appears.
Their faulty vision feeds their fears
And quite misleads them, as you see."
With that she leapt down from the tree.
    Now who is glad but January?
He kisses May, all blithe and merry,   1210
And strokes her softly on the womb,
And has his people lead her home.
Now that's my tale of January.
God bless us all, and Mother Mary!

EPILOGUE TO THE MERCHANT'S TALE

"Eh! God's Mercy!" said our Host,
"That wife would prove too much for most!

Ach, women's slights and subtleties!
They swot away like busy bees,
Just to deceive us hapless men,
And lie each day to serve their ends;   1220
This Merchant's story proves that well.
I have a wife as true as steel,
But she is poor, and loose-lipped too,
A fount of folly, and a shrew.
But let that go. I'm stuck with her.
Guess what, though? I'd much prefer
To somehow cut the marriage knot.
I'll not recount each vice she's got.
Know why? Well, she'd soon hear about it,
From one of us, and don't you doubt it.   1230
I will not name the one I fear,
But old wives blab each word they hear.
Besides, her faults exceed my wit.
I'll stop right now. I'm done. That's it!"

Heere is ended the Marchantes Tale of Januarie.

The Squire

The Squire's Prologue

"Squire" said the Host, "if it's your will,
Tell us of love, for of that ill
You know as much as any man."
    "Not true," said the Squire, "but what I can,
I'll share with you. I'll not rebel
Against your rules, good Host. I'll tell
My story. Though my words may fail,
My will is good, and here's my tale.

The Squire's Tale

The Squire tells of the birthday feast of Cambiuskan, king of Tartary and of his children: the princes Algarsyf and Cambalo, and their sister, Princess Canace. The first part of the tale brings a stranger on a brass horse into Cambiuskan's hall, wearing a gold ring and carrying a mirror and a sword.

"My master, the king of Arabia and India, salutes you," the man says to Cambiuskan, "and sends this brass horse in honor of your birthday." He explains that in twenty-four hours the horse can carry anyone anywhere, flying like an eagle. Turn a certain pin, and the horse will return at once to its starting place.

The other presents are nearly as impressive. The mirror and the ring are for Princess Canace. The mirror will show who are her friends and foes and also the secret thoughts of lovers. The ring allows her to speak with birds and gives her knowledge of medicinal herbs. The sword will cut through any armor and give wounds that cannot heal unless they are struck again by the flat of the same blade.

Cambiuskan's people are especially interested in the brass horse. "It's like Pegasus," says one. "It's like the Trojan horse," says another. "No, it's just a magician's illusion," says a third.

The court learnedly considers the other gifts and discusses how they must work, giving Chaucer a chance to display his knowledge of angled mirrors, perspective glasses, ringmaking, and ways of tempering steel for swords.

After supper, Cambiuskan learns that three pins control the horse. One makes it go, though you must tell it where; one makes it stop and stand immobile; and one makes it disappear until you call it back.

The second part of the tale opens with Canace walking in the palace gardens, where she comes upon a falcon tearing at herself and beating herself with her wings. Arriving just in time, Canace catches the falcon as the bird falls from her perch. "What is wrong here?" asks Canace. "Only love or fear could cause this behavior. There's nothing to fear in this garden, so it must be love."

It is love. The falcon's story provides us a rare description of courtly love from the woman's point of view. She was gently raised, the falcon says, and knew nothing of adversity until she was courted by a tercelet, or male hawk.

"He seemed a well of gentleness,
But that was just his courting dress.
He wrapped himself in humble cheer
And forthright manners, plain and clear,
And pleasantness and earnest care,
So no onlooker, anywhere,
Could guess his vile, deceitful powers.
A serpent hides beneath fair flowers;
You never see him till you're bit.
So worked this loving hypocrite,   10
Keeping all of Cupid's rules
With eager care, to hoodwink fools.
Ah, all was tenderness and love.
Observe a tomb: it's fair above.
Beneath's the corpse and rot and mold.
That's how he was if truth be told,
And in this way the wretch pretended—
The Devil knows what he intended—
Till he so long had wept and strained,
So many years his service feigned,   20
That my heart softened, as it ought,
All innocent of his base thought.
Half dead for love, he seemed to be.
On his strong oaths and sureties
I gave him love, with this condition:
My virtue, honor, and position
Must not be harmed in deed or seeming.
That is, his faithfulness esteeming,

I gave him love in ample store,
My deep devotion, nothing more,   30
And took his heart in trade for mine."

The false lover, all thankfulness and humility, wins the falcon over completely.

"No man, however keen his parts,
Could hope to match my suitor's arts.
Not one of them could tie his shoe!
Who could have guessed he was untrue?
You've never seen such gratitude!
Hot passion was his only mood.
No earthly she, however wise,
Could penetrate his fair disguise—
His words! His loving countenance!   40
I loved him. I had no defense
Against his faith and seeming care.
If he was hurt in some affair,
However small, and I found out,
How misery wrenched my heart about!
In short, as such things go, it went:
My will became his instrument.
I mean that I obeyed his will
In everything that wasn't ill,
Keeping my maiden's virtue clear.   50
I never held a thing so dear
As him, God knows, and never shall."

*After two happy years, the tercelet goes off on what is supposed to be a short jour-
ney, but he falls in love with another bird and forgets his first love. It's not women
who love newfangledness, the falcon says, but men:*

"Men, by their nature, covet change,
As caged birds do, although well fed.
For though you shelter them from dread,
And straw their cages soft as silk,
And feed them honey, bread, and milk,
Once they see the door is up,
They spurn your food, throw down their cup,
Fly to the woods, find worms to eat.   60
Just so, false men will change their meat."

Canace sets about healing the falcon, but the Squire's tale has a long way to go.
The Squire promises to explain how the falcon won back her lover and also to
tell about Cambiuskan's famous battles and victories, how Algarsyf used the brass
horse to win Theodora for his wife, and how Cambalo rescued Canace from two
brothers. Unfortunately, or perhaps not, Chaucer stopped at this point and left
the tale unfinished.

HEERE FOLWEN THE WORDES OF THE FRANKELEYN TO THE SQUIER, AND THE WORDES OF THE HOOST TO THE FRANKELEYN.

"In faith, good Squire, you've spoken well,
Your gentle wit has cast a spell,"
The Franklin said, "on each of us.
And you so young! I reason thus:
There's not a man or woman here
Whose eloquence you'll need to fear
If you live long. God grant you do,
And may your virtues flourish too!
Your story gave me such delight!   70
I have a son, and if I might,
I'd give up twenty pounds in rent—
Aye, let it go with full consent—
If he could match you in discretion!
For what's the use of wide possessions
Unless a man is also good?
I've scolded him, and well I should;
Yet he flees virtue, clings to vice,
Spends and drinks and plays at dice
And always loses, by my grave.   80
He'd rather court some smirking knave
Than listen to a man of sense,
Who'd favor virtue, not expense."
    "A straw for virtue!" said our Host.
"Now listen, Franklin, by my ghost,
You too, according to our game,
Must tell a tale or smirch your name."
    "I know I must," the man replied.

My tale's prepared; I haven't lied.
The Squire spoke well as we all heard."   90
     "Your story! Not another word!"
     "Gladly, Host. See me obey.
Now listen all, to what I say.
I'll play the game, and nothing loath,
With all my wit, upon my oath.
I pray my speech is not too rough.
I hope you'll find it good enough."

THE FRANKLIN

THE FRANKLIN'S PROLOGUE

    The gentle Bretons, in their lays   *of Brittany, in France*
Retell events of other days,
With each tale fashioned to their tongue
And set to instruments and sung,
Or written out to read for pleasure.
Sirs, I once learned a Breton measure,
And I'll recount it if I can.
    But as I am a simple man,
Before I start let me beseech
Indulgence for my homely speech.   10
No man knows less of rhetoric.
My words, good lords, are bare as brick.
I never slept on Mount Parnassus.   *home of the Muses*
I can't look up when Tully passes.   *Marcus Tullius Cicero, the*
The flowers of speech that art bestows?   *model of eloquence*
Plain meadow flowers are all I know,
Or flowers painted on a wall!
I have no eloquence at all.[1]
I'll tell my tale with little skill,
But you shall hear it if you will.   20

THE FRANKLIN'S TALE

    In Armorica, on the Breton shore,
A loving knight worked evermore
To serve his lady as he might.
His only end was her delight,

---

1. Of course the Franklin expects his hearers will think otherwise.

Nor could he rest till she was won.
No other girl beneath the sun
Was fairer and more gently born. *aristocratic*
He feared she'd treat his love with scorn,
But when at last he told his pain,
Behold! His suit was not in vain.   30
She thought his humble, meek submission
Deserved a fitting recognition
And offered him a great reward:
That she would take him for her lord—
Such lordship as men wield with wives.
Then, to enhance their married lives,
He gave this promise as a knight:
That he would never, day or night,
Insist upon his mastery
Or trouble her with jealousy.   40
No, he'd obey her least behest,
As lovers do who love the best.
Only the name of sovereignty
Would stay with him for men to see.
      She answered him with humbleness:
"Sir, you are gentle, I confess,
To offer me so free a rein.
I pray God never lets me stain
Our love with quarrels or other strife.
I'll be your meek and faithful wife   50
From now until death comes for me."
And thus they lived in amity.
      Here's one thing, sirs, I dare to say:
A loving spirit must obey
Its object, or love's life is brief.
Love mustn't lord it like a chief.
When mastery comes, why Love anon
Will use his wings—farewell, he's gone!
Love's a free, unfettered feeling.
No woman finds constraints appealing.   60
She won't be fenced or come at call—
Nor will her husband, after all.
A man who's mild and lenient
Is fit for love to that extent,

For patience is a sovereign virtue
That finds its way as few things do
To ends no dudgeon can obtain.
Why should we wrangle and complain?
Sirs, learn to suffer, not to chide,
Or you'll be taught, for all your pride.   70
No mortal being lives for long
In our frail world and does no wrong.
Anger, illness, adverse stars,
Wine or woe or wounds and scars,
All these can lead to evildoing,
So what's the sense of endless stewing?
A wise man's able to forgive:
To live himself, lets others live.
Just so this sage and worthy knight
Was moved to grant his love the right   80
To rule herself, and heard her swear
She'd never give him cause for care.
    Lo, here we see a wise accord.
She gained a servant and a lord,
A servant in love, a lord in marriage—
A lord who showed a servant's carriage.
Servant? Yes, but still a lord.
He gained the lady he adored
To be his lover and his wife,
To comfort and adorn his life.   90

*So much for the Wife of Bath's ideas. The knight, Arveragus, and Dorigen, his
wife, enjoy a blissful period together before Arveragus is called away to England
for two years of war. At first Dorigen is inconsolable, but gradually her friends
draw her back into their orbit and take her walking on the coast. Looking down
from the Breton cliffs, however, she is appalled by the grisly black rocks offshore.
These make her think of Arveragus, who is still overseas. She is convinced they
have no purpose but to wreck ships.*

"Eternal God, your oversight
Must lead our world toward the right.
Nothing thwarts or mocks your will.
That said, what use do these rocks fill?

They seem to rise up from the sea,
Not from design, but anarchy.
Lord, these black rocks from west to east
Can profit no one, man or beast,
By their sharp teeth. Is it your will
That they lurk here to crush and kill?   100
A hundred thousand worthy men,
A host, great Lord, beyond our ken,
Were shipwrecked here, all human souls,
Made in your likeness, set in your rolls.
We're taught to praise your charity,
But tell me, Lord, how can it be
That you permit, despite your skill,
Perils like these to work such ill?
I've heard clerks argue and protest
That your designs are for the best,   110
Though we're too dull to see just how.
But let that be, dear Lord, for now,
Save Arveragus, that's my plea.
Let clerks dispute your plans, not me.
Would God these rocks might disappear
And sink to Hell to ease my fear!"

*Seeing that the rocks distress Dorigen, her friends provide other diversions, in-
cluding a garden party where one squire dances especially for her.*

And now among the other men
One squire performed for Dorigen,
As fresh and brisk in his array
As is the welcome month of May.   120
His voice and carriage far surpassed
All other squires from first to last.
Then too he was, so might I thrive,
Among the comeliest men alive.
So young, so rich, so virtuous—
The world adored Aurelius.
This brilliant squire, this graceful youth
Loved Dorigen, to tell the truth,
For Venus held the lad in thrall,

And love to him was all in all.   130
He'd loved her for at least two years,
With secret sighs and hidden tears.
He never let bold love flare up
But drained his woe without a cup.
He wept alone. What might he say?
Only his singing could betray
His plight, his hopeless case, alack!
The girl could never love him back.
He wrote sad songs to show his pains,
Complaints with lachrymose refrains,   140
On how he sank beneath love's spell,
And languished like a soul in Hell;
How he must die as Echo did,
Who loved Narcissus but kept it hid.[2]
His songs expressed his feelings so,
But nothing else betrayed his woe,
Except sometimes at fetes or dances
Where other folk pursued romances,
He gazed too warmly on her face
As lovers will who sue for grace,   150
Though Dorigen looked the other way.
But so it chanced that on this day,
Since he lived in her neighborhood
And since his blood and name were good
And since they knew each other well,
The two conversed, and as it fell,
Aurelius drew his dear apart,
And steeled his soul and bared his heart.
    "Madam," he said, "by our creator,
If it would make your cheer the greater,   160
I wish when Arveragus went
I'd gone with him. I'd be content
To wander far and not return,
As well do that as have you spurn
My service and my bursting heart.
Dear, have some pity on my smart.

2. Echo, a nymph, loved Narcissus, who loved only himself. When he failed to reciprocate, she faded away to just a bodiless voice.

One word from you could kill or save.
Or let me die and tread my grave!
I'll say no more than I have said.
Take pity, sweet, or see me dead."   170
    Dorigen looked at him aghast;
"Is this the truth?" she said. "Alas!
I had no notion what you thought.
Now, sir, I see you as I ought.
Aurelius, by my soul and life
I'll never be an untrue wife
In word or deed, upon my head;
No, I'll be his to whom I'm wed.
And that is all I have to say."
But then she carried on in play: 180
    "My lovelorn friend, by God above,
I *might* consent to be your love,
Since you profess to love me most.
Those evil rocks along our coast—
Remove each one, now, stone by stone,
Make all those shoals a rock-free zone.
When you have cleared the rocks away
And none is left, why then, I say,
I'll love you best and, undeterred,
Reward your pains. You have my word."   190
    "Dear one," he said, "don't ask for this."
    "I do," she said, "by God in bliss—
I know it's hopeless. Sir, be taught.
Forswear this folly as you ought.
What kind of man would stake his life
In hope to gain another's wife,
Who has her body at command?"
    Aurelius groaned just as she planned.
Her comment pierced him to the heart.
What could he answer for his part?   200
    "No earthly man could do that deed.
I'll die," he said, "I cannot speed."
And with these words he turned away.

*Crushed, Aurelius can do nothing but appeal to Apollo, the sun, and his sister
Lucina, the moon, to drown Dorigen's rocks beneath the sea.*

Lord, great Lucina, chaste and bright,
Who rules the sea and walks the night
(Though Neptune is the ocean god
He answers to Lucina's nod),
Is ever moved by her desire
To be enkindled by your fire,
And so she trails you busily,   210
And as she moves, so moves the sea.
Both seas and rivers feel her power
To make the tides draw back or tower.
Therefore, Lord, grant my request
Or burst the heart within my breast.
High tides appear when you're opposed,[3]
In Leo next, as I suppose;   *the constellation*
I pray she'll raise so great a tide
That it will overwash and hide
The tallest rock that Dorigen fears.   220
Lord, let this flood persist two years.
So I can say, till it's withdrawn,
"Behold, my dear, the rocks are gone."
    Grant this, my Lord, Lucina's master,
And make her move with you, no faster.
Circle the earth in opposition
Two years, and never change position,
So that the moon is always full
And high tide floods beneath her rule.[4]

Apollo will not comply, however. Aurelius falls sick, and his condition hardly im-
proves when Arveragus returns to resume his joyous life with Dorigen. After two
more years, though, Aurelius' brother remembers a book he once saw as a student
in Orleans.

It gave the names and the locations   230
Of eight and twenty lunar stations[5]

3. The sun and moon are opposed when on opposite sides of the earth.

4. Tides vary because the moon's cycles are out of phase with the sun. Aurelius wants the sun and moon to remain frozen in the alignment that causes the highest tides.

5. The twenty-eight mansions of the moon were observational marks used in astrological calculations.

Each traced against the stars on high.
Today such things aren't worth a fly,
For now the Church's wise conclusions
Have put an end to such delusions.
When he recalled this learned book
The brother cheered and cleared his look.
As he considered it, he thought:
"My brother's cure's as good as wrought,
For able prestidigitation   240
Can work the greatest transformations.
A sound magician can unfold
Great signs and wonders, so I'm told.
One pass and, lo, a man believes
A hall is flooded to the eaves
With barges rowing up and down,
Or roaring lions prowl the ground.
Or meadow flowers spring up instead
Or vines and grapes, both white and red.
A castle rears, of solid stone.   250
One magic flourish and it's gone,
Though it was there to every eye.
    "I'll go to Orleans and try
To find my former fellow there
Who knows the moon in every lair
And other sorts of magic power.
My brother's rescued from that hour!
This man will cast illusions here
To make those black rocks disappear,
So men will think that they've receded,   260
And ships may sail there unimpeded.
We'll manage this a week or two.
Aurelius will have his due,
For Dorigen must keep her promise
Or we'll denounce her, by Saint Thomas."

*Aurelius is so encouraged by this plan he goes along to Orleans. As luck would
have it, all his brother's friends are dead, but they meet a young scholar who
proves to be an equally good master of illusion. At his house this man produces
visions for Aurelius.*

The squire saw parks with stately deer—
Well-grown stags with lofty horns;
No bigger stags were ever born.
Then scores of them were slain by hounds
And arrows whizzed about the grounds.   270
And then the deer dispersed like smoke,
And falconers and other folk
Were killing herons on a river.
Then horses plunged and lances shivered
As bold knights jousted on a plain.
And then, farewell to that again.
He saw his lady at a dance.
He grasped her hand, took up his stance—
But then the scholar at his side
Clapped his hands, and woe betide!   280
The vision melted quite away.
And there they sat in disarray
Among the scholar's books and shelves—
No visions now, but just themselves.

Impressed, Aurelius promises to pay the scholar a thousand pounds to make Dorigen's rocks disappear, and the three of them return to Armorica in the depths of winter.

The season was, as I remember,
That cold and frosty month, December.
The sun shown feebly, old and gray,
A shadow of that former day
When it burned gold in brilliant streams,
For now the Goat had dulled its gleams.   *Capricorn, in mid-December*
It looked on pale, with little heat   *to early January*
As bitter frost and driving sleet
Destroyed each lingering trace of green.
Now Janus by the fire is seen,   *god of the old and new year*
With both his faces, drinking wine.
Before him steams a roasted swine,
And each good fellow cries "Noel!"

Soon the scholar is ready to work his illusion.

He found the current lunar station
And others by extrapolation,
Forecast the rising of the moon   300
Against the zodiac, and soon
With tables, formulae, and scansion
Identified his time and mansion   *lunar position*
And found by careful observation
The hour was ripe for transformation—
Illusions used in that old day.
He felt no need of more delay,
But made it magically appear
The rocks were gone, the coast was clear.
    The anxious lover watched all this—   310
Would he win Dorigen or miss?—
Attending on the miracle.
Lord, when it came his heart was full:
It seemed that every rock was gone!
He blessed the scholar's name anon:
"Though he's a wretch, Aurelius
Thanks you, and sovereign Love no less.
For now what have I to lament?"
Then to a nearby shrine he went,
A temple Dorigen attended,   320
And found her there as he intended.
With quaking heart and humble cheer
He spoke so only she could hear:
    "Good day, my lady," he began,
"My dearest love, as I'm a man,
I know I'm tempting your displeasure,
But, dear, I love you out of measure.
I must speak, sweetheart, or I'll die.
I'd spare you my complaints and sighs,
But Venus rules my guiltless heart.   330
I can't resist her forceful art.
Now though my pains leave you unstirred,
Be mindful, lady, of your word.
Reward me, dear, by God above,
Don't let me starve for lack of love.
You said you would relieve this blight,
Not that I claim your love by right,

But of your grace. Dear lady, pardon;
I heard you say once in a garden—
You said it straight; you didn't hedge,   340
And I your servant heard your pledge—
To love me best, though I admit
My paltry gifts don't merit it.
Your honor is my chief concern
And not my comfort, though I burn.
I've done as you commanded me,
Removed those black rocks from the sea.
Remember, lady, what you said.
Yet I won't quarrel, live or dead.
Do with me, dear one, as you will.   350
The rocks are gone for good or ill."
    He left the lady standing there,
Blanched for even one so fair.
"How could I be in this position?"
She asked. "I thought that my condition
Could not be met. How could it be?
I never guessed that my decree
Might be obeyed by any shift,"
And home she went, her mind adrift,
Unnerved by shock and growing fear.   360
She wept all day with plaintive cheer,
Fainting like a deer at bay,
Yet why she wept, she wouldn't say.
Her Arveragus was away from home.
She couldn't think. Her mind would roam.
Then pale, and grieving as she must,
She tried to work out what was just.
    "Alas," she said, "I now complain
I'm wrapped in Fortune's tightest chain.
I have no earthly course, I vow,   370
But transact sin or perish now.
Two sorry fates—it's hard to choose,
But of the two I'd rather lose
My life than bear my body's shame
And blot my honor and my name.
My death might bring my soul to bliss,
For many a stalwart wife ere this,

And many a maid with this choice on her,
Has welcomed death before dishonor.
    "A host of stories say the same.   380
When thirty tyrants, full of blame,
Killed hapless Phidon at a feast,   *in Athens following the*
They mocked his daughters too like beasts.   *Peloponnesian War*
Offended by their modesty,
They stripped them bare for all to see
And made them dance there in his gore.
(God quit those brutes forevermore!)
The woeful maidens, sick with dread,
Resolved to save their maidenhead.
They threw themselves into a well,   390
And there they drowned, as authors tell.

*Dorigen knows many such stories, going on to summarize twenty or more from
a book by Saint Jerome about faithful wives and virgins. Among these are fifty
maidens of Sparta who killed themselves when threatened by their neighbors, the
Messinans; Stymphalis, a virgin stabbed to death while clinging to a statue of
Diana; Hasdrubal's wife, who burned herself and her children to death in the
sack of Carthage; Lucretia, who killed herself after being raped by Tarquin; seven
maidens of Miletus, who died rather than submit to the Gauls; and many others.
It takes her two days to consider them all.*

She grieved this way both day and night,
Till Arveragus returned and saw her plight
And asked why she wept so fearfully.
Weeping no less, she answered tearfully:
"Alas, that I was ever born!
Here's what I said—what I have sworn!"
And told him what you heard just now.
I won't repeat my tale, I vow.
Her husband, showing no dismay,   400
Questioned her as if in play:
    "What, sweetheart, Dorigen, is this all?"
    "What worse conclusion might befall?"
She answered. "God deliver me!"
    "Hush, wife," he said. "It's done, you see,
For good or ill, and yet today
You'll do as you have said, I pray.

For God have mercy on my life,
I'd rather fall to someone's knife
For love of you than have you lie—   410
What you once promised, now deny.
Truth is the chief good in our keeping."
But as he spoke he burst out weeping,
And said, "Now, wife, on pain of death,
You mustn't, while you still draw breath,
Tell others of this aberration
Or mope about your situation.
I pray God that no one may guess
And I can bear my own distress."
   He went to call a squire and maid.   420
"Go forth with Dorigen," he said,
"She has a task to do today."
And soon the three were on their way.
Only she knew why they went.
No one else caught his intent.

   Now some of you may judge or swear
The knight was wrong in this affair,
To put his wife in jeopardy,
But hold your peace. There's more to see.
She may fare better than you guess.   430
Hear out the tale. Let judgment rest.
   Aurelius, the loving squire
Whose heart was frying with desire,
When she left home contrived to meet
The little party in the street,
Proceeding to a sheltered site
Where she could yield him his delight.
The young squire guessed her destination,
And spoke in hopeful adulation.
(He watched when she went anyplace   440
And met her there as if by grace.)
He greeted her with glad intent
And asked her warmly where she went.
Her answer was distraught but candid,
"To the garden, as my lord commanded,
To keep my word—alas, alas!"
   "Ah, has she come to such a pass?"

Aurelius thought with keen compassion
To see her suffer in this fashion,
"And, Lord, her husband! What of him?   450
Who ever faced a choice more grim?
He gave his wife to save her word."
Aurelius' heart was stirred.
He thought it out on every side
And pity wouldn't be denied.
"I'll let her go, no trace of blame,"
He thought. "By God I quit my claim."
He told the lady he adored,
"Go back, my dear, and tell your lord
I'm humbled by his gentleness   460
And also by your plain distress.
He'd rather live in secret shame
Than bear a blot against your name.
I'll do without you, God above,
Before I injure such a love.
Take back your promise. You're absolved
Of every bond, for I'm resolved
That I release you free and clear.
I have no claim upon you, dear.
Don't think I'll alter this reprieve.   470
It's done. Now let me take my leave.
You are the best and truest wife
I ever met in all my life.
Think, wives, of what you promise men.
I pray, remember Dorigen,
And know squire can do a deed
To match a noble knight at need."
   The lady thanked him on her knees,
Then home she went, now blithe, at ease.
She told her husband all you've heard,   480
And he hung on her every word.
They laughed and smiled, forgot their grief.
No pen can tell of their relief.
   Let Arveragus and his wife
Now lead a happy, peaceful life.
Their words were never cross or mean;
He served her as one might a queen,

And she was true forevermore.
Goodbye to them. I say no more.
   Aurelius, though, who lost all ways,   490
Thought he was cursed, to see such days.
"Alas!" he said, "I'm obligated
To pay the thousand pounds, full weighted,
I promised this philosopher!
I'm ruined indeed, unless I err.
Now I must sell my heritage
And live a beggar all my age.
I'll shame my kindred by this act,
Unless we two can reach some pact.
And even so, this much is clear: 500
I'll need to pay him year by year,
Depend on his consideration,
And parcel out his compensation."
   He went to find his money chest,
Withdrew the gold that he possessed—
Five hundred pounds, or thereabout—
And sought his hired scholar out
To seek for terms to pay the rest.
"Master," he said, "As I profess,
I've never cheated men in trade.   510
Believe me, sir, you will be paid,
And every penny, I declare,
If I must beg upon the square.
But grant me now, upon my bond,
Two years or just a bit beyond
To meet your price, for at that rate
I may not lose my old estate."
   The scholar scanned him with one eye
And with the look made this reply:
   "Have I not kept my faith with thee?"   520
   "Of course, you have, my friend," said he.
   "And has your love lain by your side?"
   "Why no, alas!" the squire sighed.
   "And how was that?" inquired the man.
Aurelius settled and began
Upon the tale you heard before.
I told it once and will no more.

"Her husband, sir," the squire said,
"Would let the stroke fall on his head,
Before his wife should break her word.   530
And she determined, as you've heard,
Before she'd be an untrue wife
She'd find a way to lose her life.
That innocent, raised in seclusion,
Had never heard of clerks' illusions.
Should I now swindle and torment her?
No! Freely as her husband sent her,
I gave her back to him again.
That's all that I can say. Amen."

The scholar answered, "Blessed brother,   540
Each one of you obliged the other—
You a squire, and he a knight—
And now by God, who rules in might,
A clerk will do a gentle deed!
I follow where such good men lead.

"Sir, I forgive the thousand pounds.
Think that you just sprang from the ground
Or you and I had never met,
For I release you from the debt.
And for my science and my work,   550
I'll take my keep here as a clerk.
That's pay enough. Farewell! Good day!"
He took his horse and rode away.

And now, good sirs, say if you can
Which of the three was the gentlest man?
What's your opinion, everyone?
That's it. No more. My story's done.

Heere is ended the Frankeleyns Tale.

THE PHYSICIAN

THE PHYSICIAN'S TALE

"Livy, historian of Rome,
Describes one good knight's life and home:
Virginius, he was, a man of praise,
And rich in friends through all his days.

    He had one daughter by his wife,
No other children blessed their life.
The girl was dainty as a queen.
No fairer girl was ever seen,
For Nature worked with diligence
To crown this maid with excellence,   10
As if to say: "Behold my pearl!
See how I shape and paint a girl
When I try hard. Who matches me?
Pygmalion? Not that I can see,
For all his chiseling and paint.[1]
Apelles? Zeuxis? Yet more faint;   *legendary Greek artists*
They only try to ape my skill
With bronze or marble, brush or quill.
The world may hew to God's design,
But all the detail work is mine.   20
I form each being and its features.
God makes the mold, but I the creatures
(At least all those beneath the moon)   *Above the moon were the*
And ask no payment, late or soon;   *unchanging stars.*
For God and I share one accord.
I shaped this girl to praise the Lord,
Along with all my other works,
Of myriad colors, forms, and quirks.""

---

1. Pygmalion, a famous sculptor, created a statue of his ideal girl so real that, at his prayer,
the goddess of love brought it to life.

Thus Nature's thoughts, could they be seen.
  Virginia, the girl, was just fourteen   30
When she evoked such great delight.
As Nature paints smooth lilies white
And roses red—with equal art,
She touched the girl in every part
Before her birth with this intent:
Each part would have its ideal tint.
And Phoebus made her hair display
The clear refulgence of his day.
Yet though her outside shown like gold,
Her soul gleamed more, a thousandfold.   40
She lacked no touch of temperament
That makes a maid seem Heaven-sent.
Her spirit matched her graceful bearing:
Meek, upright, and chaste, yet caring;
Humble, hedged with abstinence,
Suffused with love and temperance.
Her acts were modest as her dress,
Discreet, divorced from all excess.
Though she was wise as holy Pallas   *Athena*
Her speech was plain, devoid of malice.   50
She never strained for eloquence
To seem more wise, but loved good sense.
Her words and all that she professed
Proclaimed her perfect gentleness.
As modest as a girl might be,
She made herself, as all could see,
Abstain from luscious idleness.
Most, she shunned Bacchus's excess,   *the god of wine*
To shield her heart from love's caprice.
Love feeds on wine like fire on grease.   60
Through simple goodness, never strained,
She acted tired or ill or pained
And took her leave of gatherings
Abuzz with love and idle things,
Shunning revels, feasts, and dances,
Those breeding grounds of dalliances.
Such things make girls mature too fast,
Grow forward ere their youth has passed.

Precociousness is full of peril.
Leave lavish manners and apparel
Until a girl becomes a wife!   70
    Hear me, you dames of later life
Who guard the daughters of your lords.
Don't take exception to my words.
What made you fit as governesses?
Why, holy lives, or else excesses.
Perhaps your neighbors praised your name,
Or else you fell and suffered shame
And know too well the wanton dance.
If so, you learned from your mischance   80
The cost of folly. Now, I say,
Don't let your charges go astray.
    A wayward poacher who has left
His wicked life and evil craft
Can guard meek deer from any man.
So, ladies, if you will, you can
Shield your girls against all vices.
Don't let them fall through your devices,
Or you'll be rightly called a traitor—
Rewarded now, detested later—   90
Because, God knows, no pestilence
Is worse than selling innocence.
    You fathers, and you mothers too,
Keep all your children well in view,
For you must raise them sound and whole,
Consigned by God to your control.
Beware lest your unrighteous bent
Or laxity in punishment
Should let them perish. If they do,
The reckoning will fall to you,   100
For when the shepherd's negligent,
Wolves gladly teach him to repent.
Take all this well; it's well intended.
My tale again . . . from where I ended.
    Virginia, then, of whom I told,
Was anything but overbold,
For in her, other girls might read—
As in a book—each word and deed

That makes a maiden virtuous.
She was so wise, so free of lust,   110
Her fame soon spread on every side.
Folk praised her beauty far and wide,
Acclaimed her modest virtue too—
Most folk, that is; an envious few
Begrudged her fame, as envy will,
Repulsed by good and wishing ill.
Augustine damned such vile conceits.   *Saint Augustine, 354–430 AD*
    One day the girl walked through the streets.
She and her mother went to pray,
Attend a shrine beside the way.   120
The judge who ruled their part of town
And all the countryside around
Saw Virginia as she passed,
And what he saw, he liked, alas!
For as she walked by where he stood
His heart was changed, and not for good.
His wicked eye took in the maid,
And in his lustful heart he said:
"By God, I'll have her, come what may!"
    The Devil heard and knew his prey.   130
He ran to snatch the judge's soul,
And teach him how to reach his goal.
The evil judge, his heart aflame,
Vowed he would work through bribes or blame
To wrest Virginia from her friends.
Her heart was bent toward pious ends,
And so he knew he'd never win
Her will to acquiesce to sin,
And yet he meant to have the girl.
He called a man he knew, a churl,   140
A ruffian ripe for any game,
And told his wish, devoid of shame,
But still discreet. The man must swear
He'd tell no one of this affair,
For that would cost the judge his head.
The churl agreed to all he said.
Ah, see the judge's spirits rise!
With this thief's help he'd win his prize!

They shaped a vile conspiracy
To ease the judge's lechery.   150
Both thought that they could hide their hand,
But, lords, I'll tell you all they planned.
When Claudius left (that was the churl),
The judge sat dreaming of the girl.
His name was Apius for a fact.
My tale's authentic and exact.
Its moral is true without a doubt.
This judge, I say, soon stirred about
To find a way to gain his will,
Secure the girl and work her ill.   160
It wasn't long, to tell it short,
Before he reconvened his court
And sat to issue his commands.
Soon Claudius came to start their plans.
He called, "My lord, if it's your will,
Pronounce a ruling on my bill,
A claim against Virginius!
The heavens know my cause is just.
I'll prove all things are as I say.
Grant me a ruling, lord, today."   170
      "The man's at home," the judge replied.
"You know that I must hear his side.
Call him in. We'll sound this out.
Truth will prevail without a doubt."
      The knight soon came to know their will
And heard the bailiff read the bill.
Lords, I give its contents here:
      "To you, Lord Apius, most dear,
Complains your servant Claudius
How that the knight Virginius,   180
Against all law and equity,
Detains, with no consent from me,
A servant who is mine by right.
He stole her from my house one night
When she was young, as I shall show.
My witnesses will prove it's so.
She never was his daughter, lord,
And now I pray she'll be restored.

Return the girl, lord, if you will."
This was the substance of his bill.   190
   Virginius looked on in shock.
He never got a chance to talk
Or challenge combat, like a knight,
Or summon men to prove his right
And controvert the fellow's lies.
The wicked justice seized the prize,
Refused to hear Virginius,
But rendered his opinion thus:
   "You, Claudius, shall have the maid.
Your rightful cause must not be stayed.   200
Sir, give her up into our care.
This man shall have her, I declare."
   What could he do? Virginius
Must give way to Apius.
The judge's evil treachery
Had won her for his lechery.
The knight went home with sorry cheer,
Sat in his hall and called his dear.
As gray as ashes in a grate,
He greeted her and told her fate.   210
Though scalding pity choked his voice,
He felt he had no other choice.
   "Beloved Virginia," he said,
"Too soon you will be shamed or dead.
I never thought I'd feel such pain.
The least deserving to be slain,
Yet you must die, and by my knife!
My daughter, this will end my life.
I brought you up with such delight.
You never left my heart or sight.   220
Your death will be my final woe.
Can I live on without you? No!
My chaste, dear gem, bear up, be strong.
I cannot let you suffer wrong.
I speak from love, not hate," he said.
"This hand must smite away your head.
What woe that Apius saw you pass!
He's robbed us of your life, alas!"

He told her all you heard before.
There's no need now to tell you more.   230
    "Mercy, father," said the lass,
And as she said these words she cast
Her arms around her father's neck,
Speaking as she sobbed unchecked:
"Tell me, father, shall I die?
Is there nothing else to try?"
    "No, my daughter," said the knight.
    "A moment, then, to mourn my plight.
Let me lament a little space."
Lo, Jephthah gave his daughter grace   240
To grieve before he took her life.
    The girl did not deserve the knife.[2]
She only ran as most girls would
To greet her father as she should."
And with these words, she tumbled down,
Then roused herself and looked around,
And thanked the Lord she'd die a maid.
"Kill me, father, now," she prayed,
"Keep me pure, since that's your will."
And yet she rolled her eyes aloft   250
And begged he'd make the sword-stroke soft.
Then, terrified, she swooned once more.
Her father, though his heart was sore,
Cut off her head and grasped the hair.
Back to the unjust court they fare
To show the head to Apius,
Who, when he was confronted thus,
Called for his men to hang the knight.
Now, when the people saw this spite
A thousand rallied to his cause,   260
To foil the judge and save the laws,
For they had spotted something wrong,
Suspecting Apius all along.
Claudius' challenge, so abrupt,

2. Judges 11:29–40. In return for victory over the Ammonites, Jephthah vowed to sacrifice the first creature to greet him when he led his army home. The unfortunate greeter was his daughter, who asked for a respite of two months to mourn her virginity.

And so soon granted, seemed corrupt,
And Apius' lechery was well known.
The people took the judge in hand
And had him jailed at their demand.
He killed himself there in his cell.
The mob seized Claudius as well   270
And made to hang him on a tree,
But at the knight Virginius' plea
They changed their minds and banished him
Saved only by their latest whim.
The rest were hanged, though, to a man,
Who acquiesced to Apius' plan.
   Sirs, here you see sin's true reward.
Beware, my lords, for God strikes hard
At every villain, high or low.
The worm of conscience shakes him so   280
For wicked deeds and things forbidden,
Though only God knows what he's hidden,
That he will suffer at the last.
No one of us escapes his past.
This story shows the lesson's true:
Lords, quell your sins or they'll quell you.

Heere endeth the Phisiciens Tale.

The Pardoner

The Pardoner's Prologue

Lords, said the Pardoner, when I preach,
I'm known for my resounding speech.
It rings as roundly as a bell.
I choose my words and learn them well.
Each sermon has one simple gloss:
Radix malorum est cupiditas.   *"Greed is the root of evil." (1 Tim. 6:10)*
    I show the people where I've been,
My papal bulls absolving sin   *documents signed by the pope*
And patent to regale the crowd.   *episcopal license to preach*
This proves my business is allowed   10
And no one there, not priest or clerk,
Can legally obstruct my work.
Then pardons, sirs, to stir their hopes,
From bishops, cardinals, and popes,
I lay out next, my stock in trade,
Then put my Latin on parade
To spice the air, prepare the way,
And put folk in the mood to pray.
Next I display my reliquaries
Of rags or bones—the content varies.   20
They look like relics, so they pass.
And then a shoulder set in brass
Belonging to an old Jew's sheep.
"Plant," I say, "so shall you reap.
Just soak this bone in any well,
Then if your calves or oxen swell—
Say they've been bitten by a snake—
Anoint their tongues for Jesus' sake,
And they'll be healed; and furthermore
No pox nor scab nor other sore   30
Will trouble sheep that taste that well.

A greater wonder's yet to tell:
If any man will wake and walk,
Before the crowing of the cock,
To that charmed well and wet his throat,
The old Jew taught, and men of note,
His stock and stores will multiply.
    "That water, lords, heals jealousy.
A man who's in a jealous fit,
Let him take one draught of it,   40
He'll treat his wife with love and trust
Although he knows his charge is just
And she has swived a dozen priests.
    "Next, here's a mitten from the East.
He who puts it on his hand
Will fertilize the leanest land,
Make it teem with wheat or oats.
Try it, sirs, for just two groats.   *small coins*
    "But now, good people, one small warning:
If any man in church this morning   50
Is guilty of an act so terrible
He finds his hidden guilt unbearable,
Or wedded woman, great or less,
Has practiced vile unfaithfulness,
Our Lord will never grant them grace
To touch my relics in this place.
But anyone of common blame
Who offers up in Jesus' name
Will swiftly be absolved by me.
My bulls grant that authority."   60
    By tricks like these I win each year
A solid living, free and clear.
I mount the pulpit like a clerk.
The people sit. I go to work.
I tell them all I said before—
Mere lies, of course, and plenty more.
I stretch my neck out from my gown
And bob my visage up and down,
Just like a ringdove in a tree.
My hands fly out; my tongue runs free.   70
Ah, it's a joy to see me preach.

"Flee avarice! Flee!" I beseech.
I talk that way to make them free
In tendering their coins to me.
I work to bring their pennies in
And not to chastise vice or sin.
What do I care when they stop kicking
If they're in Hell or berry-picking?
Many a scalding, righteous sermon
Comes from priests and suchlike vermin   80
Whose words are empty posturing.
Some crave the gold their speeches bring.
Some covet fame. Some preach from hate.
When I am bested in debate
I lash my enemy with words,
Preaching so that even lords
Must fear my libels; thus, you see,
It never pays to quarrel with me.
I seldom give a proper name,
But show my meaning all the same   90
By nods and hints and other signs
That all can read between the lines.
I spread my venom, yet appear
God's spokesman, holy and sincere.
     But revenge is rarely what I need.
Much oftener I'm led by greed.
My theme is yet, and ever was,
Radix malorum est cupiditas.
I preach most often on the vice
I use myself—sharp avarice.   100
You've heard that my own sin is greed.
At times my words make men take heed—
Forswear their grasping and repent—
But that is never my intent.
I preach, I say, for sheer cupidity.
Other motives? Mere stupidity!
     I give examples oftentimes,
Especially those from olden times,
For every fool loves ancient tales;
They're sure to work when all else fails.   110
Sirs, do you think, with all I've told,

How I can win men's goods and gold,
I'd pass that up for poverty?
I'd never act so fecklessly!
While I can preach in sundry lands,
I'll never need to soil my hands,
Weave baskets for my livelihood.
A beggar's life is never good.
No, I don't envy Christ's apostles.
I'll have my wool and cheese and wassails   120
If I must strip the poorest page
Or the neediest widow of our age.
Say her children starve for it;
Well, I will toss down sweet wine yet
And keep a wench in every town.
Attend me, people, now; don't frown.
It's my turn next to tell a tale,
And now I've had a drink of ale,
By God, I promise you a dish
As well prepared as you could wish,   130
For though I am a wicked man,
I've many moral tales at hand.
Here's one I use to fill my purse.
The teller makes the tale no worse.

THE PARDONER'S TALE

In Flanders once three lively lads
Chased riot, dice, and other fads
Through brothels, gaming houses, bars,
To twanging harps and loud guitars.
They danced and wagered day and night
And ate and drank beyond their might,   140
To do the Devil sacrifice
In all his wicked haunts of vice
With every form of vile excess.
This crew blasphemed with such address
You'd blanch to hear the oaths they sent
To add fresh pains to Christ's torment.

They took up where the Jews left off.
Rebuke them? Why, they'd only scoff.
  Just see the frisking dancing girls,
And pert fruit-sellers smooth as pearls,   150
And sweet-cake venders, singers, pimps—
The Devil's officers and imps—
Kindle their filthy lechery,
Close kin to greed and gluttony.
God's Bible shows us, as it must,
How drunkenness engenders lust.   *Eph. 5:18*
  Look how that sottish father, Lot,
Lay with the daughters he had got,
So drunk he didn't know his name.   *Gen. 19:33*
  And Herod, king of evil fame,   160
Well filled with wine, to please his daughter,
At his own table gave the order
To kill the guiltless Baptist, John.   *Matt. 14; Mark 7*
  Or hear from Seneca anon:
He sees no difference in kind
Between a man out of his mind
And one who's just inebriated
Before his drinking has abated.
Till then he's mad as anyone.   *Seneca*, Epistles *83.18*
The glutton's life's a life to shun!   170
It caused man's fall from Paradise.
Our bellies cost us such a price!
Christ bought us with his blood again.
We brought him suffering and pain,
And all this through our villainy!
The whole world lost for gluttony!
  Our father, Adam, and his wife
Took on a painful, scrimping life,
Expelled from Eden for their sin,
Or else, Lord God, what might have been!   180
In Paradise they lived in glee
Until a taste of that same tree
That God forbid them drove them out.
Oh, Gluttony, without a doubt,
If one but knew what wretchedness
Attends a life of vile excess,

He'd rule his stomach and take heed,
Not eat or drink beyond his need!
The greedy mouth and tireless maw
Draw workingmen by iron law　　　　　　　　　　190
To labor over hill and dale
To furnish gluttons meat and ale!
Now hear Saint Paul, and do not brood:
"Food's for your gut, your gut for food,"
He said, "but God shall rend them both."　　　　*1 Cor. 6:13*
And how disgusting, on my oath,
To think of this, much less to do it,
But flowing wine can lead one to it:
One's mouth, and not the proper place,
Spews out the belly's filthy waste!　　　　　　　200
　　The Apostle says, to score our hearts,
"Vile men there are, who for their parts"—
I say it weeping; the sentence sticks—
"Turn quite against Christ's crucifix,
Toward death. The belly is their god."　　　　*Phil. 3:18*
Oh gut! Oh belly! Stinking pod!
Swollen tight with dung and gas!
At either end eruptions pass
To foul the air, yet you're refined.
Lord, how cooks will sift and grind,　　　　　　210
Transforming simple substances
To cosset you, no other cause.
They crack hard bones, draw out the marrow,
To soothe your gullet, soft and narrow;
They scour the world like any thief
For every spicy root or leaf,
Infusing sauces with delight
To tease your jaded appetite.
Each man who lives to please his taste
Grows fat but sees his spirit waste.　　　　　　220
　　Foul lechery's set free by drink.
It makes us itch and grunt and stink.
A drunk wears a contorted face
With tainted breath and bumbling grace,
Nodding, snoring, when undone,
As if he called out, "Sampson! Sampson!"

Though Sampson never tasted wine.
He staggers like a well-stuck swine.
He cannot speak, a drooling knave.
Friends, drinking is the deepest grave   230
Of mother wit and good opinion.
The moment wine achieves dominion,
No indiscretion's left unsaid,
So hold back from white wine and red—
Especially that Spanish white
Renowned in Fish Street for its might,   *near London Bridge*
A vintage mixed in some locations
With wine from better appellations.
This stuff emits such potent gasses
That when you've swilled down just three glasses   240
Though you're at home, you'll find your brain
Thinks otherwise, that you're in Spain—
In Spain, now, mark you, not Bordeaux—
And "Sampson! Sampson!" you will go!
  But listen to my final words:
Recall men's triumphs and rewards
And victories in Holy Writ
Are fruits of God's all-knowing wit.
They rose from prayer and abstinence—
Sirs, that should sway a man of sense.   250
  Attila, that great conqueror,
Died fast asleep, as men aver,
Drunk and bleeding from the nose.
Drink ruins a ruler, as this shows.
And last of all, consider well,
The injunction laid on Lemuel—   *Prov. 31:4–5*
That's Lemuel, not Samuel—
His mother told him, as it fell,
No prince could drink and still be just.
And so my point is made, I trust.   260
  Thus I have skewered gluttony;
Turn now to gambling with me,
The very mother of foul lies
And sly deceit and faith's demise
And blasphemy, manslaughter, waste,
Lost time and substance. You're disgraced,

Reproved, reviled on every hand
Once you become a gambling man.
The more advanced your worldly station,
The greater the humiliation.   270
All men despise a prince who gambles—
No wonder if his state's a shambles.
He is, by common acclamation,
A man of evil reputation.
    The Spartan Stilboun once was sent
To nearby Corinth to present
His city's offer of alliance.
Once there, that wise man saw by chance
Their nobles playing betting games,
Out wagering, to their great shame.   280
He dropped the embassy he planned,
Returned at once to his own land,
And said, "Lords, I won't risk my name
Or have it added to my fame,
I yoked you to those gamblers.
Make others your ambassadors.
For by my faith, I'd rather die.
Than foster such a false ally.
Sparta and its great renown
Should not be linked with gamblers' towns.   290
I'll never help bring that about."
He said all this, without a doubt.
    And look at King Demetrius:
The Parthians, as sources tell us,
Sent him a pair of golden dice
To show the king, by that device,
How he had earned their scornful slur,
A trifling, lightweight common gamester.
Honest lords find better ways
To occupy their nights and days.   300
    Now let me speak of other vices
As sources teach and time suffices.
Fierce swearing is corrupt, perverse,
And swearing falsely, friends, is worse;
God told us not to swear at all,
As Matthew says. What's more, recall   *Matt. 5:34*

The words of holy Jeremiah:
"Swear truly, for God hates a liar,
And never swear without good cause." *Jer. 4:2*
All idle swearing breaks God's laws. 310
The second precept on the tablet
Of those great rules Jehovah set—
His Ten Commandments put in stone—
Was "Don't use my name as your own."
Thus God put swearing near the head
Of all the crimes that men should dread,
Like homicide and other vices.
To those who know it, this suffices
To show oaths are the graver sin.
My lords, I warn you once again, 320
God's vengeance will pursue the man
Who sins against this great command
By swearing on God's heart or nails
Or saying, "By Christ's blood at Hayles, *an abbey near Gloucester*
A seven, now, not five or three!
God's arms! If someone swindles me, *at dice*
I'll plunge this dagger through his heart!"
Such fruit comes from the gambler's art—
Swearing, raging, homicide.
So for the love of Christ who died, 330
Forswear all swearing, without fail.
And now, my lords, I'll tell my tale.
   Like many rogues these three of ours
Sat drinking in the morning hours
When from the street, as it befell,
They heard the chiming of a bell
Conducting someone to his grave.
At that, one called out to his knave. *servant*
"Go out," he said "and find for us
What man has died and stirred this fuss. 340
Be sure you get the fellow's name."
   "Sir," said the boy, "if that's your aim,
I heard it several hours ago.
The dead man was a man you know,
A friend of yours, sir. He was slain
At home and drunk, that much is plain.

A sly betrayer men call Death,
Who robs men of their life and breath,
Killed him, pierced him with his spear,
And went his way and none knows where.   350
He's killed a thousand in this plague.
Avoid him, master, please, I beg.
Do everything that's necessary
To circumvent this adversary.
And yet you'll meet him anyway,
As I once heard my mother say."
"By Mary!" said the listening barman,
"Death daunts us all, or nothing can.
I hear he slew a nearby village—
Men and women, every age.   360
I think that must be where he lives.
Well, I'll use any sign he gives,
To keep him far away from here."
   "God's arms!" roared out the rioter,
"He can't be all that fell to meet.
I'll go pursue him in the street.
I vow I will, God's skeleton!
Now, fellows, come, agree as one.
Hold up your hand before the others;
From now on we behave as brothers.   370
We'll kill this vermin with our knives.
He'll pay for taking others' lives,
As God is righteous, and today!"
   All said what he would have them say—
They'd live or die for one another—
Each serve the others like a brother—
And staggered out, drunk by the sound,
And made their way toward the town
The tavern owner lately named.
At every step they ripped and maimed   380
Christ's flesh with yet another oath.
They swore to kill Death, by their troth.
   The lads were not a half-mile thence,
Stopped, about to climb a fence,
When a ragged, poor old man
Chanced to greet the drunken band,

Saying "God guard you with his care!"
   One of the rogues, the proudest there,
Replied: "You churl, so old and base,
Wrapped like a corpse, except your face,   390
What cause have men like you for living?"
   The man looked back without misgiving
And said, "Why, sir, I cannot find
Another one of all mankind,
A younger man in town or city,
To take my years for love or pity
In trade for his. Until I do,
God wills I trouble such as you.
The grave itself won't take my breath;
Thus I live on, deprived of Death.   400
Here on the ground, my mother's gate,
I knock my staff both soon and late
And call 'Dear Mother, let me in!
Look how I waste to bones and skin!
When shall my old corpse find rest?
Mother, take my treasure chest,
The one at home—I'm no one's cheat—
Just wrap me in my winding sheet.'
But she won't grant me that much grace.
You see my suffering by my face.   410
   "But why attack an ancient man
Who neither offers harm, nor can?
You've not been injured by me yet.
Think of these words from Holy Writ:
'Stand up and honor gray-haired men.'   *Lev. 19:32*
That's sound advice, you apprehend:
Don't mock old people now or do
What you'd have no one do to you
If you should ever reach my years.
Now God attend you and your peers.   420
I must continue. Let me pass."
   "No!" said the other. "Not so fast!"
He might be drunk, but he had brawn.
"You'll stand and answer, by Saint John!
You mentioned Death, the one we want.
He's killed our friends in every haunt

Throughout this country. You're his spy.
Say where he is, old man, don't lie,
By Jesus and his sacrament.
Death does his work with your consent.   430
You help him. You're as bad as he!"
    "Ah," cried the old man, "let me be!
You'll find Death up this crooked way.
I swear I left him there today,
Beneath a tree. He'll wait for you.
He's not afraid of what you'll do.
See that big oak? He's sitting there.
I hope God saves you all, I swear,
And turns you into better men."
    The gamesters ran off there and then.   440
Beneath the spreading oak they found
A pile of florins, bright and round,   *gold coins*
Almost eight bushels, so they thought.
What? Was it ever Death they sought?
The gleaming gold so took their sight—
That store of florins, polished bright—
They threw themselves upon the ground.
The worst spoke first, while looking round.
    "Brothers," he said, "you've heard me joke.
No joking now, or may I choke.   450
This gold is ours, belongs to us,
And we'll enjoy it as is just,
And spend it lightly, as it came.
Who guessed, in God's almighty name,
That this much luck was on our side?
If we could sack it up and ride
Home to my house or, brothers, yours—
The gold's not his or mine, but ours—
We'd live in high felicity.
By daylight, though, that cannot be.   460
We'd never prove we weren't thieves
And men would hang us up like leaves.
We'd better, therefore, if I'm right,
Convey it home by dead of night.
For now, though, we'll draw straws and then
Send one man to the town again

To bring back bread and wine to us.
Leave two to watch, as someone must,
Lest others come and steal the treasure.
Tonight we'll cart it home at leisure   470
And stash it where we think is best."
    He held three straws out to the rest
And bid them draw. When they were done
The cut fell to the youngest one,
Who set out for the nearby town.
His boon companions looked around
As soon as he was out of sight.
"Now," one expounded with delight,
"We own this gold, as you may see,
And we're to share the lot, we three.   480
Say, friend, if I explained to you
A way to cut the shares to two,
Would that not be a friendly turn?"
    "How?" said the other with concern.
"He knows it's here, and in our care;
Our hands are tied in this affair."
    "In confidence?" his friend replied.
"Come, brother, say you'll take my side.
Give your pledge you won't betray me,
And let me say how this may be."   490
    "I swear," said the other, "as you demand."
    "Well,' said his friend, "look how things stand.
Two men are twice as strong as one.
When he comes back, stand up in fun.
Grapple him as if for pride,
And let me knife him in the side.
Grip him well as if in play.
You stab him too; we'll win the fray
And then farewell to shares for three.
We'll have it all, just you and me.   500
Ah, how we'll live upon that hoard—
We'll dice and play like any lord."
And so each cruel reprobate
Agreed for gold to kill their mate.
    Meanwhile, their fellow in the town
Recalled the heft and chinking sound

Of all those florins, rich and bright.
"Oh if," he thought, "by any slight,
I could enjoy that wealth alone,
I swear no man was ever known   510
To match my joy in any nation."
With that he had an inspiration—
The Devil put it in his mind—
To add strong poison to the wine.
The fiend could shape his thoughts this way,
For vice had made him Satan's prey.
He had no mercy. His intent
Was kill them both and rest content.
He hastened, in no mood to tarry,
To the town's apothecary.   520
"Please sell me something for my pests.
I've rats," he said, and then professed
A weasel plagued his chicken stock,
Annihilating half his flock.
"I need the strongest thing you've got.
I'll kill those pests and let them rot."
    The man mixed powder in a bowl.
"Take this," he said, "and by my soul
No mortal thing that tastes of it
Can live. It only takes a bit   530
No bigger than a grain of wheat.
That much will sap all life and heat.
Death comes in just a little while,
The time you'd take to walk a mile;
The poison is that stark and strong."
    The gamester paid and went along,
With poison now, into the street.
Almost at once he chanced to meet
A bottle-vender, just the man
To sell three bottles for his plan.   540
He poisoned two, but not the third.
Two were for murder, as you've heard.
The other bottle was for him.
The gold was heavy. The spot was dim.
Sure, it would take him hours to shift it.
Strong drink would help him haul and lift it.

Committed to the Devil's work,
He filled each bottle to the cork,
Then journeyed back to find his lot,
Awaiting him with their own plot.   550
    Well, what's the use of further talk?
They killed the man. They didn't balk.
Two renegades of evil lives,
They slaughtered him with hidden knives.
"Now drink," said one, "and count our gains,
And then we'll hide our friend's remains."
He grasped a bottle close at hand,
One poisoned, as the dead man planned.
He drank. His fellow took no less.
And soon they died, as you must guess.   560
    But not at once. No Avicenna   *Arab physician, 980–1037*
Ever saw such anguished sinners,
More signs of poison undisguised,
Than met at these two men's demise.
They had scarce leisure to condemn
Their dupe, the man who poisoned them.
    Oh cursed, sinful wantonness!
Oh homicide, oh wickedness!
Oh gaming, lust, and gluttony!
Oh Christ's-side-piercing blasphemy!
Oh oaths of habit or of pride!   570
Say, where can wretched humans hide
Who dare to wound their own Creator?
Christ bled for you, unworthy traitor!
Oh thankless and unnatural!
    That's it, good men, God save us all,
Especially from avarice!
I've pardons and indulgences
For golden nobles, sterling pence,   *coins*
Or rings or spoons, a small expense.   580
Bow down before my holy bull!   *papal document*
Come up, you wives, and offer wool!
I'll write your names upon my rolls,
Record your gifts and save your souls!
Let me absolve you by my power.
Just give, dear friends, and from this hour

You'll shine as clean as driven snow.
That's how I preach, sirs, where I go.
May Christ, who is our souls' physician,
Forgive your sins and grant remission.   590
      Still, I have one more thing to say—
I've writs and relics here today
To match the best in all the land.
I had them from the pope's own hand.
If you are sinful but abhor it,
Give up some thing of value for it.
I'll cleanse your souls. Just kneel and give!
My pardons let your spirit live.
Or gain forgiveness as we go—
Fresh pardon every mile or so!   600
But then one payment won't suffice;
Each pardon has its separate price.
Good fortune smiles on each one here
To ride with me, a pardoner,
Who can absolve you as we go.
Death strikes us when it will, you know!
Come, come, and let the Host begin,
For he's the deepest steeped in sin.
Come, offer, Host, and don't be slack.
Come kiss each relic in my pack   610
For just a groat! Unlatch your purse!"
      "No!" said the Host, "or else be cursed!
Give gold to you or any riches?
Why, you would make me kiss your britches
And swear a martyr wore them last
Though they were shitty from your ass!
By Helen of the Holy Land,   *Saint Helen, said to have found*
I wish I had your balls in hand—   *the true cross*
Not sacred relics, by my oath!
Just cut them off! I'll carry both,   620
Fitly mounted in a turd!"
      The Pardoner answered not a word,
He was too mightily provoked.
      "Bah," said the Host, " I will not joke
With you or any angry man."
"No more," the worthy Knight began

When he heard the people's laughter,
"Don't plague the man, now or hereafter.
Sir Pardoner, regain your cheer,
And Host, you know I hold you dear.   630
Come close and kiss the Pardoner,
And, Pardoner, don't you demur.
Let's have more tales before we sup."
And so they kissed and made it up.

Heere is ended the Pardoners Tale.

THE SHIPMAN

THE SHIPMAN'S TALE

A wealthy businessman near Paris,
Thought wise as every financier is,
Maintained a wife of noted beauty.
This wife thought flirting was her duty,
Yet brought the merchant more expense
Than she fetched in through trade or rents
By charming men at feasts and dances.
Such men and their admiring glances,
They pass like shadows on a wall.
God spare the man who pays for all!   10
But husbands were put on earth to pay
And deck us[1] out in fine array
To make a show of their success.
No wonder, sirs, we live to dress.
The fate of spouses who lack gold,
Or hold it back, is quickly told:
Say our husbands grudge our spending.
Why, admirers make it up by lending
Amounts they hope will strain our vows.
  This merchant kept a noble house   20
That swarmed with people every day.
He welcomed them; his wife was gay;
And that's the setting of my tale.
Among his comrades, stout and hale,
There was a monk—good-looking, bold—
A man just thirty winters old,
Who seemed to live about the place.
This manly monk, so fair of face,

---

1. At one point Chaucer seems to have intended this story for the Wife of Bath.

Had made himself so fast a friend
That once he started to attend,   30
The house became his daily haunt—
As staunch a friend as one could want.
    Because the wealthy businessman
And this same monk, so much on hand,
Hailed from a hamlet of some dozens,
The monk insisted they were cousins.
The merchant sang the selfsame song,
As cheerful as a bird at dawn.
His "cousin" suited him, he thought.
He vowed to treat him as he ought,   40
And each of them assured the other
They loved each other like two brothers.
    The monk, Don John, was openhanded
And quick to do all life demanded
To spread complacence and well-being.
He tipped the servants, guaranteeing
Each member got the proper wage,
From major domo to the page.
He scattered presents when he came,
So all there smiled to hear his name.   50
As birds rejoice to see the sun . . .
But that's enough. This part is done.
    Well, once it happened, as things may,
The merchant planned to go away
To Bruges. He had some business there,
And meant to buy some Flemish wares.
He sent to Paris for Don John
To come and grace his next salon,
And stay a while and share his bread—
His wife would like that too, he said—   60
Before he rode out with his folk.
    The noble monk of whom I spoke
Enjoyed his abbot's broad permission,
As one of prudent disposition
To oversee, within, without,
The abbey holdings round about.[2]

2. That is, he was free to come and go, not confined to the monastery.

He rode to see his friends anon,
And how they ran to greet Don John,
A man so courteous and fine!
As always he brought Malmsey wine,   70
Another red wine (Fie to thrift!),
And sundry wild fowl as his gift.
Now let them eat and drink their fill,
And celebrate as good friends will.

    The third day, though, the merchant went
To tally up his deals and rents.
Shut up at his desk he sat,
Reviewing notes on this and that
To see how well he fared that year,
Whether he was in the clear   80
And if his wealth had grown or not.
His books and bills and coins were brought
And spread out on his counting board,
No little pile, a chinking hoard!
He looked about and locked the door.
No one must bother him before
He could account for every dime.
And so he sat till after prime.   *after 9 AM*

    Don John was up betimes as well
And walked about to read and tell   90
His prayers beside the merchant's house.

    The good wife came without her spouse
To where he strode there like an abbot
And greeted him as was her habit,
She and a small child in her care.
This girl went with her everywhere,
Still subject to the wife's command.
"My dear Don John," she teased the man,
"Say, why were you so quick to rise?"

    "Niece," he said, "five hours suffice.   100
That's sleep enough for any buck,
Except old feeble ones, my chuck.
Ancient husbands squeezed by care
Lie in as still as any hare
Oppressed and worried by the hounds.
But dear, whence these pale looks and frowns?

I think my cousin, that good man,
Has worked you so since night began
That now indeed you need to rest."
The monk laughed gaily at his jest, 110
But also reddened at the thought.
    The wife was not at all distraught
But said, "There's nothing God can't see.
He knows, sir, how it goes with me.
As sure as Christ sustains my life,
Nowhere in France does any wife
Get less joy from that sorry dance.
But all that is my own mischance.
I mustn't say a single word
About my troubles. How absurd! 120
I swear I'd like to run away,
Or end my dreary life today!
My life of sorrow and despair!"
    This made the monk turn round and stare.
"Alas," he said, "high God forbid
You kill yourself for care or dread!
Trust me, dear lady, tell your grief;
Sometimes just telling brings relief.
Speak out, madam, that's essential.
Say what you like; it's confidential. 130
I swear here on my book of hours
No threat of any earthly powers
Shall make me tell a word of it."
    "And I swear too—it's only fit—
She said, "by that same breviary
That imps may take me all unwary
Or men may pull my limbs apart
Before I utter or impart
To magistrates or family
A word of what you say to me." 140
They kissed one time to bind the oath,
Then told away, and nothing loath.
    "Cousin," she said, "if I had space,
As I have not, here in this place,
I'd tell the story of my life,
What I've endured here as a wife,

Although your cousin is my spouse."
   "No!" said the monk. "For by my house,
That man is no more kin to me
Than any leaf upon this tree!   150
I claim he is, I witness here,
To gain access to you, my dear.
Ah, there, it's out! I'm yours, my dove.
No other woman shares my love!
I swear! Now, sweetheart, speak your piece
Before he comes and we must cease.
Dear, tell me all before we part."
   "Don John!" she said, "you have my heart!
You do, my dear; I'd keep it hidden,
But I must speak as you have bidden.   160
My husband is the poorest man
The world has seen since it began.
Yet I'm his wife, for all my cares,
I shouldn't speak of our affairs,
Not in our bed or in our hall.
Not even now will I tell all.
A wife can't carp, you understand,
No matter how she finds her man.
Yet here's the sum of things, I say:
He's worthless, much to my dismay.   170
I'd rather have a fly to keep!
Sir, most of all the man is cheap.
You know, my lord, there are six traits
That women look for in their mates:
To please his wife a man must be
Hardy, wise, and rich and free,
Pliable, too, and fresh in bed.
Sir, by Our Lord, who wept and bled,
To bring him credit by my dress
I need by Sunday, I confess,   180
A hundred francs, or I'll be shamed.
I'd rather be unborn or maimed
Than let my rivals slander me,
But should my husband guess, you see,
I'm lost. And so, my lord, I pray,
Let me have that sum today.

I promise for your hundred francs
You'll soon enjoy my warmest thanks.
My dear Don John, come to my aid,
Then pick your day to be repaid.   190
You'll have my service, I attest.
I'll do whatever you request.
If not, then let my hurt be greater
Than God gave Ganelon, the traitor."   *He betrayed Roland to the Saracens.*
    The monk replied with little thought,
"My dear, I'll help you, as I ought.
I pity you, I swear. I do!
I'll prove my deep devotion too
When he departs as he intends.
Count on me, dear, to serve your ends.   200
You'll have your precious hundred francs!"
With that he seized her by the flanks
And kissed away with no pretense.
    "Now go," he said, "all innocence,
And let us dine soon, as we may,
For now it is the prime of day.
Dear, be as true as I shall be."
    "I will by Holy God," said she,
And skipped off jolly as a pye.   *magpie*
She bid the cooks to stir and fry   210
So all might dine with no delay,
Then to her husband made her way,
And boldly knocked upon his door
To call him from his counting chore.
    "Ha, sir," she said, "your dinner beckons.
Say, how much longer can you reckon
Your sums and books and bills and things?
The devil take these reckonings!
You have enough of what God sent.
Come out and leave your bags and rent.   220
Aren't you ashamed to leave Don John
To fast while you count all you've won?
Let's hear a Mass and then go eat."
    "You little know," he said, "my sweet,
The ticklish state of our affairs.
For God will ruin despite their prayers

Ten merchants out of every twelve.
No matter how we drive ourselves,
Luck rarely lasts us all our lives.
Each merchant must pretend he thrives　　　　230
But many just hang on, alas,
Put up a front, like all our class,
Until they die or quit the game.
Some must leave town to save their name
And give their creditors the slip.
Success is slippery, hard to grip;
Pitfalls lurk on every hand.
God save the harried businessman!
　　"To Flanders I must make my way,
But I'll be back soon as I may.　　　　240
So, wife, here's my behest to you:
Act for the best in all you do.
Be diligent for our estate.
Preserve our goods at any rate.
You have enough, and more, my dear,
To run the household for a year.
You've got good clothes and all supplies
And cash as well. That must suffice."
With that he locked his counting house
And went away beside his spouse　　　　250
To hear a muttered, hasty Mass.
The board was laid with plate and glass,
And they enjoyed a hearty feast,
The merchant and Don John the priest.
　　Meat done, Don John said privately:
"My cousin, do one thing for me.
I'll tell you plain, no subterfuge,
I see that you must go to Bruges.
God and Augustine be your guide.
Beware, dear cousin, how you ride　　　　260
And keep an eye on what you eat,
For that's important in this heat.
We two can speak what's in our hearts.
God shield you, cousin, in those parts!
What you require by day or night,
I swear if it's within my might,

Just name it, cousin, and you'll see
Your wishes are like laws to me.
    "But you must toss your friend a bone:
I pray you, cousin, for a loan. 270
A hundred francs, a week or two.
I have some purchasing to do,
Some cattle for a farm of ours.
God knows I wish that farm were yours!
I'll get the money back to you,
And nothing lacking, every sou,
But please tell no one of the debt.
I haven't made my offer yet.
May you fare well, my cousin dear,
God keep you safe and give you cheer!" 280
    The merchant answered back anon:
"O noble cousin, brave Don John,
Surely that's a small request.
You'll have your francs at my behest.
Take freely of my gold or wares.
God knows I love to ease your cares.
    "But here's the thing, as you'll allow.
Full coffers are a merchant's plow.
Our credit's good with gold at hand,
But not without, you understand. 290
Still, pay when it's convenient,
And I will count the sum well spent."
    And so to win the sly monk's thanks
The merchant rendered up the francs.
No one from Paris to Cologne
Knew anything about this loan
Except these two, who now are gay,
And just at dawn John rode away.
    That morning, too, the merchant went
Flanders-ward just as he meant, 300
Until he came to Bruges at length.
He bought and sold with all his strength,
With cash or credit as it chanced.
He neither drank nor diced nor danced,
But drove his business every day.
And there at Bruges we'll let him stay.

Within the first week he was gone,
Lo, to his house came Cousin John,
Head and beard full freshly shaved.
No one in the house behaved   310
Less than pleased in any way
To have the monk come back to stay.
That night with all the curtains drawn
The wife accorded with Don John
That for his francs he'd feel no lack.
She'd entertain him on her back.
And what she said, she did, this wife.
That night they led a busy life,
Till morning came and off he went.
He left the household well content,   320
For no one in the neighborhood
Suspected him of less than good.
We'll leave him riding to his cell.
That's all I'll say of him. Farewell!
      Our merchant, when Bruges Fair was done,
Came back to France with what he'd won,
Rejoined his wife in all good cheer.
But he'd found Flanders ware so dear,
That he had often bought on credit,
And now was bound to pay his debt,   330
Twenty thousand shields, no less.   *a very large sum*
He soon went off to town to press
His friends for loans and to call in
Such sums as others owed to him.
Yet once in Paris, his first thought
Was for Don John, and so he sought
His friend the monk, for fellow-feeling—
And not for any business dealing.
He yearned to see how his friend thrived
And tell how he himself contrived   340
To make his mark in Flemish ware.
Don John seemed glad to see him there,
And heard the merchant tell the tale
Of all his doings, each detail,
Thanking God his luck had held,
Except that now he was compelled

To meet his bond as best he might;
That done, he swore, he'd be all right.
    Don John answered, "What good news!
Your journey went as you would choose.   350
If I were rich, God save my soul,
You'd have the shields to see you whole.
I know full well the other day,
You lent me gold, and let me say,
God thank you, friend, upon my life.
I gave the gold back to your wife.
She had it, every franc, from me
As she'll remember, certainly,
By tokens known to me and her.
But now, my cousin, I must stir.   360
Our abbot's riding out, you see,
And I must bear him company.
Remember me to my sweet niece.
God bless you, cousin. Go in peace."
    The merchant found his credit good.
He transferred money, as he should,
To those who held his Flemish debt.
They cleared him once his bond was met,
And home he went, all blithe and gay.
He knew things stood in such a way   370
That he must win, and not long hence,
A thousand francs, plus his expense.
    His wife was waiting at the gate,
Less cold than she had been of late
And pleased to pass the night in mirth
To celebrate his new net worth.
At dawn his spirit roused again;
His kisses made his feelings plain.
He pressed her hotly, somewhat rough.
    "No more," said she, "You've had enough!"   380
But wantonly she did his will.
The merchant said, when they grew still:
"By God, my dear, I'm somewhat miffed
With what might seem your lack of thrift
Or social grace. Dear, I complain,
I think you caused a bit of strain

Between me and my cousin, John.
You might have told me early on
He'd given you the hundred francs
He owed to me. Instead of thanks,   390
He thought I meant to jog his purse
As if it slipped his mind, or worse,
When I spoke of my Flemish debt.
We parted friends, I hope, and yet
I saw him frown. But Christ the King!
I wasn't asking for a thing.
I pray, dear wife, you'll let me know
When any man, well placed or low,
Repays a debt when I'm not here.
If not, as you can see, my dear,   400
I might call in the same debt twice."
     The woman answered in a trice,
While looking somewhat put-upon,
"Dear, I defy that false monk, John,
Yet I must give the man his due.
He brought the coins to me, that's true.
But, damn his silly monkish snout,
He let me think, the careless lout,
He gave me gold to honor you,
To spend on clothing with a view   410
To please us both and give us cheer
For all his entertainment here.
My God, this is a pretty pass.
Forgive me, dear; don't stand aghast.
If I'm your debtor now, suppose
I pay you with my *quelque chose*   *French: "something"*
From day to day, and if I fail,
Why, you shall score it on my tail,   *my tally (pun intended)*
And make me pay with interest.
By God, I spent the gold on dress—   420
I never wasted half a groat—
To make you seem a man of note.
It's for your honor, lord, I say,
So don't be angry, dear, be gay.
I pledge you all my choicest parts.
I'll pay my debt with loving art.

Forgive me everything, my dear,
Turn this way now, and make good cheer."
　　The merchant knew the gold was lost.
Complaints would just extend his cost.   430
The hundred francs were gone indeed.
"All right," he said, "but, dear, take heed:
Don't fritter all our wealth away,
But guard your goods and mine, I say."
That ends my fable, may God send us
Tail enough, the saints defend us!   *credit (and pun)*

Heere endeth the Shipmannes Tale.

Bihoold the murie wordes of the Hoost to the Shipman and to the lady Prioresse.

"Well told, by *corpus dominus,*"   *"the Lord's body"*
The Host called out, "keep sailing thus,
My Shipman, gentle mariner.
And give that monk an evil year!   440
Ha, my fellows, what a jape!
This monk has made the man his ape,
His wife as well, unless I'm drunk.
The lesson? Never trust a monk!
　　"But onward, now, and let us see
Who next of all this company
Will tell a tale." And then he said
As sweetly as a lady's maid,
"And now, dear Prioresse, your leave—
I swear I'd never make you grieve—   450
Your story, lady, if you would,
But only if you think it good.
Won't you honor us, my dear?"
　　And she obliged, as you shall hear.

The Prioresse

The Prioresse's Prologue

Oh Lord, dear Lord, thy holy name is known
Through every land by wondrous means, said she.
Besides your priests and soldiers fully grown,
The mouths of children voice your sovereignty
And praise your power and goodness as we see.
For even infants suckling at the breast
May magnify your fame among the rest.

Therefore, to praise you, Lord, oh grant me grace—
Yourself and that white, tender lily flower
Who gave you birth, although a maiden chaste.   10
Support me, Lord, augment my little power,
Though she needs naught I have, although she tower
As mankind's highest honor and the source,
With Jesus, of forgiveness and remorse.

Oh Mother Maiden, Maiden Mother free!
Oh shrub that flamed unburned in Moses' sight!
You caught a living spark of deity,
The Holy Spirit's fructifying might.
His blessed virtue, radiant and bright,
Made you conceive Lord Christ, the Father's Son.   20
Come, help me tell the tale I have begun.

Your bounty, lady, your magnificence,
Your blameless life, your sweet humility—
These far surpass all human tongues and sense,
For often, well before we pray to thee,
You sweep away the darkness that we see
And bring God's light to lead us through your prayer,
My lady, to your son, so dear and fair.

My knowledge is too weak, dear blissful queen,
To praise your holy wonders as I ought. 30
Your worth's immense; my wit is mean.
I'm like a helpless infant child, untaught:
Almost without a useful word or thought.
I'm that, no more, and so, dear one, I pray,
Join with me now and teach me what to say.

The Prioresse's Tale

   In Asia once, a wealthy city stood,
A Christian town, but with a share of Jews
Maintained there by a lord for his own good.
These thrived on usury, a foul abuse
God's people shun as noisome in their views. 40
Throughout their ghetto men could freely ride.
It opened to the town on every side.

A Christian school taught little children there,
Hard by the Jewry, at its farther end,
With many tender pupils, young and fair,
Who worked from year to year to comprehend
Such skills as Christian parents most commend,
Practicing their singing and their letters,
As little children must, to please their betters.

Among them was a widow's only son— 50
A cheerful little boy of seven years—
Who studied there until his term was done.
The lad was rightly taught, as it appeared.
Wherever he saw Mary's image reared,
He knelt at once to cross himself and say
His *Ave Mary* there upon the way.

The little fellow's pious mother taught
How that great lady, Christ's own mother dear,
Should always have the first place in his thought.
And he was meek and reverent of cheer; 60

Indeed, his childish faith reminds me here
Of blessed Nicholas. From infancy   *Even as an infant at the breast,*
That saint knew God and served him faithfully.   *Nicholas fasted two days a week.*

This little boy, too small to join the chorus,
Sat in the schoolroom working at his slate
And heard the strains of *Alma Redemptoris*   *"beloved Mother of Our*
As older children sang that hymn of weight.   *Redeemer"*
Drawn by the sound, he sat beside the gate
And listened as the others tuned their throats,
And thus he learned the first verse, words and notes.   70

Of course the Latin terms were far beyond him;
He had no earthly notion what they said.
He asked the older students to expound them,
To fix the anthem's meaning in his head
And learn the sacred truths to which it led.
He earnestly besought them not to tease
And begged them all for help, upon his knees.

One student somewhat older than the boy
Relayed what he had heard another say:
"This song salutes God's mother in her joy.   80
It celebrates her triumphs and it prays
For her sweet help against our final day.
At least that is the meaning in summation.
My Latin can't afford a full translation."

"You say this is a song of supplication
To Christ's dear mother?" asked the pious lad.
"Well, then, I pledge to work without cessation
To learn it all by Christmas. I'll be glad,
Though teacher says my primer work is bad
And beats me for my faults three times an hour,   90
To study Mary's song with all my power."

His fellow taught him daily after school,
As they went home, to know the song by rote.
Soon he could sing each part of it by rule.
He had it word for word and note for note,

And twice a day it graced his piping throat.
He walked to school and homeward every day
And sang Our Lady's anthem on the way.

As I have said, throughout the Jewish ghetto
This little child, rejoicing as he passed,   100
Sang out aloud to everyone he met so
The *Alma Redemptoris,* first and last.
His voice and heart up to Our Lady cast
His unrestrained devotion, warm and sweet,
Extolling her by name in every street.

Our dark Satanic foe, that hellish snake,
Who builds his waspish nest in Jewish parts,
In fury called, "Now, Hebrews all, awake!
A plague on this and on all Christian arts!
Shall one small boy thus flout your heathen hearts?   110
Say, do you grant this little lad the right
To sing Our Lady's hymn in your despite?

Stung by his taunts, the wicked Jews conspired
To purge the little scholar from this life.
A vile, remorseless murderer was hired
And stationed at a spot where crime was rife
To slaughter our young schoolboy with his knife.
This wretch attacked the student for their sakes.
He slit his throat and cast him down a jakes.   *toilet*

I say it was a privy where he fell,   120
A fulsome pit where Jewish people purged.
Oh cursed race of Herod, who can tell
What help you gained from all the harm you urged?
Murder will out; it will not stay submerged,
Especially where God's honor is involved.
Blood calls aloud to see a murder solved.

Young martyr wedded to virginity,
Now may you sing, now that your life is gone.
There is a Lamb in Heaven's fields, trust me,
Proclaimed in Revelations by Saint John.   *14:3–4*

From Patmos he once told the world how one
Who dies before enjoying women's love
Would sing before this godly Lamb above.

The wretched widow wore away the night
In waiting for her son, but all for naught,
So she went out as soon as it was light,
Pale and anxious, shrinking from her thought.
At school and in the crowded streets she sought
Until, at length, comparing all the clues,
She learned he'd last been seen among the Jews.   140

Distraught and breathless with a mother's pity,
She ran the streets and alleyways, half-mad,
Asking all she met throughout the city
If they had heard or seen her little lad.
Christ's mother was the strongest hope she had,
And so she cried to Mary as she passed
Until she reached the Jewry, saved for last.

She fawned and pleaded, prayed most piteously
To every Jew who went about that place,
"Oh, tell me, did you see my son?" said she.   150
They all said no, but Jesus by his grace
Determined her direction and her pace
So that she came as if by her own wit
To where they cast her son into the pit.

Oh God, who showed your works of old
By innocents, we celebrate your might.
This chastest gem of yours, this emerald,
This precious, martyred ruby, clear and bright,
Although his throat gaped open, reared upright,
Sat up to sing his *Alma Redemptoris*   160
In ringing tones no privy could suppress!

Now Christians ran in clusters to the site
And stood in awe to marvel at God's deed.
They called the judge, an honest local knight,
Who came at once and made all men take heed.

He praised great Christ, the lodestone of our creed,
His mother, too, with virtues so profuse,
And then he sent his men to bind the Jews.

Lamenting, he exhumed the little child
And took him up, still caroling his song.   170
The Christians formed a long and pious file
To bear him to an abbey in a throng;
Of course his grieving mother came along.
The abbey gained, she would not leave the room
But clung like Rachel to her small son's tomb.   *Matt. 2:18*

With lively torments, lingering shameful ends,
The provost punished all the guilty Jews,
Who plotted murder with their bitter friends.
"Kill us," he said, "as Christians, if you choose,
But now each man of you will have his dues."   180
His pulling horses split the Jews in four,
And then he hanged the pieces in their gore.

Then for the boy they said a Holy Mass.
His body lay in state before the altar.
The abbot and his monks brought this to pass
With prayers for his salvation from the Psalter.
One wonder more from Christ, mankind's exalter:
The body roused when it felt holy water
To sing *O Alma redemptoris mater!*

The abbot was a pious, holy man,   190
As all monks are—at least they ought to be—
He heard the young lad singing and began
To conjure him: "Now, child, I call to thee,
By virtue of the sacred Trinity,
How can you sing before the people here
When, as we see, your throat's slit ear to ear?"

"My throat is cut down to the white neck bone,"
The small boy said, "and as is nature's way
I should have died without another moan,
And yet Lord Jesus Christ, as good books say,   200

Will put his righteous power on display.
His glory and his mother's, just as dear,
Let me sing out my *Alma* loud and clear.

"That well of mercy, Our Lord's mother, Mary,
I always loved, as much as children can.
When death struck me, my lords, she didn't tarry,
But came at once, as she might to a man.
"Now sing for me, dear child" was her command.
I sang my anthem, and when it was sung
I thought she laid a seed upon my tongue.   210

"And thus I sing before you, lords. I need
To hail Our Lady's triumphs over sin,
At least until you take away that seed.
But now I hear her loving voice again,
Explaining how my real death will begin:
She says, 'I'll fetch you when the seed is gone.
Don't fear that hour; a better life will dawn.'"

Thus said the boy. The abbot in his stole
Caught out his tongue and took away the seed.
The little body rendered up its soul   220
And when the abbot saw him dead indeed,
His salt tears ran to vent his heart-felt need.
The man fell flat, face downward on the ground,
And lay as still as if he had been bound.

The other monks stretched out their lengths beside him,
To weep and praise Christ's holy mother there
And then they rose and busily applied them
To move the martyr's body and prepare
A fitting tomb of marble, clean and fair,
And in it close the little schoolboy's dust.   230
That tomb is there today, or so I trust.

Oh blessed Hugh of Lincoln, you were slain   *hero of a similar story*
By wicked Jews like those I've told of here.
Not long ago they reveled in your pain.
Oh pray for us, inconstant but sincere,

So that the loving God whom we revere
May grant us his forgiveness here on earth
In honor of the mother of his birth.
Amen.

Heere is ended the Prioresses Tale.

Chaucer's Tales of Sir Thopas and Melibee

The Prologue to Sir Thopas

Now when this wondrous tale was done, *the Prioresse's Tale*
A rather somber mood descended
Until our Host revived the fun
And said to me, as if offended:
"My friend, I hope your sulks are ended.
Is downward-gazing just your habit,
Or are you searching for a rabbit?

"Come near" he added, "do not sigh.
Stand back, all. Give him a place.
He fills his clothes as well as I, 10
A proper armful to embrace
For any woman. What a face!
He looks a little like an elf.
That's why he hangs back by himself.

"Now sir, present, like all the rest,
A mirthful tale, and don't be slow."
"Host," said I, "don't be distressed.
I'll tell the only tale I know—
A rhyme I first learned long ago."
"Ah, good," said he. "Now we shall hear 20
A proper story. Never fear."

CHAUCER'S TALE OF SIR THOPAS

The First Fit

Listen, lords, with good intent
And I will tell in merriment
   A tale of mirth and solace
About a knight, of high descent
In battle and in tournament.
   His name? It was Sir Thopas.

He was born a young grandee,
In Flanders, far beyond the sea,
   In a town called Popering.   30
His father was of high degree,
A regal man and lord full free,
   As was, God knows, the proper thing.

Sir Thopas was a sturdy lad,
His face as white as risen bread,
   His lips red as a rose.
His cheeks as well were scarlet red,
And, judging by what I've heard said,
   He had a seemly nose.

Golden hair fell from his crown   40
Below his waistband all around.
   His shoes were from Cordova.
From Bruges they brought his hose of brown,
Of costly silk his well-cut gown—
   A handsome swain all over.

Ah, he could course the swiftest doe,
Ride the woods and hunting go
   With his fine gray hawk.
A keen performer with his bow;
No man around could wrestle so;   50
   He made the others gawk.

Full many a maiden in her bower
Longed for Thopas by the hour,
   Whenas she should be sleeping.
But he was chaste, though far from sour,
But sweeter than the bramble flower
   That bears the rose hips peeping.

And thus it happened on a day,
For so it mentions in my lay,
   Sir Thopas wished to ride.   60
He stepped astride his noble gray,
Took up his lance, and fared away,
   A long sword by his side.

He rode until the clearings ceased,
Into a wood of many beasts,
   Indeed, both buck and hare.
And as he jangled north and east
The perils in his path increased,
   Though he was unaware.

There sprang up herbs both great and small,   70
Like licorice and cetewale,   *a ginger-like spice*
   Along with scented cloves.
And nutmeg sweet to flavor ale,
Whether it is new or stale,
   Or sprinkle on one's clothes.

The small birds sang throughout the day,
The sparrow hawk and popinjay,
   So it was joy to hear.
The brown thrush cock intoned his lay
And each wood dove along the way   80
   Descanted loud and clear.

Sir Thopas felt a love-longing
Just as he heard the thrush cock sing,
   And spurred like one demented.
His good horse ran to ease the sting,

Its sides bled red as anything,
  Before the lad relented.

But now the knight himself was tired
From galloping upon the sward,
  So fearsome was his will.
So he lay down, as it transpired,
And freed his mount as it desired
  To roam and eat its fill.

"Oh, Blessed Mother, hear," said he,
"Why should hot love so gnaw at me
  And blind me with its smoke?
My dreams last night were bold and free,
An elf queen would my lover be
  And lie beneath my cloak.

"That elf queen will I love, I swear.
No other woman anywhere
  Is fit to be my mate.
My elf queen is beyond compare,
I'll have no other, I declare,
  No matter what her state."

Onto his horse he climbed anon
And rambled over stile and stone
  To find his elvish queen.
Till he so long a space had gone
He found a place much farther on
  Where fairies might be seen,
      So wild
That in that country there was none
That dared to walk or ride alone,
      Neither wife nor child.

At last there came a frowning giant,
A big one, called Sir Elephant,
  A perilous man indeed.
He swore, "Now, by Mohammed's aunt,

90

100

110

Unless you turn and leave my haunts, 120
  I shall brain your steed.
        My mace
Shall now defend the Queen of Fairie
With her harps and pipers merry,
    Dwelling in this place."

Our knight defied the man's decree.
"Tomorrow I will meet with thee,"
  He said, "and wear my armor.
And then I hope, by all my creed
That you shall feel my lance indeed, 130
  And mourn those words full sore!
      Your belly,
I'll lay open, if I may.
Just before the break of day,
    Your guts will run like jelly."

As Thopas turned and drew back fast,
The giant took up stones to cast
  With the sling that he was bearing.
The youngling got away in haste,
Through the working of Christ's grace, 140
  And by his own great daring.

The Second Fit

Listen further to this tale,
Merry as a nightingale,
  And hear me now explain
How Thopas then reversed his trail,
Cantering over hill and dale,
  Back to his domain.

His merry men, their courage whetted,
Saw him fitly fed and feted.
  They knew that he must fight 150
Against a looming brute three-headed,
By his love and hope abetted,
  For a fairy queen full bright.

"Come with me," he told his minstrels,
"And jesters all, come bring your tales,
   To tell me, as I arm,
Of high romance and broken hopes,
Of cardinals and splendid popes,
   And love and lovers' charms."

They plied him then with sweetened wine   160
And mead in wooden bowls, combined
   With royal, precious spice,
Then gingerbread fit for a shrine
And licorice and cumin fine
   And sugar sifted twice.

He wore against his snowy skin
Small clothes of linen, fine and thin,
   His drawers a work of art.
A padded jacket to his chin,
A coat of mail to scrimmage in   170
   And cover up his heart.

Finally, his armor plate,
Jewish work of sober weight,
   Polished steel of proof.
A crest to show his high estate
Adorned his surcoat, crisp and straight,
   An emblem of his truth.

His shield was gold enameled red
Around a golden wild boar's head
   With a dark red gem.   180
He stood and swore by ale and bread
He'd see the loathsome giant dead,
   Which no one could condemn.

His greaves were made of hardened leather,   *shin guards*
His sheath, of ivory altogether,
   His helmet bright as brass.
His saddle was of narwhale bone;
His bridle jingled clear and shown
   Like moonlight unsurpassed.

His spear was made of chosen cypress;
For warlike shafts, that wood is best.
    The head was sharply ground.
His steed was sleek and dappled gray.
It ambled gently on its way,
    Walked slow and looked around
    The land.

Well, my lords, that ends a fit.
If you wish any more of it,
    I speak at your command.

The Third Fit

Now hold your tongues for charity,
Both knight and noble lady free,   200
    As I resume my tale
Of battle and of chivalry
And lady-love beyond the sea.
    I'll tell you without fail.

Men give divers tales the prize,
Of good King Horn and Ipotys,
    And Bevis or Sir Guy,
Or Lybeux or Pleyndamour,   *heroes of medieval romances*
But Thopas is the very flower
    Of royal chivalry!   210

His steed Sir Thopas now bestrode,
And forth upon his way he rode,
    Like sparkles from a coal.
Upon his crest he bore a tower
And on the tower a lily flower.
    May God preserve him whole!

Because he was adventurous
He would not sleep inside a house
    But lay down in his hood.
His helmet pillowed his fair head,   220

His horse stood at his side and fed
   On forage from the wood.

The knight drank water from a well,
As did the famous Percival,   *Aurthurian hero*
   The worthiest of men.
Till on a day—

The Host Intervenes

   "No more of this!" our Host exclaimed.
"I've never heard a tale so lame.
Why serve us such a jangling mess?
As I pray God my soul to bless,   230
My ears ache from your rigmarole.
The Devil swallow such rhymes whole!
Not rhymes, I say, but doggerel!"
   "How so?" said I. "Why can't I tell
This tale I have begun so well?
Can others speak when I cannot?
I swear this is the best I've got."
   "By God," he said, "in simple words,
Your crappy tale's not worth a turd.
It's too naive, a waste of time.   240
I order you to cease this rhyme.
Now prose might suit our congregation,
Or verse based on alliteration,
But give us mirth or good advice."
   "I will," I said, "by suffering Christ!
I'll tell a little thing in prose,
That you will like, as I suppose,
Or else your tastes are hard to suit.
It offers moral aid to boot,
Though it's been told in different words,   250
By other folks you may have heard.
   "You know though each Evangelist
Who tells the pain of Jesus Christ,
Speaks not exactly like the others,
It's still the truth that each one utters.

Although their words diverge at times,
Their underlying meaning chimes.
Some say more and some say less
As all the Gospels will attest
Of Matthew, Mark, and Luke and John,
And yet their message is all one.
And so, my lords, I must beseech,
If it appears I swell my speech
By adding some few details more
To episodes you've heard before,
In the treatise I have mentioned,
Credit me with good intention.
Though my words are not the same
You may have heard, in Jesus' name,
Don't think of me as one who mocks.   270
I swear my meaning's orthodox.
I pray, my lords, remember this
So you won't take my tale amiss.
Please listen then to what I say
As I begin and tell away.

CHAUCER'S TALE OF MELIBEE

*Chaucer's replacement story, the tale of Melibee, is a lengthy prose narrative about
a rich young lord, Melibee, whose enemies break into his house and beat his wife,
Prudence, and wound his daughter, Sophie. Melibee's first reaction is to rend his
clothes and weep, but his wife convinces him to call in his friends for their ad-
vice. Finding their opinions mixed, Melibee decides in favor of going to war
against the evildoers. But then Prudence herself weighs in—with a multitude of
references and authorities—and persuades him not to fight. First she has to con-
vince him that women should be listened to, a task that takes her over much of
the same ground the Wife of Bath covers in her prologue. Then she delivers a long
lecture on practical politics, which eventually satisfies Melibee and persuades him
that he should let her negotiate a settlement. Prudence holds a meeting with the
enemies, who are so impressed with her that they apologize and ask for peace.
Then she persuades Melibee to grant it on the most merciful terms, just as God
freely forgives men's sins if they are truly repentant.*

THE MONK

THE MONK'S PROLOGUE

Hearing this of Melibee
And Prudence, with her charity,
Our Host said, "I'm a faithful man
But swear by holy Madrian   *unidentified, perhaps a mistake*
I'd give an untapped barrel of ale   *on the Host's part*
If my wife, Goodlief, heard this tale.
For she is hasty, on my life,
Not like this high lord Melibee's wife.
Say I decide to beat my knaves;
She brings me heavy clubs and staves.
"Kill them all, the idle drones,"   10
She cries. "Go, crush their backs and bones!"
Or if a neighbor, I allow,
Meets her in church and will not bow,
Or slights her in some other way,
She makes my tavern ring all day
With "Coward! Sneak! Avenge your wife!
Or if you won't, I'll take your knife,
And you sit at my wheel and spin!"
She never stops, to my chagrin.
"Alas!" she says, "a sorry scrape,   20
To wed a milksop, coward ape,
Who's overawed by everyone
And lets his wife be put upon!"
    That's what I hear unless I fight.
No force at all who's wrong or right—
Her side or none. She wants to see
A lion's mindless rage from me.
She'll work me up, I swear, to slay
A neighbor, some unlucky day;
For I'm a bad man with my knife,   30

295

Afraid of nothing but my wife.
Ach, she's bruiser, big and wide.
Lords, few have done her down, or tried.
But that's enough. Back to our stories!
    "Sir Monk," he said, "by Heaven's glories,
You shall tell a tale, I say,
Rochester's not a mile away!
Come, come, my lord, observe our game;
But truly, I don't know your name.
Tell me, are you called Don John?   40
Or Thomas, James, or Solomon?
What's your house, by all your kin?
By God, you have a milk-white skin.
You eat your fill. You pasture well.
You're not all spirit, I can tell.
In faith, you are an officer,
A sexton or a cellarer.   *supervisor of buildings or kitchens*
My father's soul, what makes you roam?
Sir, you must wield some force at home:
No cloisterer or puny novice—   50
A governor, discreet and wise.
Then too, just note your brawn and bone.
You're well set up and fully grown!
I swear the man's not worth a pigeon
Who first consigned you to religion.
You could have trod some hens all right!
If you had will to match your might
And spent yourself begetting sons,
By God, you'd sire some noble ones!
Why do you wear so wide a cope?   *meaning unclear*
I tell you, sir, if I were pope,
Manly men of your estate,
No matter how they shaved their pate,   *wore a monk's tonsure*
Should wive, or else all mankind's cheated.
Religion leaves the world depleted
Of mighty humpers, while we shrimps
Beget limp reeds and chinless wimps.
Our heirs are so emaciated
They're weaker than their sires when mated.
And wives are so dissatisfied   70

They ask religious men astride.
Lord, monks like you were surely meant
To see Dame Venus gets her rent.
God knows your coins aren't counterfeit!
Now, don't be angry, lord. I'll quit."
    The Monk knew what these words were worth
And said, "Host, I'll advance your mirth,
As far as sorts with decency—
Recount a tale, or two, or three.
Perhaps I'll tell, to spread his glory,   80
Our noble monarch Edward's story.   *Saint Edward the Confessor,*
Or maybe something else will please.   *King of England 1042–66*
I know a hundred tragedies.
A tragedy's a narrative
Of how a certain person lived:
A man of great prosperity
Who sadly falls from high degree
To misery and wretchedness.
The most are written, as is best,
In bold hexameters, six-foot lines,   90
Or else in prose of sundry kinds.
But prose or meter's just a dress.
The tale's the meat, as you must guess.
    Now listen, if you care to hear,
But, lordings, don't be too severe
If I don't always order things—
That is, my heroes, popes, and kings—
In strict succession, first to last,
But jumble stories from the past
Just as they chance to come to mind.   100
I'm not a scholar, as you'll find.

THE MONK'S TALE

The Monk tells seventeen tragic stories, set in an interlocking stanza form based on French ballades, before the knight stops him and he has to make way for the Nun's Priest. Although "The Monk's Tale" isn't usually regarded as Chaucer's finest work, some of the stories give interesting views on issues raised by other pil-

*grims. For instance, the Monk's account of Zenobia, a Middle Eastern queen of
the third century AD, adds another striking perspective to the pilgrims' discus-
sion of women's roles and the marriage theme.*

Zenobia ruled Palmyra as its queen,   *ancient city in Syria*
And Persians still recall her nobleness,
A warlike, worthy monarch, and so keen
No man could match her sovereign hardiness.
Her ancient blood and perfect gentleness
From many famous Persian kings descended.
There may have been a fairer maid, I guess,
But none whose queenly bearing was more splendid.

From childhood on, this regal maiden fled
A woman's duties. Through the woods she went,   10
And many a wild deer's bright heart's blood she shed
With sharp-edged arrows, mortal bolts well spent.
She coursed them through the wilds, swift and intent.
As she grew older and advanced in skill,
Her hounds tracked bears and lions by their scent.
The girl herself would dress them at the kill.

She dared to rouse the wild beasts from their dens
And run rough mountain traces through the night
And sleep beneath a bush far from her friends.
And she could wrestle with a hero's might,   20
Match any of her retinue in fight.
Not one of them could best her in a race.
And all the while she kept her virtue bright.
She welcomed no man's wooing or embrace.

But then at last her good friends wedded her
To Odaenathus, a man as royal as she.
The match took longer than they would prefer:
He needed urging too. It happened he
Was also half-determined to live free,
But nonetheless they married, as you'll hear,   30
And lived together in felicity.
Through all their trials they held each other dear.

In one thing, though, the queen would not relent:
She gave the man one chance to lie with her.
One chance, because the sum of her intent
Was to conceive. No other longings stirred.
She'd please him once, no more till she was sure
That she was not with child from that one deed,
Then she would let him do as he preferred
One time again and hope that would succeed.   40

But if she was with child from that first cast,
No more! They wouldn't play the married game
Until her term of forty weeks was passed.
Then once again she would endure the same.
Let Odaenathus wheedle, rage, or blame,
He got no more from her. Zenobia said
It made a wife a harlot, to her shame,
To work for love, not children, in her bed.

Two sons the royal couple had this way,
Two boys she raised to flourish and live well.   50
She was, to praise her merits as I may,
As great a queen as any tongue could tell,
Wise and just, grand but also fell,
Tireless in war, and noble over all.
No rival king of many could excel
Zenobia before her tragic fall.

Each thing about her spoke of wealth and might:
Her clothes, her weapons, all her household gear.
Her gold and jewels dazzled plain men's sight,
Yet she held knowledge, not just hunting, dear.   60
She had an eye for language, and an ear,
And studied when she could, and not for sport.
It pleased her most to read about her sphere:
Books helped her rule herself and all her court.

To give her story in its shortest form,
So strong were Odaenathus and his queen,
They battled down their neighbors like a storm,
Subduing all the towns near their demesne—

Rich desert cities where Rome held a lien.
Palmyra spread and flourished in its pride;   70
No limits to its power were then foreseen.
That is, until King Odaenathus died.

Her battles are set down for all to read:
How she subdued the Persian king Shapur,   *Shapur I, 241–72 AD*
Her strategies and hopes for every deed:
How she conquered, what her reasons were,
And later how she felt misfortune's spur.
Her city was besieged until it fell.
It's all in Petrarch; therefore I defer   *Chaucer means Boccaccio,*
The full account to him. He treats it well.   *De claris mulieribus, 98.*

When Odaenathus died, the grieving queen
Took up Palmyra's reins in either hand.
Her aptitude for war was sharp and keen.
Soon every prince or king throughout the land
Was praying nightly that his luck would stand,
And Zenobia would wage some other war.
They all acceded to the queen's demand
That they must rule their kingdoms under her.

Not Gallienus, who ruled Rome till he died,   *253–68 AD*
Nor Claudius, the man who followed then,   *268–70 AD*
Dared brave Zenobia's martial skill and pride—
Nor any man of Egypt or Armenian.
Arabia and Syria cringed before her men.
No one cared to face her host and fight
For fear the queen would best them once again
And scatter all their forces with her might.

Zenobia dressed her sons for kingly show
As princes each and each his father's heir:
Hermmano, one, the other, Thymalao,
As Persia learned to call the royal pair.   100
But honey's often mixed with gall and woe.
For all her might, the queen could not endure.
Fortune revoked its favor at a blow
And sent her tumbling down, disgraced and poor.

Aurelian succeeded to the throne.   *Aurelianus, emperor of Rome,*
He grasped the reins of Rome and bore the sway.   *270–75 AD*
He vowed to make Zenobia atone
For her incursions; thus he took his way
Toward Palmyra—there's little more to say:
She had to flee. He caught her as she fled,   110
And made her and her royal sons his prey,
No longer royal, but prisoners instead.

Among her other things, Aurelian seized
Her chariot, aflame with gems and gold.
As this expressed her riches, he was pleased
To lead it in his triumph, where it rolled
Behind him, while Zenobia, once so bold,
Went first in golden chains for men to see.
A precious prize, as if she might be sold,
In jeweled clothes that suited her degree.   120

Alas, Dame Fortune! She that one time was
A scourge to mighty emperors and kings
Is now a slave to mock and chide for flaws.
And she who once went armed for battle's stings
And won strong towns and towers with all that brings,
Must wear a humble veil and sew and sweep.
And she who blazed with dazzling jewels and rings
Must now spin yarn and weave to pay her keep!¹

---

1. Zenobia spent the rest of her life in Italy, actually in comfortable circumstances.

THE NUN'S PRIEST

THE NUN'S PRIEST'S PROLOGUE

"Hoo!" said the Knight, "no more of this!
While no one story seems amiss;
It's just too much—your tales of grief,
Sir, wring our hearts without relief.
I know myself I hate to hear
How men enjoy good luck for years,
And then lose everything, alas!
How about a tale of some solace,
As when a man of poor estate
Thrives and sees his wealth grow great   10
And lives in long prosperity?
Now there's a tale to gladden me,
The sort of story we should tell."

"That's right!" the Host said, "By Paul's bell!   *bell of St. Paul's Cathedral*
This Monk goes maundering on and on
Of happy fortune wrecked and gone,
Always carping on that theme.
There's not one thing here to redeem
Bad luck. He just complains,
'Alas, alack!' dispersing pains.   20
Who wants to hear these tragedies?

"Relent, Sir Monk. Grant us reprieve.
Don't go on droning like a gnat.
Your stories aren't worth a sprat;
Each sad rehearsal is the same,
And so, Dom Piers, (I know your name),
I pray you tell us something else,
For, sir, the jingling of the bells
Hanging from your horse's bridle,
By Christ the King, who's never idle,   30
Is all that's keeping me awake

302

And safe from falling in some lake.
Suppose I did; what of your stories?
Clerks know the finest oratory
Is lost without an audience.
That can't surprise a man of sense.
   "Come, sir, discourse of better stuff.
I see you're able, right enough,
To tell of hunting and your prey."
   "No," said the Monk, "I won't be gay.   40
Let someone else now take his turn."
The Host peered round him, looking stern,
And called upon the Nun's poor Priest.
"Ha, John," he said. "This Monk has ceased.
Give us a tale to make us glad.
No matter that your horse is bad—
A bony plug fit just for glue.
Rejoice! He's good enough for you!
Be merry now and evermore."
   "Ah," said the Priest, "No need to roar.   50
I'll be as merry as I can."
He drew a breath and then began,
And thus he said to everyone,
This good and pleasant Father John:

THE NUN'S PRIEST'S TALE

   A widow long without a spouse
Lived humbly in a narrow house
Beside a grove, sirs, in a dale;
It's she of whom I tell my tale.
She'd led, since she was last a wife,
A burdensome, hardscrabble life   60
With few possessions and less rent.
By husbanding what goods God sent
She fed herself and her two daughters.
She kept three sows, for breed, not slaughter,
And three thin cows and Moll, the sheep.
Her house was sooty, hard to keep,

And there she served, despite her wishes,
No piquant sauce nor far-fetched dishes.
No dainty morsels passed her throat;
Her diet matched her threadbare coat.   70
No fats and feasting made her sick;
Strict moderation was her physic,
With hard work and a patient stance.
Gout never made her miss a dance,
Nor apoplexy shook her head.
She took no wine, not white or red.
Her table favored white and black:
Milk and dark bread she rarely lacked.
These and eggs sustained her life,
A hard-subsisting widowed wife.   80
    In her yard fenced round about
With sticks and with a ditch without,
She kept a cock named Chanticleer.
In all that land he had no peer.
His voice outdid the ample organ
That rang out when the Mass began.
His crowing kept the hours as well
As any clock or abbey bell.
He knew the stations of each sphere
Above that town throughout the year.   90
For each hour that the heavens turned,
He crowed as if his wattles burned.
His comb was red as brightest coral
And scalloped like a castle wall.
His beak shone black as finest jet.
His legs and toes were blue, and yet
His nails were white. Above, I'm told,
His feathers shone like molten gold.
This cock had in his governance
Seven hens to do his pleasance.   100
Each matched his color and his lines,
His sisters and his concubines,
But none so gold or fair of throat,
As his beloved Pertelote.
She'd been so fresh and debonair,
So gracious, condescending, fair,

Since she was only one week old,
She had his very heart to hold,
His greatest love, and all his duty;
He fairly doted on her beauty.   110
Ah, what a joy to hear him sing
Just as the sun began to spring:
"My love is faring far away"!
For, lords, it happened in that day
That beasts and birds could speak full clear.
    One day at dawn as Chanticleer,
The cock on whom my tale depends,
Perched sleeping with his flock of hens,
Beside his charming Pertelote,
A horrid groan escaped his throat,   120
As if he suffered in a trance.
Dame Pertelote looked up askance
And said, "Alas, my husband dear,
What's happened? Are you feeling queer?"
    "I dreamed," he said, "I pray your grace,
That I was caught in such a place,
That even now my heart is pounding.
God save me from the fiend's confounding,
And let me flourish in the clear!
I dreamed while I was roaming here,   130
In our own yard, a dog-shaped beast
Would grab me roughly at the least.
I think he really wished me dead!
His color mingled gold and red,
With black tips to his tail and ears.
That fiery color stoked my fears—
A slender snout and glowing eye—
My heart beat so I thought I'd die!
It made me croak like any raven."
    "Fie, sir," said she, "you heartless craven!   140
Alas, my lord, by God above,
You've sunk in my regard and love.
I can't abide a coward, sir.
Whatever other hens aver,
We want bold husbands, all agree,
Tactful, openhanded, free,

Not over-rash, of course, and yet,
Not trembling at every threat,
No boasters, either. God above!
How dare you say to me, your love,   150
That you're appalled by burning eyes?
A person's heart should match his guise.
Why should you be afraid of dreams,
Where nothing *is,* but only seems?
Dreams are born of overeating
And heady fumes, diversely meeting.
When humors struggle and contend,[1]
The vapors swirl and dreams ascend.
Indeed, the dream you had just now,
Sprang from a strong excess, I vow,   160
Of hot red choler in your system.
It took your sleeping thoughts and mixed them
In its own ways, producing dreams
Of arrows, fire, and blood in streams,
And bright red beasts that snarl and bite,
Or strife and wars and headlong flight—
Just as a surfeit of melancholy
Can cause a sleeping man to cry
For fear of fierce black bulls or bears
Or coal-black devils with their snares.   170
The other humors work as well
At breeding dreams, as I've heard tell:
The vapor spreads, the dream reflects it.
    "Dionysius Cato, well respected,   *third-century Latin author*
Said no one should be swayed by dreams.
    "This leads me on to other themes.
For God's love, take a laxative,
A healthy dollop, stark and stiff,
To purge yourself of all this folly,
And choler too, and melancholy.   180

---

1. The four humors were gaseous essences given off by bodily fluids: blood, phlegm, yellow bile, and black bile. When out of balance, they affected a person's health and temperament. We still talk of people being sanguine (hopeful, dominated by blood), phlegmatic (sluggish, too much phlegm), melancholy (despondent, cast down by black bile), or choleric (irascible and bilious).

Take it soon; you mustn't tarry.
Don't wait for an apothecary.
I'll show you simples round about,   *herbs*
To sort these noxious humors out—
Many a healthful plant and leaf
To cool your fears and bring relief
And purge your bowels and your brain;
These herbs will see you right as rain.
Because your nature's choleric,
The rising sun could make you sick   190
When you are overfull and hot.
I pray you, lord, make sure you're not,
Or you'll contract a tertian ague.   *recurring fever*
Take steps to head this off, I beg you.
You'll need a day of smooth digestives,
Bland worms, before your laxatives
Of spurge, euphorbia, fumitory,
Or centaury, or rhamus berries,
Or twining ivy growing near.
Eat all or some of these, my dear,   200
And you'll soon be yourself again.
No silly dream will cause you pain."
   "My thanks," said Chanticleer, "for your leeching,
But touching Cato and his teaching,
Although he's held in great esteem,
And though he set no store by dreams,
Many an old book testifies
That better men thought otherwise,
Men of double Cato's weight.
The soundest authors all relate   210
That dreams are full of revelations
Of happiness or tribulations
That folks will meet throughout their life.
This can't be doubted, darling wife,
And here's a proof of it indeed:
   "As great an author as men read   *Cicero, or perhaps Valerius Maximus*
Tells how two honest fellows went
On pilgrimage with good intent
And made their way into a town
So filled with people all around   220

They couldn't find along the way
A single place where both could stay.
And therefore, of necessity,
That night they parted company,
And each man went from house to shed,
Throughout the place to find a bed.
One joined some oxen in a stall,
Curled up among them by a wall.
The other's fortune was less rough;
A tavern lodged him well enough.   230

    "It came to pass ere it was day,
The well-lodged pilgrim where he lay
Seemed to hear his fellow call,
Lying in the oxen's stall:
'Alas, this night I'll murdered be.
Now help me, friend, come succor me.'
The man was startled wide awake,
But then he gave his head a shake
And told himself the dream was vain.
He slept, but dreamed the same again.   240
The third time that his fellow came,
He came to say that he'd been slain.
'Behold these bloody wounds,' he cried.
'You'll soon admit all you've denied.
Tomorrow at the town's west gate
You'll see a cart with dung for freight.
My body's hidden in that cart.
Arrest it there, upon my heart.
They killed me for my purse of gold.'
Each detail of the crime he told   250
With piteous voice and ashen look,
And this time every detail took.
His friend went swiftly to his inn
And peered inside the oxen's pen,
And shouted out his fellow's name.

    "The hostler heard him call and came.
'Your friend is gone away,' he said,
'He left before the first light spread.'

    'My dream was true!' the pilgrim cried,
Suspecting that the hostler lied.   260

He hastened to the gate and found
A cart with dung to spread the ground,
A cart that matched on every side
The dung cart that his friend described.
He summoned all his heart to cry,
'Vengeance! Justice! Felony!
My friend was murdered overnight.
He's buried here by wicked sleight.
I call upon the magistrates
Who keep this city and its gates.
Harrow! Alas! My fellow's slain!'   270
The upshot, Pertelote, is plain.
The people rose up for their part
And overturned the dung-filled cart
And there they found the murdered man,
As he foretold, you understand.
　　"Oh blissful God, Thou art so true,
No bloody villain cozens you!
Murder will out. We see it's so.
No crime is more accursed and low.   280
Let him roam loose two years or three,
No murderer is really free.
The carter was bound by every limb.
The hostler too. Men tortured them
Till they confessed their evil deed
And swung from gibbets for their greed.
　　"So here you see how dreams come true,
And later in the same book too,
The very chapter after this—
Don't think I lie or speak amiss—   290
Two other men would cross the sea
On business with a consignee,
But while the wind remained contrary
They had no choice except to tarry,
Lodging in the harbor town.
At last just as the tide went down,
The winds that blocked the harbor ceased.
Well, they were jolly then, and pleased,
And planned to sail next day at dawn.
But, lo, a sending came to one.   300

He dreamed when it was nearly day
A man stood by him as he lay,
And warned him to put off his sailing
Despite the better wind prevailing.
'Sail now and drown, you and your friend,'
He said. 'This trip will be your end.'
The man relayed what he had heard,
Unto his fellow, word for word,
And prayed him to postpone his trip.
That man began to joke and quip   310
Against his friend. 'What, wait?' he said.
'No dream can fill *my* heart with dread,
Or make me change my plans a whit.
I don't respect these dreams a bit;
They're naught but vanities and japes.
They fill our heads with owls and apes
And darkness and perplexities
And puzzles and absurdities.
Stay if you like, but I am loath
To waste this welcome wind by sloth.   320
I'll go at once now that it's day.'
He left the inn and went his way,
But long before his course was sailed
His luck expired; his fortune failed.
The bottom of his bark was rent,
And down the ship and all hands went
In sight of other boats that tried
To cross the sea on that same tide.
You see, Dame Pertelote, my dear,
Both these examples make it clear   330
That no one should dismiss his dreams.
No matter how it sometimes seems,
Many a dream deserves our fear.
    "In holy Kenelm's tale you hear   *ninth-century British saint*
How that sweet martyred Mercian[2] prince
Received a vision to evince
The power of dreams the day he died.   *in 821 AD*

---

2. Mercia was an early kingdom in central Britain. Kenelm disregarded a dream-warning
that sister would have him killed.

He saw his death from every side.
His nurse construed his dream with reason
And bid him to beware of treason,   340
But he was young, no more than seven,
And all his thoughts were fixed on Heaven,
A hopeful lad, but not alert.
By God, I'd give my finest shirt
If you could read his doleful tale.
    "Or will Macrobius[3] avail,
My dear, expounding long ago
The vision of great Scipio?   *in* The Dream of Scipio, *400 AD*
He says such dreams are true portents
Of otherwise unknown events.   350
Or, dear, you could consider well
The witness left by Daniel.   *Dan. 1:7–28*
Does he think dreams are vanity?
Or read of Joseph. There you'll see   *Gen. 37 ff.*
How certain dreams—I don't say all—
Warn us of things that will befall.
Lord Pharaoh, the Egyptian king,
Soon learned to dread the power of dreams.
His servants learned with him as well.
The books of many peoples tell   360
The wonders that arise from dreams.
When Lydian Croesus ruled, it seems,
He dreamed he sat upon a tree,
And he was hanged, as you may see.
Andromache, Prince Hector's wife,
The day her husband lost his life,
Had dreamed it all the night before.
He'd taste defeat that day, she swore,
If he went out among the ranks.
But Hector gave her little thanks.   370
He heard her out, then went his way.
Achilles killed him that same day.
There's plenty more, as you must know,
But day's at hand, and I must crow.
Still, dear, remember my belief

---

3. Macrobius edited Cicero's original work and added his own commentary.

This dream will cost me pain and grief.
That said, I add a furthermore:
I hardly trust your herbal lore.
All laxatives are venomous.
They kill as soon as healing us.   380
    "But let's have mirth, no more of this.
Dame Pertelote, as I have bliss,
I must be thankful for God's grace,
Each time I look upon your face—
The scarlet rings about your eye!
My comfort spreads; my worries die.
For surely, *In principio*
Mulier est hominis confusio—   *"From the first, woman has*
The meaning of this Latin is   *been man's ruin."*
'Woman is man's joy and bliss.'   390
Ah, when I feel your side in bed
Though I can't mount you there or tread—
Our perch is far too small, alas!—
I welcome all that comes to pass,
And scoff at ill portents and dreams."
With that he flew down from the beams,
And clucked to summon forth his wives.
The weak man fails, the strong survives.
He found them grain, and undismayed
Surveyed them royally, unafraid.   400
He treaded Pertelote twenty times,
Enjoying her ere it was prime.   *around 9 AM*
He glared about him like a lion
And on his toes stalked up and down,
Scarcely setting foot to earth.
Where he found food (there was no dearth)
He clucked to gather up his hens,
As regally as any prince.
Now I leave Chanticleer there scratching,
To tell the plot that fate was hatching.   410
    After the month the world began
(It's March I mean, when God made man)   *a traditional belief in*
Had ended, and sweet April too,   *Chaucer's day*
And May had made her fresh debut,
Chanticleer in all his pride,

His sleek hens clustered by his side,
Cast up his eyes unto the sun,
That by then in the Bull had run   *the constellation Taurus*
Twenty-one degrees and more.
He knew by instinct, not by lore,   420
The hour was prime, and crowed aloud.
"The sun is shining," he allowed,
"Forty-one degrees in height.
Dame Pertelote, God save my sight,
Listen to the small birds singing
Amid the buds and fresh flowers springing!
My heart is bathed in joy and solace!"
But then his fortune turned, alas,
For every bliss concludes in woe;
Joys quickly come and quickly go.   430
Wise authors know and often tell
How sorrow strikes when all seems well.
This is a sovereign observation.
And well borne out by my narration,
A tale as true, I undertake,
As those of Lancelot du Lake,
That women hold in reverence.
Enough of that. I'll recommence.

 A coal-fox, sly, iniquitous,
Who'd lived nearby three years at least,   440
The one of whom the cock had dreamed,
Had made his way that night, it seemed,
Into the yard where Chanticleer
Had lived a life devoid of fear.
In a bed of herbs it lay,
Lurking till the height of day,
To snatch our hero in his pride,
A gleeful, wicked homicide,
Like those who plot to murder men.
Confound you, villain, in your den!   450
Iscariot! New Ganelon!   *1)Judas; 2)betrayer in* The Song of Roland
Dissimulating Greek Sinon,   *Sinon convinced Troy to take in*
Who brought the Trojan ramparts down.   *the Trojan horse.*
Chanticleer! Cursed be that dawn
You left your perch among the beams!

You had good warning in your dreams,
The day was full of peril, alas,
But what God has foretold must pass,
Or so we're told by certain clerks.
True, many other learned works   460
Have brought this point into contention,
A doctrine shrouded in dissention
Among a hundred thousand men.
I cannot sift it to the bran,
Like Saint Augustine, that man of trust,
Or Bradwardine or Boethius: *British theologians*
Whether God's knowing what I'll do
Constrains my will and others' too
To do it of necessity;
Or whether we in fact are free   470
To do an action or refuse,
Though God knows well which way we'll choose;
Or whether there's a middle way—
"Conditioned necessity," as men say.[4]
I'm not the man to speak of this;
Simple fables suit my wits,
How Chanticleer went forth despite
The warning in his dream that night.
Of course Dame Pertelote said he should,
But women's counsel's seldom good.   480
A woman heard the Prince of Lies   *Satan*
And Adam lost us Paradise,
Where he was blithe and full of ease . . .
But I don't know whom I'll displease
If I go further with this theme.
Still, lest you think my words extreme,
Read authors I will gladly name
For what they say about the same.
But now my tale's of Chanticleer;
I won't discourse of women here.   490
    Pertelote settled in the sands
To dust-bathe with her sister hens,

4. Common answers to the seeming conflict between God's foreknowledge and humans'
free will.

While Chanticleer sang out with glee
Like any mermaid on the sea
(*Physiologus,* the bestiary,   *an 11th-century Latin work*
Says mermaids sing full blithe and merry).
A scrap of movement caught his eye
Above the herbs—a butterfly—
But then he saw the fox below
And quickly lost all will to crow.   500
"Cluck! Cluck!" he cried, and back he started,
Unstrung by terror, hollow hearted,
For every creature knows its foe;
Its instinct works to make this so,
Though they have never met before.
    The cock saw something to abhor.
He would have fled, but first the fox
Said, "Wait, good sir. Please listen. Pax!
I swear to you I am your friend,
There's nothing here to apprehend.   510
I'd never do you any harm.
Dispense with this misplaced alarm.
My only thought in coming here
Was to meet great Chanticleer.
They say you sing as sweet and loud
As any angel on a cloud.
With feeling, too—I've heard you must
Match singers like Boethius.   *Boethius wrote a treatise on music.*
My lord, your father, may God bless him—
Your mother too, so sweet and prim—   520
Deigned once or twice to visit me,
A signal honor, you'll agree.
But singing, now . . . I've heard men say
No one but you can match the way
Your father praised the shining dawn.
He sang with passion, each note drawn
From fullest heart, and Heaven knows,
He always sang with both eyes closed,
On tiptoe for the loudest tones;
And furthermore to stretch his bones,   530
He thrust his slender neck far out.
No man or rooster round about

Could sing like him or think as fast.
One tale in *Brunellus the Ass*   *a satirical poem*
Concerns a heady, vengeful cock.
A priest's son bruised him with a rock,
But later by a clever twist
He cost the boy his benefice.[5]
Even this bird could not compare
With your brave father, I declare,   540
For wisdom or for subtlety.
Now sing, dear sir, for charity.
Recall your father. Sing as sweet!
     Chanticleer's wings began to beat.
No thought of treason now dismays
Our vain young cock, puffed up with praise.
     You lords beware! You fall by right
Through flatterers and parasites,
Whom you prefer, through wrongful vanity,
To downright truth and modest sanity.   550
Read in Ecclesiasticus   *12:10 ff.*
How flatterers devour us.
     Chanticleer tottered on his toes,
His neck stretched out, his eyes squeezed closed,
And crowed full loudly for the nonce.
Russell the fox rose up at once
And grabbed his throat in brisk attack.
He tossed the cock across his back,
And bore him off toward the wood.
     Fate works this way for bad or good.   560
Alas, that Chanticleer left his beams!
Alas, his wife distrusted dreams!
On Venus' day, Friday, by mischance!
     Oh Venus, goddess of love's dance,
Since you held Chanticleer in thrall—
For heady love he did his all,
More for delight than generation—
Why bare him to such vile predation?

---

5. A boy called Gundulfus hit a cock with a stone. Later when Gundulfus was a priest and about to be assigned to a parish, the rooster crowed late. Gundulfus overslept and lost the position.

Dear Geoffrey, every poet's master,
When good King Richard met disaster
And you deplored his grievous death—
Why haven't I the art and breath
To chastise Friday half so well?
For it was Friday Richard fell.
If I were you I'd scorch the air
With Chanticleer's extreme despair!
    I'm certain no such lamentation
Arose from all the Trojan nation—
When Pyrrus, whom the Trojans feared,
Grasped old King Priam by the beard
And butchered him, as Virgil tells,
As rose from Chanticleer's demoiselles
When they all saw their lord was gone.
Pertelote made the harshest moan,
Louder than Hasdrubal's wife
The day her husband lost his life,
And Romans burned royal Carthage down.
She mourned her husband and her town,
And threw herself into the flames,
And thereby won the world's acclaim.
    Oh, woeful hens, the selfsame sound
Was heard when Nero burned Rome down
From wives of guiltless senators,
Whom Nero slew despite their tears.
Now I'll resume this tale of slaughter.
    The helpless widow and her daughters
Heard their hens shrieking with dismay
And saw the red fox run away
With Chanticleer upon his back.
"Out!" they cried, "Harrow, alack!"
And ran headlong to save the cock.
Their outcry made men run amok,
And dogs as well—Gerland, and Coll—
And Mistress Malkin in her shawl.
Cows galloped madly with the hogs,
Dismayed by shouting and the dogs.
Up went their tails; they ran pell-mell,
Bellowing like fiends from Hell.

Geoffrey de Vinsauf, who wrote
a treatise on poetry
King Richard the Lionhearted

Achilles' son
580

Carthaginian king

146 BC

590

64 AD

600

The ducks were panicked, and the geese
Swirled in arcs above the trees.   610
Out of the hives roared bees in swarms,
The air was filled with such alarms,
Jack Straw himself was not so loud,   *a peasant revolutionary*
Killing Flemings with his crowd,   *immigrant laborers*
As all these friends of Chanticleer.
They sounded horns of bone and brass
And shrieked and hallooed to surpass
The loudest revelry or brawl.
It seemed the sky itself would fall.

　　Yet now, I pray you, learn from me   620
How Fortune can turn suddenly
Against us when her favor slacks!
The cock upon the fox's back
Summoned all his heart to speak:
"You've won, Sir Fox. So why be meek?
Shout to those churls, 'I spurn you all!
No matter how the truth may gall,
I have this cock, though you repine;
Accept defeat—the bird is mine,
And I will feast on him anon.'"   630

　　"In faith," said the fox, "it shall be done."
But speaking made him lose his grip.
The cock pulled free, gave him the slip,
And flew at once into a tree.
Now when he saw the bird go free,
The fox said, "Ah, my Chanticleer,
You've lost all trust in me, I fear.
I snatched you, true, and used you hard,
I bore you roughly from your yard,
But it was done with good intent.   640
Come down. I'll tell you what I meant."

　　"Not I!" said Chanticleer, "Spite us both!
And spite me first. I give my oath,
I'll not succumb repeatedly
To wheedling and flattery.
You made me sing and shut my eyes!
He who blinds himself to lies
Deserves his fate. God curse his head!"

"No," said the fox, "curse him instead
Who's moved by arrogant caprice   650
To speak when he should hold his peace!"
    My lords, this fable helps us see
The evil done by flattery.
    But if perchance you will not hear
Of talking hens and Chanticleer,
Accept the moral anyway.
Paul said no writing goes astray
If readers search for fruit, not chaff.   *Rom. 15:4*
Dear God, I pray on our behalf
That you will make us all good men   660
And save our souls at last. Amen.

Heere is ended the Nonnes Preestes Tale.

EPILOGUE TO THE NUN'S PRIEST'S TALE

"Priest," said our Host in ringing tones,
"God bless your britches and your stones!
A merry tale, we'll all agree!
If you were of the laity,
You'd tread some hens, and never fear it.
If you had might to match your spirit,
You'd win your own and other men's—
A multitude of willing hens!
Of what a build are you possessed—   670
So thick a neck, so deep a breast!
No sparrow hawk could match that eye!
You needn't paint your cheeks or dye
With colors fetched from overseas.
God bless your tale and expertise."
    And after this with merry cheer,
He spoke again, as you will hear.

THE SECOND NUN

THE SECOND NUN'S PROLOGUE

The Minister of Vice, and sin's chief nurse,
Is in our English tongue called Idleness.
This gateway to all things we hold perverse
Eschew, my lords, and its contrary bless—
That is to say, all lawful busyness.
We do right well to keep ourselves employed
Lest Satan draw our souls into the void.

That fiend deploys a thousand silken cords
Continually to bring our souls to grief,
And, sensing idle deeds or idle words,   10
Ensnares us so that we refuse relief.
Until a man is trussed up by that thief
He scarcely knows he's in the Devil's hand,
So work we must, and idleness withstand.

Even those who think they'll never die
Can see, if they but use their share of reason,
A fallow, empty state's a state to fly;
It never bears good fruit in any season.
Sloth leashes sluggish men. It means them treason.
They drink and sleep and feed without remission,   20
At others' cost, unstirred by fit ambition.

Thus to preserve us from all idleness,
The cause of many fallen souls' damnation,
I have a holy martyr's story dressed
According to the legend in translation.
I tell of your great grace and exaltation,
Cecilia, with your lilies and your roses,
A tale that sacred martyrdom discloses.

Invocation to Mary

And you, the brightest flower of virgins all,
Of whom Bernard wrote often with delight,   *Saint Bernard of Clairvaux,*
To you, as I'm beginning, let me call,   *c. 1090–1153*
You comfort of us wretches without light.
Please tell through me your martyr maiden's plight,
Her life, her death, and her great victory,
Her selfless will, dear Lady, help us see.

You maid and mother, daughter of your Son,
You well of mercy, doleful sinners' cure,
In whom Christ's earthly trial was begun,
You humble Empress, awesome and demure,
In you, our human nature shone so pure   40
That God himself revered you, chose your womb,
To start Christ's path on earth toward his doom.

Within the blissful cloister of your flesh
The mighty lord of earth and sea and air
Took on man's shape, man's spirit to refresh.
This world of creatures burgeons in his care
And praises him in one unceasing prayer.
You bore him, yet remained a spotless maid,
Your helpless Son, in Heaven's might arrayed.

You flood the world with your magnificence   50
And also mercy, goodness, inspiration,
So that despite your peerless excellence
You answer not just humble supplication
But oftener with fond anticipation
And open hands you tender us your aid
Before we've shaped our wants ourselves, or prayed.

Support me, Queen, from Heaven's towering height;
Please help me in this vale of bitter gall.
Reward me like the trusting Canaanite   *Matt. 15:22–8*
Whose faith made Jesus hear her humble call.   60
Like her, I'll take whatever crumbs may fall
From Our Lord's table. Grant eloquence, I pray.
Though I'm unworthy, tell me what to say.

And since all faith is dead without good works,
To do your will, oh, give me wit and scope.
Free me from this waste of darksome murk,
Dear Saint, our brightest reservoir of hope.
Yea, plead for me from Heaven's highest cope,
Where glad hosannas rise on every hand,
Christ's mother, blessed daughter of Saint Anne!   70

And with your light, oh, set my soul afire,
Now trapped within my body's thick contagion.
Oh, free me from the clinging clay and mire
Of earthly appetites and false affection.
Dear place of refuge, undeserved salvation
Of those who toss in sorrow, weak and faint,
Please help me tell the marvels of your saint.

And may all you who read my tale the while
Accept my true contrition and repentance.
I haven't thought to gloss or gild the style,   80
For I obtained each word and moral sentence
From him who in the purest reverence
Wrote down this story, following her legend.
Where I have erred, may you yourselves amend.

Brother Jacobus Voraigne's interpretation of the name *Cecilia* in his *Golden Legends*[1]

Now let me start with Saint Cecilia's name,
Expounded in the book that tells her story.
That it means "Heaven's lily" is a claim
Well suited to her chastity and glory.
The flower it names may be an allegory:
White honesty; green conscience of good fame;   90
Sweet-scented holiness—thus "lily" is her name.

1. What follows is a medieval etymology, not so much meant to trace the real derivation of *Cecilia* (the suggestions are all wrong) as to show the sacred "rightness" of the name. This was a common technique in sermons and pious books such as the one cited here: Jacobus de Voraigne's *Legenda Aurea,* c. 1260.

Or *Cecilia* means "the way unto the blind,"
As her brief life points us toward salvation;
Or then perhaps her name is two words twined:
Caelum for Heaven's sacred inspiration,
And *Leah,* meaning "constant occupation":
"Heaven," to show the holy martyr's spirit,
And "effort" for the care she took to steer it.

Or *Cecilia* may denote a *lack* of blindness,
Recalling how her soul was filled with light,   100
Her wisdom, courage, probity, and kindness.
Or then again its antecedents might
Be two more words: *caelum,* as is right,
With *leos* to complete the combination—
"Heaven of people, example to each nation."

For *leos* means but "people" in our tongue
And as above we in the heavens see
The sun and moon and constellations throng,
Just so, within her spirit Heavenly,
Her faith and wisdom shine out fair and free.   110
Against her faith and wisdom—that's her sky—
Her doings gleam like Heaven's lamps on high.

And just as great philosophers describe
A swift and burning Heaven ever turning,
We may those selfsame qualities ascribe
To Cecilia, adding works to all her learning,
Keen and full and fervent in her yearning
And burning with a pure and constant flame.
And so, my lords, you understand her name.

THE SECOND NUN'S TALE

This maiden, bright Cecilia, as I've read,   120
Derived from Romans of the noblest kind,
But from her cradle she was raised instead
To hold Christ's Holy Gospel in her mind.

She never ceased, as far as I can find,
To pray to God on high in love and dread,
And most, that he might save her maidenhead.

At length she must be wedded to a man,
One her own age, for so they thought was best,
A likely Roman youth, Valerian;
But when the day was come to see them blessed   130
She, in the humble sorrow of her breast,
Beneath her robe of shining golden mesh
Put on a pinching hair shirt next her flesh.

And while the organ pealed its melody,
Cecilia sang to God with little art,
"O Lord, please let my soul and body stay
Unblemished, lest my virtue should depart"—
A prayer she'd said for years with all her heart,
Repeating her devotions as she might
With frequent, painful fasting day and night.   140

That night Cecilia meekly went to bed
With her young husband, as a new bride must,
But privately unto the boy she said,
"Oh honored spouse, so well beloved and just,
Let me invoke your charity and trust.
I've something now to tell you while I can
In confidence, as you must understand."

Valerian meant to honor her and swore
That not for any cause that he could see
Would he betray the trust she asked him for.   150
She spoke up quickly on this guarantee:
"I have," she said, "an angel watching me.
No matter whether I'm awake or sleeping,
That angel has my body in his keeping,

"And if he feels by any happenstance
You mean to touch me in a lover's fashion,
He'll kill you, my young husband, with a glance—
An early death will be your final ration.

But if you learn to chastely curb your passion,
He'll grant you that same love he gives to me,   160
A wholesome love that you may taste and see."

Valerian, constrained as great God planned,
Spoke grudgingly: "Before I trust in you,
Show me the angel. That's a just demand.
If it's in fact an angel, right and true,
Then I will do whatever you command.
But if I find you love another man,
Lo, with this sword I'll slay you as you stand."

Cecilia was forthright in her reply:
"If that's your wish, then you will see him clear,   170
But first you must consent to be baptized.
Go out the Appian Way—the gate is near—
You'll find a village just three miles from here.
Then tell the ragged people living there
That they're to be your guides in this affair.

"Explain that I, Cecilia, pray they'll lead you
To good Pope Urban, whom they all revere,   *Urban I, d. 230 AD*
Upon a sacred errand. They will heed you.
And when at length that saintly man is near,
Recount the promise I have made you here.   180
He'll purge you of your sins, if you agree,
So you can see the angel guarding me."

Valerian proceeded as she planned
Upon the Via Appia that same day.
He found the pope, an old and feeble man,
In hiding where the Christian bodies lay
Among the catacombs along the way.
When Urban heard Cecilia's wise prediction,
He raised both hands in joyful benediction.

Warm, thankful tears burst from his aged eyes.   190
"Almighty Lord, Oh Jesus Christ," said he,
"Oh counselor and shepherd of the wise,
The fruit of that same seed of chastity

Thou sowed in her has now returned to thee!
How like a guileless, holy, loving bee,
She serves you, Lord, this righteous Cecily.

"For she this spouse she took because she must,
This fiery lion, turns into our way,
Meek as a lamb and hoping to be just!"
Now with these words the place grew bright as day   200
To show an ancient man in white array.
A book of golden script was in his hand,
A book he held out to Valerian.

Valerian tumbled down like one struck dead,
But the old man set him back upon his feet
And, watching him intently, sternly read:
"One Lord, one faith, one God without deceit,
One Christendom, one Father of all, complete,
Above and over all in every place."
Those golden words adorned his page by grace.   210

This read, the white-clad figure spoke again:
"Do you believe these words? Say yes or no."
"I do, good father," said Valerian.
"The world has not a truer rule to show
This side of Heaven. That I surely know."
The old man vanished, no one could say where;
The pope baptized the young one then and there.

At home Cecilia met her transformed spouse
Inside his chamber, where an angel shone,
Holding a glowing crown in either hand,   220
With crimson roses and snow-white lilies sown,
Crowns meant for him and his pure bride alone.
And so the angel crowned Cecilia's hair,
And then the boy's with flowers beyond compare.

"With bodies clean and with unspotted thoughts,
Keep well these flowery crowns," he said to them.
"From Paradise I have them freshly brought.
These flowers will never droop upon their stems

Or lose their holy fragrance or grow dim,
And yet no earthly man can see them plain   230
Unless he's just, and chaste without a stain.

"And you, Valerian, seeing you so soon
Made room for Heaven's truth within your soul,
Ask what you like and you shall have that boon."
"Tiburtius, my brother," the boy said, clear and bold,
"I'd have him hear all this that I've been told.
Give him the grace, although I know not how,
To see the truth as I perceive it now."

The angel said, "God favors your request
And wills that as two martyrs most revered   240
You both shall come unto his blissful feast."
With that, behold, the man himself appeared.
Tiburtius smelled the savor that adhered
To those unfading flowery crowns, thrice blessed,
And marveled much within his honest breast.

He said, "I wonder at this time of year
How I can smell the perfume all unknown
Of roses and of lilies hovering here
As if those fragrant blooms were freshly blown.
Surely no sweeter flowers have ever grown!   250
Their odor fills me with a wondrous passion.
I feel transformed, but can't say in what fashion."

Valerian answered him: "Two crowns have we.
Their whiteness shines and deep red colors glow,
But you, my brother, have no power to see.
Only my prayers have let you smell them so,
But you'll behold them too, that much I know,
If you can reach a faith, unfeigned and whole,
In holy truths that will preserve your soul."

Tiburtius answered, "Have I heard you right?   260
Do I wake, brother, or is this a dream?"
"We've dreamed," Valerian said, "all night—
Dreamed all our lives, my brother, as it seems,

But now at last the truth will show supreme."
"You've learned the truth?" Tiburtius said. "What is it?"
"My truth," his brother said, "will cap your visit.

"The angel of the Lord unsealed my eyes;
You'll see him for yourself if you renounce
All heathen gods, but never otherwise."
Now for the holy couple's flowery crowns,   270
Saint Ambrose mentions these and then expounds   *d. 347*
Their meaning in a full and telling way.
That Doctor of the Church has this to say:

"In order to receive a martyr's blessing,
Cecilia was infused with God's rich grace.
All ordinary worldly goods suppressing,
She made these Roman brothers mend their pace,
So God, accepting their sincere embrace,
Sent down two noble crowns of fragrant flowers,
Their just reward and earnest of his powers.   280

"The maid thus brought Tiburtius to bliss,
Revealing to the world the saving might
Of chastity, which never is amiss."
Cecilia showed the Roman lad outright
How vain his idols were in her God's sight,
How they were deaf and dumb, not things of power,
And said he must renounce them from that hour.

"Whoever doubts you is a hopeless beast,"
The boy proclaimed. "You've made my spirit burn."
She kissed his breast at once and wished him peace,   290
As one so soon enkindled, quick to learn.
"From this day forth, your soul is my concern,"
Declared the holy, spotless, blissful maid,
And added this, in Heaven's truth arrayed:

"Just as the love of my God, Jesus Christ,
Made me your brother's wife, the selfsame way,
I hold you, brother dear, of equal price,
Seeing you cast your heathen gods away.

Go with your brother, be baptized today.
Make your soul clean so that you may behold   300
That angel's face of which Valerian told."

Tiburtius spoke up roundly, "Brother dear,
Please tell me where to go and whom to see."
Valerian answered him with guileless cheer:
"Pope Urban is the man who wields God's key."
"Pope Urban, brother, is this your decree?"
Tiburtius said. "Petition such a one?
He seems instead a rebel to be shunned.

"Tell me this pope is not the selfsame man
Condemned by Rome to execution's flames,   310
Who now is hunted up and down the land.
He hides his face, denies his very name!
If he is found, to his eternal shame,
He will be burnt at once, I guarantee.
If we befriend him, brother, so shall we.

"And while we seek your new divinity
Well hid above the clouds as I presume,
The men of Rome shall burn us, as you'll see!"
But Cecilia spoke up boldly in that room:
"Ah, well might mortal men shrink from the tomb   320
And shield themselves full anxiously from strife,
If breath on earth were all there is to life.

"But life is better in another place
And never will be lost there once attained.
God's Son Himself has taught us through his grace
How God the living world at first ordained
With mortal creatures in whom reason reigned,
Each one of whom the Holy Ghost enrolls
Among the host of bright immortal souls.

"For such as us, God's Son has testified   330
When he was in our world, by word and deed,
There is another life once we have died."
Tiburtius answered, "Sister, now take heed.

A god called Christ at one time filled your creed,
But now you talk of Fathers, Sons, and Spirits.
A flock of gods like Rome's, or something near it."

"One God" said she, "and here's the explanation.
As human minds divide themselves in three—
Remembrance, reason, and imagination—
Just so in undivided unity,   340
The God you seek contains three faculties."
Then she began to set forth and attest
The store of Christian doctrine in her breast.

She touched upon the details of Christ's story,
How God's own Son was born into this world
To open up the way to Heaven's glory
To human souls in stifling darkness hurled.
And so the maiden God's great plan unfurled
Before Tiburtius, listening rapt and charmed.
The boy went seeking Urban, quite disarmed.   350

The pope rejoiced to christen yet another,
A noble Roman swayed to Christian ways.
He made the boy as perfect as his brother,
A yearning heart with sacred fire ablaze.
The angel shone before Tiburtius' gaze,
And every gift the lad required of Christ
As his reward was granted in a trice.

It would be hard to set down without fail
The wonders that Christ worked among these three
But at the last, to tell you all my tale,   360
Rome's sergeants brought the boys—who would not flee—
To hear the prefect Almachius' decree.
He questioned them, discerning what they were,
Then sent them to an idol, Jupiter.

"Who will not sacrifice to Jove," he said,
"Cut off his head, and that's my final word."
So forth these pious Christian lads were led,
But one official, Maximus, who heard

The prefect found his heart was stirred.
He led the budding saints toward Jove's altar,   370
But, weeping, felt his resolution falter.

When Maximus was told the martyrs' lore,
He made the executioners agree
To lead them to his house and furthermore
To let them preach there unrestrained and free;
Thus he and all the others came to see
The Christian truth, and more than that, deny
False faiths, and on God's sovereign word rely.

Cecilia met them there as well that night,
With priests to christen all of them as one,   380
And afterward, as day began to light,
She saw the brothers' race was nearly run:
"Dear knights of Christ, at last you see the sun,"
She said, "Now throw off darkness as you should
And arm yourselves with light and truth and good.

"Your strife is over; your worst trials are passed,"
She said. "You've proved our faith's true power.
Go take the crown of life you've earned at last.
The rightful Judge will bless your final hour
And welcome you to his eternal bower."   390
These words were Saint Cecilia's last advice;
Next came more men to make them sacrifice.

But when the boys approached the shrine of Jove—
To tell you shortly how their lives played out—
They would not add an offering to his trove,
But knelt unyielding, faithful, and devout.
That each lad lost his head there is no doubt,
But as heads fell and bodies crumpled down,
Their souls went flying up to true renown.

Now Maximus, who saw this, standing by,   400
Told later one more detail of the story:
He saw both souls, released, to Heaven fly
With angels, trailing clouds of light and glory,

To cheat the cruel Romans of their quarry.
To stop his talk, the prefect had him battered
With leaden scourges till his life was shattered.

Cecilia soon retrieved the good man's bones
To bury in Valerian's family plot
Beneath the martyred brothers' marble stone.
Almachius heard and ordered she be sought   410
And brought to him as soon as she was caught.
He hoped his power over Cecilia would suffice
To make her bow to Jove and sacrifice.

He little knew his troop of officers
Saluted Saint Cecilia as the dawn
And, weeping, vowed to give their lives for hers.
"Christ is our God," they said. "The line is drawn.
This is the God we worship, three in one.
We know Cecilia serves this God on high;
With her we'll sing his praises, though we die."   420

As all these doings reached the prefect's ears,
He had the maiden fetched into his court.
When she appeared, he greeted her with sneers:
"What thing are you?" and questions of that sort.
"One born as well as you," was her retort.
"I ask you, wench, and answer me with speed,
What is your true religion and your creed?"

"You start your inquisition like a fool,"
Cecilia said. "To mix two separate questions
In one demand is not to ask by rule."   430
Almachius gathered all his self-possession.
"Why bandy words with me without discretion?"
He asked. "Why mince my words for you?" said she.
"I'm unafraid, and so my words should be."

The prefect asked her to recall his power.
Cecilia answered him with steady eyes:
"Your might," she said, "will not outlive your hour.
Man's largest sway dies with him when he dies.

Your might's a blown-up bladder I despise.
One needle prick against it at its greatest,   440
Behold! Your precious power lies deflated!"

"You started ill and now proceed to worse,"
The prefect said, "impairing your own good.
Have you not heard our mighty princes' curse
On heretics who won't do as they should?
Christians are traitors, that's well understood.
You'll suffer for your faith if you pronounce it.
To live beyond today, you must renounce it."

"Your princes err," she said, "and you as well,
To make us guilty through such sick decrees.   450
We wish your Rome no harm. We don't rebel.
We only hope to live in common peace,
Revere our God, and celebrate his feasts.
But just because we bear the Christian name,
You outlaw us and threaten us with shame.

"But we protest our goodness with one voice.
If you have other evidence, supply it."
Almachius said, "Enough! Make Jove your choice:
Now sacrifice against your faith; deny it.
Even here, so near your end, you still can fly it."   460
At that the holy, virgin martyr maid
Laughed cheerfully, as to the judge she said:

"O Judge, I fear your mother wit has flown.
Would you have me renounce my innocence?
Hold wickedness? Embrace it for my own?
Surely what you say is just pretense.
Gainsay it now. Speak like a man of sense!"
Almachius started up: "Proud impudence!
Against my power you've not the least defense!

"The law is in my charge. How to apply   470
Its terms is well within my rightful scope.
I am the man to bid you live or die.
I am the man to grant despair or hope!"

"In truth," replied the girl, "I will not grope
For favor. That is steadfastness, not pride.
There is no vice more Christians have decried.

"Supposing you can bear a further truth,
Let me set right another great mistake:
Your claims of might are foolish and uncouth—
Saying your princes gave you power to make   480
A person live or die, as for your sake.
In truth, you've shown you have the power to kill.
But life? Life doesn't lie within your will.

"Say, rather, you're the minister of death,
And if you claim a greater role than this,
You lie, and your claims vapor with your breath."
"Enough!" the prefect said, "Our gods exist.
Now sacrifice to them or feel Rome's fist.
I've strength enough to bear your disrespect
As rooted in the teachings of your sect,   490

"But those same wrongs I cannot overlook
Heaped on our gods, and in a Roman court!"
"Ah fool," Cecilia said, "I undertook
To make you understand at last how short
These doctrines fall that are your law's support.
Every word you've spoken here proclaims
How weak your precious system is, and vain.

"It seems as well that you're completely blind
To things that every common man can see.
This stone is stone, from center point to rind,   500
Yet you proclaim it your chief deity!
Just touch it with your hand, and you'll agree.
Or lick it! You'll perceive the taste of stone!
Yet you can't see. Ah, Lord, how blind you've grown!

"The true shame is that men will laugh at you
And scorn to hear such unmixed foolishness,
For every common person holds it true
That God wears highest Heaven for his dress,

While these poor, stony images attest
Their powerlessness to serve themselves or men.   510
Take all together, they're not worth a pin."

These words and more the fearless maiden uttered
As Almachius heard with ever-growing rage.
At last he bid her bath at home be shuttered
With her inside, so it became her cage.
"Burn her," he said. "Although it won't assuage
My wrath, I'll see this stubborn girl a cinder."
His men obeyed and stoked the fire with tinder.

Through all that night and then a day as well,
Beside her bath, although it smoked and boiled,   520
Cecilia sat serenely in her cell,
All cool, although the room around her broiled.
When Almachius saw his bad intentions foiled,
He sent a man, since nothing else availed,
To take her life with steel where fire had failed.

Three strokes he gave Cecilia on the nape,
But though he struck with malice as she saw,
Her neck was never severed, though it gaped,
And then she heard the hired churl withdraw.
Three strokes were all allowed by Roman law.   530
He left the virgin, living, on the floor;
He didn't dare to give her one stroke more.

Half-dead and swooning now, neck hacked and torn,
Cecilia lay at length upon the mud.
The folks about her took no time to mourn
But soaked what cloths they had in her warm blood.
Three days she lingered there, the virgin bud;
She never ceased to pray and talk and teach,
While all her converts came to hear her preach.

To these she gave her clothes and household things,   540
And sent some to her friend, the saintly pope,
And wrote, "I've had my gift from Heaven's King,
A short reprieve from death of three days' scope

To recommend to you, with all my hope,
These needy souls, and give, for what its worth,
My house to you to be a Christian church."

Pope Urban and his deacons secretly
Fetched Saint Cecilia's body to its rest
Among his other saints of each degree.
Her house, just as she hoped he would, he blessed   550
And named it Saint Cecilia's. This impressed   *still a church in Rome*
Her fame in Christian records. To this day,
Men go to Saint Cecilia's Church to pray.

Heere is ended the Seconde Nonnes Tale.

THE CANON'S YEOMAN

THE CANON'S YEOMAN'S PROLOGUE

Soon after the story of Saint Cecilia ends, near the village of Broughton-under-Blean, or about six miles from Canterbury, the pilgrims are overtaken by a Canon and his Yeoman, riding fast on sweating horses and hoping to join the company. The Yeoman does most of the talking for both of them. His master, he says, is such an able scientist he could turn all the ground on which they ride from there to Canterbury upside down and transform it into gold.

"Well, that's a wonder," says the Host. "So why does he go about in those dirty, worthless clothes?" The Yeoman explains that the Canon is too caught up in his science to prosper, and so the two of them usually lurk outside towns with robbers and thieves. "And why is your face so strangely colored?" asks the Host. "From poring over fires and bellows," answers the Yeoman, going on to say that he and his master have been practicing alchemy without success. They borrow gold, promising to double it through their experiments, but the experiments never work because the science is too difficult. They will wind up beggars.

The Canon overhears most of this and tries to shut his Yeoman up, but the man has had enough of the life they shared. As the Canon flees, the Yeoman says he will tell all he knows of the alchemical art.

THE CANON'S YEOMAN'S TALE

The First Part

He spent seven years with the Canon, says the man, losing everything he owned and all he could borrow. Now he is ruined, as anyone else will be if he takes up alchemy. Success is always coming, but never arrives.

The Yeoman's involvement with alchemy is at least somewhat serious and betrays a good deal of knowledge on Chaucer's part. The man talks at length of arsenic, burnt bones, ground-up iron, mercury, sealed pots, lead, red clay, crucibles, yeast, and fire, among a host of other things. Combined the right way and using the four "spirits"—vapors of quicksilver, arsenic trisulphide, sal ammonia, and brimstone—it ought to be possible to transmute the seven "bodies"—gold, silver, iron, mercury, lead, tin, and copper—into one another. But it never works!

What is missing is the elixir, or philosopher's stone—the catalyst that would trigger the proper reactions. Alchemists go mad with sorrow searching for it, says the Yeoman, but though they spend all they have in the process, they never find it. They are left penniless, dressed in rags, and reeking of brimstone. You can recognize them by these signs. If you ask why they don't live better, they whisper in your ear that if they are found out they will be killed for their knowledge.

The Yeoman knows, from watching his master, that there is always an explanation for failure: the fire was too hot, the crucible was not strong enough, the metals bury themselves in the ground or go through the roof, and so on. But though they never succeed, alchemists always hope for better luck next time.

The Second Part

The Yeoman's story concerns an alchemist who is a canon, but not, he insists, his former master. This man is an outright thief, though that does not mean all canons are. He would poison a town if he saw a reason. His victim is a prosperous priest, a man he reels in skillfully.

The canon begins by borrowing gold from the priest and paying it back promptly. To show his appreciation for the loan, he offers to show the man a wonder. He has the priest send out for three ounces of quicksilver (mercury). Hot coals are brought, and the priest himself puts an ounce of mercury in a crucible. The wicked canon adds a special powder (perhaps chalk or ground glass, the Yeoman says) that he claims will produce the desired reaction, and they heap the coals around and over the crucible. Up his sleeve, the canon hides a false coal holding an ounce of silver behind a wax plug. He puts this "coal" on top of the crucible, where it burns and releases the silver into the flask as the mercury is boiling off. The two men pour what is in the crucible into a mold, cool the mold in water, and voila! an ounce of silver!

The canon plays two more variants of the same trick, using his special powder on another ounce of mercury and an ounce of copper. This is enough to convince the priest the transformations are legitimate. The upshot, of course, is that the priest pays forty pounds for the special powder, which doesn't work, and never sees the canon again.

Such lust for gold and swindling is the reason, the Yeoman believes, that gold is so scarce. At any rate, no one knows how to start with nothing and make gold of it. That transmutation, he says, works only the other way:

A person's gold, if he has aught,
Can quickly be transformed to naught!

No one knows how to change base metals into gold, the Yeoman says, and no one ever will. He ends his tale with a strange anecdote concerning Plato (d. 347 BC): when one of his disciples asked Plato the name of the philosopher's stone, the great man refused to tell because Christ (!) did not want it known. God is against the whole project of alchemy. No wonder alchemists never thrive!

The Manciple

The Manciple's Prologue

At another little village near Broughton-under-Blean, this one called Bob-up-and-down, the Host notices the Cook falling asleep on his horse and orders him to tell a tale. But the man really does look bad. The Manciple offers to tell a story instead, and then he notices the Cook is drunk. The man's breath smells so bad, the Manciple says, it is as if the Devil's foot was in his mouth. Angry, the Cook tries to reply, but he is too drunk to speak. He shakes his head and is thrown from his horse.

The Host agrees the Manciple should tell his tale, but warns him that when the Cook sobers up he may get the Manciple in trouble. It seems the Cook knows an embarrassing thing or two about the Manciple's accounts. To get back in the Cook's good graces, the Manciple offers him a drink, and the man accepts. Chaucer memorably compares the Cook's tipping action as he drinks to someone blowing a horn.

At any event, the drink patches up the quarrel, to the Host's delight, and the Manciple begins his tale.

The Manciple's Tale

The tale concerns the god Phoebus, who the Manciple says was the best archer and musician and the handsomest and most courteous man who ever existed. Phoebus lived with his wife, whom he loved more than anything else, and a talking pet crow, white as a swan. If the god had a fault at all, it was jealousy. He worried his wife might deceive him and watched her carefully. But that's a fool's game, says the Manciple; a good woman doesn't need watching, and with a bad one, watching does no good.

Phoebus treated his wife well, but that isn't helpful either. Feed a caged bird the finest food, and it still longs to go free. It would 20,000 times rather eat worms in the rude forest. Or give a cat a silk cushion and the finest milk and meat—the minute it sees a mouse all that goes by the board, for appetite banishes good sense and discretion. A she wolf is just as bad. When she wants a mate she will take the stupidest male or the one with the worst reputation.

And thus it was that Phoebus' wife took a low, inconsiderable man for her lover. Phoebus, only too aware of his own merits, suspected nothing, but women often take up with inferior men. Though it seems crude to say so, there's little difference between unfaithful women, whatever their rank. Men lay them each just as low.

In fact, there's not much difference between criminals of any sort. A man who burns down whole towns is called a captain or tyrant; someone who can do only lesser harm is called a thief.

It happened that once when Phoebus was away his wife called her lover for a tryst in the god's house—in fact, in his bed. The white crow saw everything. It said nothing, but when Phoebus returned it greeted him with the cuckold's song, "Cuckoo! Cuckoo!"

"What sort of song is this?" asked Phoebus.

"The only one that fits the case," said the crow and went on to describe what it had seen. Phoebus' wife had betrayed him, and with a man of no reputation, one worth no more than a gnat.

Enraged, Phoebus mounted an arrow and killed his unfaithful wife, but then in grief he broke his harp and lute and guitar and psaltery and his arrows and his bow as well.

"Traitor," he said to the crow. "Scorpion-tongue!" He should never have believed the crow's story, he said, for there his wife lay, plainly innocent. He took away the crow's whiteness and its voice, leaving it able only to croak. And since that time all crows have been black.

The lesson? Never tell any man someone else has slept with his wife, says the Manciple. In fact, never tell scandal or bad news under any circumstances. As the Manciple's mother once told him, men commonly get into trouble by saying too much, almost never by saying too little. Whoever says something he shouldn't becomes the slave of his hearer. When he is tempted to spread bad news, the Manciple's mother told him, he should remember the crow.

THE PARSON

THE PARSON'S PROLOGUE

By now the Manciple's tale had ended,
And now the southern sun descended
So low it seemed to my best sight
Twenty-nine degrees in height.
It was four o'clock, I guess,
My shadow, eleven feet or less:
About two times my body's height.
The scales were the prevailing sign.   *Libra; the details point to Good Friday, 1394.*
A hamlet rose along our line,
Just as our Host, our jolly guide,   10
Looked back from where he sat astride
And said, "My lords, we're almost there;
Just one more story as we fare
Will do for now, if you agree;
So far we've heard from each degree
And nearly filled the pact we made.
May God provide that man his aid
Who tells the next. Sir Priest,
Are you a vicar, now, at least,
Or parson? Be what may,   20
You must fulfill the game we play.
You'll be the last, no holding back,
Come, show us what is in your pack,
For sure, now, judging by your looks
You know as much as many books.
Recite a fable, by God's beard!"
The man was nettled, it appeared,
And said, "You get no jests from me.
As Saint Paul writes to Timothy,
Woe to those not strong enough   30
To foreswear fables and such stuff.   *for example, 1 Tim 1:4*

342

Why should I sow worthless weeds
When I have wheat to serve your needs?
No, I'll give you, as I think I should,
A glimpse of evil and of good.
That is, in memory of Christ,
I'll serve you plain fare, simply spiced.
I'll entertain you if I can,
But know I am a southern man
And cannot rum, ram, ruf, by letter.[1]   40
And, God knows, rhyme is little better.
Yet, lords, I'll manage, I suppose,
To tell a merry tale in prose
And knit up all our tales at last.
Dear Jesus grant, as in the past,
That I may show you all the way,
The true way, lords—attend, I pray—
To that holy city in the sky.   *Heaven, the new Jerusalem*
So if it suits you all, now I
Will start my tale with your permission,   50
But, sirs, I make one last condition:
  Everything that I shall say
Might be denied, for I may stray.
I do my best, but I'm no clerk.
My little learning suits my work.
I hope to bring you to reflection,
But, lords, I'm subject to correction."
  Upon this word, we all agreed.
His offer seemed to suit our need.
We'd end the day with Godly thoughts,   60
Attend him, as we knew we ought.
We told the Host, who said, "Tell on!
We'll listen till the light is gone."
  The Host, I say, spoke for us all.
"Priest," he said, "tell, by Saint Paul,
Everything you have to say.
But hurry, for the close of day
Is coming. Now before it's here

---

1. The Parson is from the south of England, not the north, where alliterative writing, "rum, ram, ruf," was still in favor.

Sir, pour some nectar in our ear.
Say your piece; that's my decree."   70
This launched the Parson's homily.

THE PARSON'S TALE

The Parson delivers a protracted sermon on the sacrament of penance, or confes-
sion, and the seven deadly sins, which he considers in detail. Envy, for example,
is denounced by Saint Augustine and the Holy Ghost, for it leads to malice, which
is opposed to the bounty of the Holy Ghost. Malice can be conscious or uncon-
scious and can lead to bad deeds or simply to regret that certain things are true
or that God grants grace to certain people. In this way envy works against all the
virtues, because it resents them all. Indeed, envy is unique in that while all the
other deadly sins bring some delight (even if it is sinful delight) envy offers no
pleasure whatever, only anguish. And so on . . . and on.

Despite the Parson's admission that he is unlearned, his "tale" is complex and
bristling with fine distinctions and authorities. And despite the Host's urging him
to be brief, his talk would have taken about three hours to deliver aloud.

CHAUCER'S RETRACTION

Heere taketh the makere of this book his leve.

Now I pray to all those who hear or read this little treatise[1] that if they like any-thing here they thank the Lord Jesus for it. From him proceeds all goodness and true learning. And if anything offends them, I pray they blame my ineptness and not my will. I would have written better if I could. Saint Paul says, "All that is written is written to teach us,"[2] and that was my intent. Therefore, I beseech you meekly, for the mercy of God, to pray Christ have mercy on me and forgive my sins. Among these sins I include my writing and translations of worldly vanities, which I now renounce: my book of Troilus and Criseyde; *my* House of Fame; *my* Legend of Good Women; *my* Book of the Duchess; *my* Parliament of the Fowls; *my* Canterbury Tales *(a book conducive to sin); my* Book of the Lion,[3] *and many others I can't recall here, and many songs and lecherous lays. May Christ in his mercy forgive them all.*

But for my translation of The Consolation of Philosophy[4] *and other books of saints' legends, homilies, morality, and devotion, I thank our Lord Jesus Christ with his blissful Mother and all the Saints of Heaven, beseeching them from now unto my life's end to send me grace to bewail my guilt and study the salvation of my soul, and to grant me the mercy of true penitence, confession, and satisfaction for sin before I die. I pray this through the benign grace of Him who is King of Kings and priest over all priests—Jesus Christ, who bought us with the precious blood of his heart—so that at the Judgment Day I shall be one of those who are saved.* Qui cum Patre et Spiritu Sancto vivit et regnat Deus per omnia secula.[5] *Amen.*

Heere is ended the book of the tales of Caunterbury, compiled by Geffrey Chaucer, of whos soule Jhesu Crist have mercy. Amen.

1. "The Parson's Tale," with which the Retraction is associated in Chaucer manuscripts.

2. 2 Tim. 3:16.

3. Now lost.

4. A book of pious reflections written by Boethius (d. 524), one of Chaucer's favorite au-thors.

5. Who, with the Father and the Holy Spirit, lives and reigns, God forever and ever.

345

SELECT BIBLIOGRAPHY

Editions

Benson, Larry D., general editor. *The Riverside Chaucer.* 3rd ed. Boston: Houghton Mifflin, 1987. The standard modern edition of Chaucer's work.

Donaldson, E. Talbot, ed. *Chaucer's Poetry: An Anthology for the Modern Reader.* 2nd ed. New York: Ronald Press, 1974. Helpful commentary.

Kolve, V.A. and Glending Olson, eds. *The Canterbury Tales: Nine Tales and the General Prologue.* A Norton Critical Edition. New York: Norton, 1989. Good background, commentary, and critical essays.

Middle English Glossary

Davis, Norman, et al. *Chaucer Glossary.* Oxford: Clarendon Press, 1979.

Critical Books

Boitani, Piero, and Jill Mann, eds. *The Cambridge Chaucer Companion.* Cambridge: Cambridge University Press, 1986.

Brewer, Derek. *A New Introduction to Chaucer.* 2nd ed. London and New York: Longman, 1998.

———. *Chaucer and His World.* 2nd ed. Cambridge: D.S. Brewer, 1996. Well illustrated.

Cooper, Helen. *The Canterbury Tales.* Oxford Guides to Chaucer. Revised ed. Oxford and New York: Oxford University Press, 1991.

Crane, Susan. *Gender and Romance in Chaucer's Canterbury Tales.* Princeton, Princeton University Press, 1994.

Dinshaw, Carolyn. *Chaucer's Sexual Politics.* Madison: University of Wisconsin Press, 1989.

Donaldson, E. Talbot. *Speaking of Chaucer.* New York: Norton, 1970.

Hansen, Elaine Tuttle. *Chaucer and the Fictions of Gender.* Berkeley: University of California Press, 1992.

Howard, Donald R. *The Idea of the Canterbury Tales.* Berkeley: University of California Press, 1976.

Mann, Jill. *Chaucer and Medieval Estates Satire: The Literature of Social Classes and the General Prologue to* The Canterbury Tales. London: Cambridge University Press, 1973.

Muscatine, Charles. *Chaucer and the French Tradition: A Study in Style and Meaning.* Berkeley: University of California Press, 1957.

Pearsall, Derek. *The Canterbury Tales.* London: Allen & Unwin, 1985.

———. *The Life of Geoffrey Chaucer: A Critical Biography.* Oxford: Blackwell, 1992.

Phillips, Helen. *An Introduction to the Canterbury Tales: Reading, Fiction, Context.* New York: St. Martin's Press, 2000.

Robertson, D.W. *A Preface to Chaucer: Studies in Medieval Perspectives.* Princeton, Princeton University Press, 1962.

Websites

The Chaucer Metapage. http://www.unc.edu/depts/chaucer/index.html. A University of North Carolina page with a wide array of information and Chaucer links. Includes audio files of Chaucer's language read by professors.

Duncan, Edwin. An Electronic Edition of the General Prologue to Geoffrey Chaucer's Canterbury Tales. http://www.towson.edu/~duncan/chaucer/indexn.htm. Elegant, useable interactive edition of the General Prologue.